THE EXECUTION OF JESUS

THE EXECUTION OF JESUS

*A Judicial,
Literary and
Historical
Investigation*

by William Riley Wilson

CHARLES SCRIBNER'S SONS
New York

Library of Congress Catalog Card Number: 70-123334
SBN 684-10674-4 (cloth)
SBN 684-13114-5 (paper, SL)

TO M.M.W., K.W.H., K.W.S. AND J.W.T.

CONTENTS

Preface   ix

1: THE JEWISH LEGAL SYSTEM AND THE DEATH
   OF JESUS   1
   "It is not lawful for us to put any man to death."
2: PONTIUS PILATE   17
   ". . . unbending and recklessly hard . . ."
3: THE EARLIEST RECORDS OF JESUS' DEATH   25
   ". . . these are written that you may believe . . ."
4: THE TRIAL IN MARK AND MATTHEW   41
   ". . . and they all condemned him . . ."
5: THE TRIAL IN LUKE   53
   "He stirs up the people . . ."
6: THE TRIAL IN JOHN   63
   "Are you the king of the Jews?"
7: THE JEWS, THE ROMANS AND
   THE GOSPEL RECORDS   75
   "Let his blood be upon us . . ."
8: JESUS AND THE POLITICAL CRISIS   85
   ". . . these men sowed the seed of every kind of misery . . ."
9: THE CLIMACTIC DAYS IN JERUSALEM   95
   "Have you come out as against a *lestes*?"
10: THE JEWISH PROCEEDINGS AGAINST JESUS   113
    "What further testimony do we need?"
11: THE ROMAN CONDEMNATION   129
    ". . . perverting our nation . . ."
12: THE EXECUTION   145
    "And they brought him to the place called Golgotha . . ."
Conclusion: LEGALITY AND RESPONSIBILITY   167
   ". . . he delivered him to be crucified."

Notes   175
Appendix I   211
Appendix II   215
Bibliography   227
Index   241

PREFACE

This book is an attempt to solve the historical riddles surrounding the trial and execution of Jesus of Nazareth. Even the most optimistic author recognizes that, on a subject of such perplexity, his book will hardly be the last word. Yet I do hope to reach one goal: I have tried to explore this fascinating historical problem in terms which the untrained reader can follow easily. Too many issues of religious and historical importance are discussed only in the rarefied atmosphere of ivory towers, where scholars communicate with one another in footnotes. My aim is to bring this subject down to earth where that elusive person, the "average reader," can share in the excitement of piecing together the puzzle of those few days in Judaea which have had such a profound effect on us all. This effort is all the more important because so many misconceptions have developed in the popular mind on this difficult subject. I hope that this book will clear away many of these misconceptions.

In a sense, I have sought to write two books in one. The text itself is addressed to those who have only a general knowledge of the Bible and ancient history; I have made an effort to explain any historical or literary references which might not be understood by the nonprofessional reader, even though they are obvious to the scholar. I hope the professional reader will bear with these explanations as they appear. The material which is important only to serious students has been reserved mostly for the footnotes; these may be omitted entirely by anyone not concerned with the more detailed issues and the scholarly literature surrounding this inquiry.

This book had its beginning several years ago in a doctoral dissertation written in the Department of Religion at Duke University. I wish to thank Dr. Kenneth W. Clark of Duke, recently retired, for his very helpful guidance in that effort. I am also indebted to Dr. Robert S. Rogers of Duke. Although I had often confronted the problem of the trial of Jesus in earlier studies, it was Dr. Rogers' graduate seminar in Ancient Greek and Roman History which first awakened my serious interest in this subject.

Anyone who attempts to write on this problem should express his thanks to the vast number of scholars who have explored it before him through the years. On almost every page of this book I have drawn on the research of others. I hope I have adequately documented this dependence.

Finally, the Christian reader should be reminded that this book is not a devotional treatise but an analytical one. The religious significance of the death of Jesus is not the issue here. But it seems to me that a serious grasp of the historical facts of Jesus' trial and execution is an essential basis for an intelligent faith.

WM. R. WILSON

Dallas, Texas, 1969

THE EXECUTION OF JESUS

1

THE JEWISH LEGAL SYSTEM AND THE DEATH OF JESUS

"It is not lawful for us to put any man to death."

John 18:31

On a spring morning in about the year A.D. 30, in a minor province on the fringes of the Roman Empire, the resident Roman governor completed brief judicial proceedings. Then he turned a young man over to the attendant soldiers with instructions that he be taken out to a nearby site and executed.

The governor had no way of knowing that his instructions would change the direction of history. He would have been stunned by the suggestion that this decision on an annoying and somewhat trivial problem, which had interrupted his daily work schedule, would cause him to become better known than all the Caesars, and would make him an integral part of a story which would profoundly influence the lives of untold millions of people.

Yet the death of Jesus of Nazareth was to become one of those events which radically alter the course of human affairs. This death, and the conviction that Jesus had overcome it by rising from the

1

grave, launched the faith around which the spiritual life of western civilization has revolved for 1700 years.

Small wonder that the circumstances which resulted in the execution of Jesus are of such intense interest to us now. Yet, ironically, few if any of the landmark events of the past are so inadequately understood as this one. Today almost every sort of supposition still swirls about the causes of Jesus' death. Speculation has reached such limits that there is hardly any imaginable theory which has not gained some acceptance as an explanation of this pivotal event.

What is the reason for this failure to reach a reasonable consensus of opinion? Two answers can be found. First, since the trial and execution of Jesus are subjects of such widespread interest, they are continually interpreted in books and articles of a "popular" kind by writers who have no special training for this task. As a result, all kinds of farfetched opinions, based on preconceived notions rather than on serious research, have surrounded this subject with confusion.

Yet even when this subject is approached with careful scholarly preparation, the problems it presents are extremely complex. To solve them one has to maneuver expertly in three separate and very difficult areas of study. A blunder in any one of them will almost certainly lead us astray in attempting to reconstruct what actually occurred. These three areas are:

1) *The study of the legal problems surrounding Jesus' trial.* The most common errors made in interpreting Jesus' death arise from confusion over judicial questions. Such questions include: Was Jesus' trial legal? On what grounds was he executed—was he convicted of violating Jewish religious laws or Roman civil laws or both? If the Jewish leaders wanted to do away with Jesus, why did they not simply execute him themselves instead of delivering him to Pilate? These and similar questions must be answered correctly in order to establish both the causes and the responsibilities for Jesus' death.

2) *The analysis of the Gospel sources.* The New Testament contains not one but four separate accounts of Jesus' trial and death.

These records often disagree, even at the most fundamental points, and they are not complete. These four versions must be unravelled and then rewoven into one consistent and reliable account. This task requires the best tools of modern Biblical scholarship. It is made all the more difficult by the fact that the religious convictions of the early Church had a serious effect on the historical reliability of these New Testament records.

3) *The study of Jesus' death within the context of contemporary Jewish history.* This death was not an isolated event, unrelated to the time in which it occurred. It resulted directly from an intensive struggle then going on within the Jewish nation. Jesus died because he fell victim to a prolonged national crisis when he journeyed to Jerusalem at the time of the Passover feast. Understanding this crisis and its bearing on the life and death of Jesus is our third major task.

The aim of this book is to explore these three areas of study and to piece together the evidence gained from all three. If the information gained from these three sources were conflicting, it would be necessary to discount part of it and to take a calculated guess about what happened to Jesus. But these investigations supplement and clarify each other to a remarkable degree. Together they provide a picture of the arrest, trial and crucifixion of Jesus which lays strong claim to being an accurate historical description of these monumental events.

We begin by investigating the judicial background to the execution of Jesus. Over the years, every sort of judicial theory has been suggested as an explanation of Jesus' trial and death. Many of these explanations draw on modern Anglo–Saxon law rather than on the judicial realities of Jesus' own world. To understand the course of Jesus' prosecution it is essential to clear away the debris of these unfounded judicial theories and to determine what can be known about the system of authority under which he was seized and indicted in Jerusalem. This task occupies us in the present chapter. The starting point is to recall the turn of events which had placed a Roman governor on the seat of power in Jesus' homeland.

. . . . .

It was some six decades before the birth of Jesus when Roman legions brought a final end to the freedom of the Jewish state. In 63 B.C. General Pompey entered Jerusalem after a three-month siege and closed one of the brighter epochs in Jewish history: the period of Maccabean independence during which the Jews had governed themselves for the first time in centuries.

For a generation thereafter Palestine was in a state of political turmoil. This small and somewhat insignificant nation lay on the far edge of the empire and as a result, the Romans were not greatly concerned about its internal administration. Eventually, in 40 B.C., the Romans brought order to the country by designating Herod as a native puppet-king who was responsible directly to Rome.

Herod's rule proved brutal but effective. He satisfied his Roman sponsors and succeeded in expanding the territories assigned to him. All the while, his Jewish subjects despised him—partly for his half-Jewish blood, partly for his introduction of foreign practices and ideals, partly for his excessive cruelties. Despite his varied administrative successes he was not mourned when he died in 4 B.C., at about the time Jesus was born.[1]

At his death the Romans did not consider any of his family strong enough to control his entire kingdom, so they divided the territory among three of his sons—Philip, Antipas, and Archelaus.[2] Philip received the area north and east of the Sea of Galilee. Antipas was given Galilee and the area just east of the Jordan River. Of these two sons, Philip plays no role in our Gospel records, but Antipas appears in several stories because he ruled the area in which Jesus lived and worked. According to the Gospel of Luke, Antipas even shared in the final prosecution of Jesus. In any case, both these brothers fared well in office and ruled throughout the lifetime of Jesus.

The most crucial portion of Herod's kingdom was assigned to the eldest son, Archelaus. He inherited Judaea, with its capital city of Jerusalem, plus the neighboring areas of Samaria to the north and Idumaea to the southeast. Unfortunately, Archelaus' task soon proved too much for him. He was unable to control the Jews in

Judaea, where opposition to Roman domination was most intense.[3] After ten years the Romans tired of his ineffectiveness and exiled him. At this point Augustus, the first Roman emperor, made a decision which later proved fateful for the Jewish nation and also for Jesus. He refused to place another of Herod's relatives on the throne and he rejected the request of the Jews that the nation be restored to independence. Instead he drew Judaea more closely into the confines of the Roman Empire; he converted the country into a Roman province and appointed a Roman governor as ruler.

Roman provinces in the first century A.D. were of two kinds, senatorial and imperial.[4] The former were controlled directly by the Roman Senate, but the latter were under the personal control of the emperor and were administered for him by governors whom he himself appointed. The major imperial provinces were governed by legates, who were officials of high standing in the Roman bureaucracy. But a few imperial provinces were too unimportant to justify the services of such a high-ranking administrator. In these cases, the emperor placed the control in the hands of a lesser official, called a *procurator*.[5] In A.D. 6, Judaea became one of a handful of small provinces which were ruled by such procurators.[6] This form of government continued in Judaea until the Jews launched their full-scale revolt against Rome in A.D. 66.[7] During this sixty-year period there were fourteen successive procurators of Judaea. The fifth was Pontius Pilate, A.D. 26–36.

What powers were entrusted to Pilate and the other Roman governors of Judaea? Each procurator held the supreme authority over all the internal affairs of the province, answering only to the emperor himself.[8] The military garrison of the country was at his command and he was responsible for the collection of taxes. More important, he also possessed full judicial authority and administered the country's laws. The Jewish historian Josephus, the chief source for the study of the Jews in this period, states specifically that the governor of Judaea had the right of life and death over the populace.[9] Such power was commonly entrusted to governors throughout the empire.[10] There is no doubt that the governor of Judaea held this supreme judicial authority; it is understanding how and when he exercised it which creates a problem for us in interpreting Jesus' execution.

To begin with, it is clear that the procurators delegated a large measure of judicial control to the Jews themselves. When thinking of the Roman government of Judaea one must not imagine any parallel to the military occupations of our own day. In Judaea, as in most parts of the empire, the Romans showed a remarkable talent for bringing order and stability with a minimum of control. They were not concerned with fitting the widely diverse peoples of the empire into the mold of Roman law, culture and religion.[11] Their goal was to maintain peace while exercising a minimum of direct interference in the internal affairs of the provinces. Judaea was one of the most turbulent and rebellious areas of the empire, yet its procurators controlled the country with a skeleton military force of only some three thousand men. Although we have no clear evidence, it is extremely unlikely that the Romans interfered in the more routine judicial affairs of the Jews. There is no reason to doubt that the native Jewish courts were free to pass judgment on religious, civil and even criminal infractions by native Jews—at least up to a point.

Of these native courts, only one is important for interpreting the last days of Jesus. That is the central judicial body in Judaea, the supreme Sanhedrin of Jerusalem. The make-up and functions of this body are of special significance for the study of Jesus' trial.

In earlier times this supreme Jewish Council had been composed entirely of the nation's leading priests.[12] But by the time Judaea was made into a Roman province, members of a different group, the Pharisees, had made their way into the Council. The Pharisees were laymen who had an intense interest in religion and who exercised great influence among the common people. The priests belonged to a smaller and more conservative religious party, the Sadducees. In Jesus' day, the balance of power among the Council's 71 members[13] may have swung to the Pharisees, although the priests continued to hold the chief offices.[14]

The leading members of the Sanhedrin were the high priests;

this title heads all the New Testament lists of the Council's members.[15] The title refers chiefly to the individual who served as president of the Council.[16] But it was also given to all former holders of this office,[17] and even to the male relatives of the high priest.[18] That is why we meet this term in plural form (often translated "chief priests") in the New Testament, even though only one man filled the presidency of the Council at a given time. Throughout most of Jesus' lifetime, all the high priests were members of a single family, that of Ananus, who exerted a powerful influence over the Council during Jesus' lifetime.[19] The man who filled the high priesthood during Jesus' public ministry was Caiaphas. The Gospels describe him as a central figure in Jesus' trial.[20] The rest of the Council's membership was made up of "scribes," who were the most educated interpreters of the law, and the "elders." This latter designation covered the majority of the members, both Pharisees and Sadducees. These various titles are important, because they reappear continually in the Gospel records of Jesus' death.

The Sanhedrin was the central governing body of the Jewish religion. Its spiritual authority extended to Jews throughout the world. Within Judaea itself the Council also held extensive political and judicial powers, and some of these powers undoubtedly continued in effect during the rule of the procurators.[21] The governors relied on the Sanhedrin—and particularly on the high priest and the other Sadducean leaders—for the maintenance of order within the country.

It is this fact which brings us face-to-face with the central legal question in the trial of Jesus. *During the rule of the Roman procurators, did this supreme Jewish Council have the legal right to try and to execute Jesus, or any other native Jew, on a capital charge?*

. . . . .

This question is the most celebrated legal problem connected with Jesus' death. It becomes so because of a perplexing sequence of events which occur in his trial.

The Gospels all agree that certain Jewish officials—the full Sanhedrin, according to Matthew and Mark—arrested Jesus and initiated legal proceedings against him. But at the end of these proceedings the officials took no direct action against Jesus. Instead they simply delivered him to Pilate. Here Jesus' prosecution continued, and at the end of these Roman proceedings Jesus was led away and executed. The question which arises is obvious: Why did the Jewish officials take Jesus to the Roman governor? If they regarded Jesus as guilty of some capital offense, why did they not convict and sentence him, then carry out that sentence themselves?

The most obvious answer is that the Romans had taken away the Sanhedrin's right to pass and to execute capital sentences. The Jewish officials were forced to take Jesus to Pilate because they lacked the power to put him to death themselves. This view is explicitly stated in the Gospel of John. In this Gospel the officials present Jesus to the governor as an "evildoer"; then we read:

> Pilate said to them, "Take him yourselves and judge him
> by your own law." The Jews said to him, "It is not lawful
> for us to put any man to his death." (John 18:31)

So Pilate proceeds to hear the case, and the end result is the crucifixion. If John's account is correct, the course of Jesus' trial was determined by the legal restraints which the Romans had imposed upon the Jews. If John is mistaken, as many believe, we apparently have to search for some other explanation for the transfer of the case to Pilate.

It is clear, then, why this question of the Sanhedrin's authority has become so central to the study of Jesus' death. To solve this problem we have to dig patiently through scattered bits and pieces of testimony from our ancient sources, since no official Roman or Jewish documents describing the administration of the province of Judaea have survived. Opinion is far from unanimous, but if we assess the available evidence carefully it is possible to attain reasonable certainty on this famous problem. Understanding this evidence is essential to a clear grasp of the trial and death of Jesus.

First, some scholars are convinced that the Gospel of John is incorrect and that the Jews actually retained the right of capital punishment under the Romans.[22] The evidence for this view is drawn from four sources: (1) the Jewish historian Josephus, (2) the ancient Jewish rabbinic literature, chiefly the *Mishnah,* (3) the writings of Philo Judaeus and (4) the New Testament itself.

1) Josephus has two significant references which seem to indicate that the Jews retained the right of capital punishment. First, he reports that a formal notice was posted on the grounds of the Jewish temple in Jerusalem, declaring that non-Jews might not enter the temple's inner courts on pain of death.[23] He adds that the Romans had officially granted this right of execution to the Jews. Second, he records the martyrdom of the Apostle James, the brother of Jesus, who was stoned to death by the Jews after having been convicted by the Sanhedrin.[24] Josephus also records several lesser items which may bear on this subject. He mentions that the Jews throughout the empire were granted special privileges by the Romans, although these privileges are somewhat vague.[25] He notes that the Romans granted the Jews in Cyrene (in North Africa) the right to follow their own laws without restriction.[26] And he comments that the Essenes, the small Jewish sect now known to us more fully through the Dead Sea scrolls, enforced some of their regulations by executing violators.[27]

2) The *Mishnah,* a compilation of Jewish traditions which dates from the third century A.D. (and which forms the core of the larger collection, the *Talmud*) contains a full section on the composition and practices of the supreme Sanhedrin. This section gives detailed judicial regulations which were to be followed by the Sanhedrin in trying capital cases. According to some scholars, the existence of these detailed and formal rules of procedure proves that the Sanhedrin had the legal right to try capital cases.[28] In addition, the *Mishnah* specifically reports an instance in which the daughter of a priest was burned to death for committing adultery.[29]

3) The writings of Philo Judaeus, the Jewish philosopher of Alexandria who was a contemporary of Jesus, contain some pertinent references. Philo comments more than once on the special privileges which the Jews enjoyed under the Romans.[30] He also specifically describes the rights of the Jewish courts in Alexandria, which were apparently empowered to carry out death penalties—

although the approval of the Romans may have been required before the sentence was executed.[31]

4) Finally, the New Testament itself is a rich source for evidence for this theory. The most vivid is the story of the death of Stephen, recorded in the book of Acts (Chapters 6–7). Stephen was accused of blasphemy and was taken before "the Council," presumably the supreme Sanhedrin. At the conclusion of his lengthy statement he accused the Jews of having murdered Jesus, who had since ascended to the right hand of God. These remarks so enraged the Council members that, in a frenzied mob, they hauled Stephen outside the city and stoned him to death. At several other points in Acts we read also of arrests and physical punishment suffered by Christians at the hands of Jewish officials.[32] Paul, before he became a follower of Jesus, is also reported to have pursued Christians "unto death." [33] Then, after Paul's conversion the Jewish officials and some of the populace made repeated attempts to kill him.[34] Some scholars believe that these references prove that the Jews freely exercised capital powers in the time of Jesus.

.   .   .   .   .

However, when all this evidence is added together it does not amount to very much. Most of it is simply irrelevant, on one of four counts. Some of the references do not relate to Judaea itself, and there is no good reason for applying them to the very distinctive situation in the province. Some do relate to Judaea but they cannot be shown to date from the *time* of procuratorial rule. It is obvious that the rule of Roman governors brought special judicial conditions into existence in Judaea; evidence which dates from other periods is of very little use. Some of the incidents described above are obviously lynchings or other illegal acts; they do not prove that the Judaean Jews had *legitimate* capital authority. Finally, some of the references merely indicate the existence of *partial* judicial privileges, not the right of capital punishment, which is the only issue at stake.

As an example, the lengthy regulations in the *Mishnah* governing the Sanhedrin's conduct of capital cases have little bearing because their date and authenticity are uncertain. The material accumulated in the *Mishnah* covers a period of several hundred years. We have no way of knowing whether the judicial powers implied by these regulations were in force during the period of the Roman governors. In fact, it is quite possible that they were never in force. It is now certain that many of these rules were only idealistic and theoretical and do not reflect actual practice in any period.[35] As for the *Mishnah's* record of the burning of the high priest's daughter, this reference is also of no use because we have no idea when it occurred. It is clear that in *certain* periods the Jews freely executed offenders against their laws; the question is, did they have this right under the procurators? Besides, we are told specifically that the girl's execution occurred because the court was "unskilled." Apparently the execution was illegal.

The remarks by Josephus and Philo about the "special privileges" of the Jews in the empire are much too vague to support any judicial theories. Apparently these special concessions related to the observance of religious customs[36] and the exemption from certain taxes.[37]

The only evidence which seems to carry serious weight is the rule allowing the Jews to execute Gentile trespassers in the temple area, a rule which clearly dates from the time of Jesus. This regulation was a concession to the Jews on an issue which had particular importance to them. The sanctity of the temple was a matter of profound historic concern to the Jews. The Romans customarily granted provincial citizens as much freedom as possible in practicing their religion, and they evidently showed the Jews special considerations of this kind, as just observed. The license to preserve the religious purity of the temple is an example of this tendency. This notice cannot be used to prove that the Jewish courts *routinely* exercised capital powers as part of their authority. The temple regulation is clearly a specific exception, not a statement of ordinary judicial privilege.[38]

Most important, in dealing with the ancient evidence we must not confuse instances of lynching and mob-justice with legitimate judicial authority. There is extensive evidence that throughout the empire in Jesus' day native provincial courts, or private citizens, frequently took matters into their own hands and illegally executed natives on criminal charges. The Romans were totally unable to police the internal life of the provinces closely, and would not have done so if they had been able. Roman officials often winked at the excesses of the provincial courts in dealing with alleged offenses, as long as Roman citizens were not involved. There is no doubt that some, if not all, of the executions mentioned above are to be explained in this way. For example, Josephus makes it clear that the execution of the Apostle James was illegal. He states that the event occurred during a brief interim between governors, and that when the new governor arrived the high priest (Ananus II) was removed from office because he had condoned this judicial murder.[39] In fact, Josephus indicates that it was illegal for the Sanhedrin even to meet during this period without the procurator's permission; this certainly suggests that the Sanhedrin's powers were seriously restricted under the rule of the governors.

Such instances should be kept in mind when we read about the Jewish persecution of the early Christians, both in Judaea and beyond. It must not be supposed that every reference to the intimidation of Christians in the book of Acts is evidence of formal judicial privilege. The Jewish animosity toward the emerging Christian sect expressed itself chiefly in extra-legal suppression, not in authorized court proceedings.[40] A prominent Christian writer of the second century complained: "You (Jews) do not have the power (i.e., legal right) to kill us, because of those now in control; but as often as you could, you did this too." [41] The death of Stephen is almost certainly to be interpreted in this way. There is no indication that Stephen was duly convicted and sentenced by the court. Instead, he so angered the assembled Council members that they lost control of themselves and swarmed over him, then dragged him out and killed him. This account cannot be taken too literally, since there is obviously a strong anti-Jewish bias in the story. But at least the evidence indicates that Stephen's death was not the result of formal judicial procedures but of a lynching. If this single incident is discounted there is no reference in the New Testament which justifies the belief that the Jews held the right of capital punishment during and after the time of Jesus.[42]

In short, the evidence that the Jews could legally have put Jesus on trial for his life is very weak. On the other hand, there is substantial evidence to indicate that the Romans definitely did not make it a practice to grant capital powers to native provincial courts around the empire.

Regrettably, information about criminal jurisdiction in the Roman provinces is very scarce, in contrast to the full details available concerning Rome itself. The limited evidence which has survived indicates that, while the Romans freely delegated most judicial authority to local native courts, they very carefully restricted the power of capital punishment to the Roman governor himself. No evidence from any Roman source indicates that the Romans ever granted the right of capital punishment to provincial courts.[43] Two important examples of this Roman restriction of capital powers in the provinces have been recovered. A decree of Augustus, addressed to the proconsul of Cyrene in 7–6 B.C., specifically states that jurisdiction could be delegated to the native courts *except in capital cases*.[44] The restrictions were even more severe in Egypt, which, like Judaea, was governed by procurators.[45] The native courts in Egypt had very little authority under Roman rule. These courts served only a grand-jury function and prepared the evidence for itinerant Roman officials who then judged the cases.[46]

The laws which applied in Cyrene and Egypt were probably customary, in varying form, throughout the rest of the empire.[47] The only exception was the small handful of free states which were given extraordinary judicial (and other) privileges because of their meritorious service to Rome in previous years. Judaea was certainly not a free state and, as the noted Roman authority A. N. Sherwin-White remarks, hardly any area in the empire was less likely than Judaea to receive special privileges on the basis of loyalty to Rome.[48] Considering the tumultuous state of affairs in Judaea during the Roman occupation, and the repeated insurrections launched by the Jews, it is hard to believe that the Romans made a special exception and allowed the Jews to carry out executions at their own discretion.

These deductions can be substantiated by more direct evidence. A statement in the *Talmud* declares specifically that the Jewish nation had lost the right of capital punishment during the procuratorial period. The Jerusalem *Talmud* notes that the Jews had lost this privilege "forty years" before the destruction of the Jewish temple in A.D. 70.[49] The forty years must be interpreted loosely, according to normal Jewish usage, but the statement makes it clear that for most or all of the procuratorial period the Romans deprived the Jews of this legal power.[50] Coupled with the reference in the Gospel of John, this notice gives a second direct statement from the primitive sources which contradicts the notion that the Jews possessed this important right at the time of Jesus' death.

.   .   .   .   .

To sum up:

1) No available evidence from any source clearly testifies to the legal right of the Jewish courts of Judaea to pass or to execute capital sentences under the Roman governors. Several of the references cited above illustrate the *violation* of legal authority rather than its legitimate use.

2) The best evidence suggests that the Romans reserved the right of capital punishment for Roman governors alone. Judaea would hardly have qualified for any special exception to this rule.

3) Finally, specific statements in the New Testament and the *Talmud* declare that the Jews had lost capital authority at the time of Jesus. It is hard to see how or why both these sources could be mistaken.

Only the unlikely discovery of some official document from these years could remove all doubts. But there is good reason to believe that Jesus could not have been legally tried and put to death by the supreme Sanhedrin.[51] This means that any explanation of the trial and death of Jesus which is based on the presumption that the Jews could legally have executed Jesus themselves is built on very shaky ground. Two such theories have cropped up repeatedly through the years:[52]

1) *That the Jewish officials had the power of capital punishment, but delivered Jesus into the hands of Pilate because they did not want to bear the blame for killing him.* According to this view, the Jewish leaders did not lack the authority to kill Jesus, they lacked the nerve. They were afraid to face the wrath of the Jewish populace or of Jesus' followers. There is no evidence, either in the Gospels or elsewhere, to support this strange view. Even leaving aside the question of judicial power, it is foolish to suppose that this supreme national Council arrested and tried Jesus, and then suddenly became too timid to carry out its own sentence.

2) *That the Jewish officials could pass death sentences, but needed the ratification of the governor before executing these sentences.* This theory has proved attractive simply because it explains why the Jewish authorities might have tried and sentenced Jesus, then transferred the case to Pilate. However, this explanation is shattered by the testimony of the Gospels. There is no doubt that Jesus died by crucifixion, which was an exclusively Roman means of execution. If Pilate had merely approved a Jewish condemnation of Jesus for religious crimes, he would have released Jesus to the Jewish authorities to execute him according to their own customs. Those customs did not include crucifixion; there is no record in all Jewish literature of any Jew being crucified by his own people, and no modern writer has ever suggested that the Jewish officials crucified Jesus. Further, under no circumstances would a Roman governor himself have executed a provincial citizen simply because he had violated some native religious law. Pilate put Jesus on trial and executed him for reasons of his own; he did not merely ratify a Jewish sentence.

A final question is in order.

If the Sanhedrin lacked the authority to execute Jesus, does that fact alone explain why the Jewish officials took Jesus to Pilate?

It is natural to assume that since the Jewish officials *could not* legally execute Jesus, they *must* have taken him to Pilate so that he would act in their behalf. But such an assumption overlooks one important alternative. From both a judicial and historical standpoint, it is conceivable that Jesus was delivered to Pilate not because the

Jews lacked the right to deal with religious offenses, but because *the fundamental charges against Jesus were never religious in nature.* If Jesus was seized in Jerusalem for alleged violations of the *Roman provincial laws,* rather than the Jewish religious laws, then his case properly belonged before Pilate, not before the Jewish Council. That in itself would explain why the Jews took Jesus to the governor instead of attempting to sentence and execute him themselves.

In the coming chapters we will see that this alternative possibility fits the historical evidence very closely. The Jewish officials evidently could not have done away with Jesus legally themselves, but it was never in their minds to do so. They expected Pilate to deal with Jesus, because they believed that Jesus' actions had brought him into conflict with the governor and the interests of Rome.

2

PONTIUS PILATE

". . . unbending and recklessly hard . . ."
Philo, *Leg. ad Gaium*, 38

The events told in our Gospels were unfolded in one of the remote corners of the Roman world. That is why the people who fill these pages are virtually unknown in the secular literature of the period. This applies even to Jesus himself; his name attracted only the briefest mention in the non-Christian writings of the first century. The same is true of Simon Peter, the Apostle Paul, and all the other Christians who seem to us so intimate a part of this era in history.

A remarkable exception to this rule is Pontius Pilate. It is extremely interesting that of all the people who play a prominent role in the career of Jesus, he is the best known to us from secular history. Indeed, although it was Jesus' trial which has made his name famous, most of our information about him comes from sources outside the New Testament. Surprisingly, this information relates directly to our study of his actions in the trial of Jesus.

In order to understand Pilate's conduct in the trial, we naturally

begin with the information supplied in the Gospels. In their accounts of Jesus' death the Gospels give a poor picture of Roman
administrative practice, but they paint a vivid portrait of the individual who filled the procurator's office at the time. The Bible is a
book about people, not about governments and laws, and this fact
is illustrated in the records of the Roman proceedings. The Gospels
are far more interested in Pilate's character than in the judicial principles by which the trial was conducted.[1] In fact, the description of
Pilate is one of the few points at which the Gospel records all agree.

Pilate is presented in the Gospels as weak and vacillating, a man
caught between his personal conviction that Jesus is innocent and
his pathetic desire to appease the Jews. He recognizes that the
charges against Jesus are fraudulent and he wants to release him,[2]
but his judgment is swayed by the insistence of the officials and the
angry mob, who vehemently demand Jesus' execution.[3] Finally,
Pilate can resist no longer. He is coerced—even frightened—into
giving in to the Jews.[4]

So the Gospels explain the execution of Jesus not from judicial
processes but from human frailty; not by Pilate's convictions but by
his weakness. He crucified a man whom he believed guiltless because
he lacked the courage to do otherwise. This description has been so
elaborately detailed that it is common to portray Pilate as the very
model of cowardice. Yet although he is despised for his weakness,
his guilt in Jesus' death is considered to be only passive; the Jews
were actually responsible for the crucifixion.

Since the Gospels make Pilate's personality and character central
in their explanation of the trial, it would be very helpful to have
further information on this subject from other sources. Here we are
unusually fortunate. In his histories, Josephus gives more attention to
Pilate than to any other governor.[5] He records three major events
which occurred during Pilate's rule, all of which provide an excellent basis for judging Pilate's character.

The first episode concerns the introduction of Roman insignia
into Jerusalem.[6] From his headquarters in Caesarea, Pilate dispatched
part of his troops to Jerusalem so that they could establish winter
quarters in the city. The military standards carried at the head of

the column bore busts of Caesar. This act created an uproar among the Jews, because their laws prohibited the admission of any pagan religious objects into Jerusalem, so a large group of Jews hurried to Caesarea and demanded that Pilate remove the ensigns. Despite their pleas Pilate adamantly refused, and as a result the Jews prostrated themselves on the ground for several days. Finally, from his tribunal in the market-place, Pilate called the protesting Jews before him and encircled them with his soldiers, threatening to kill them all if they did not accept the images. But the Jews threw themselves to the ground and exposed their necks to the swords, crying that death was preferable to sacrilege. Pilate was so surprised at the extent of their superstition that he stopped short of a wholesale slaughter and ordered the standards withdrawn.

In the second incident we are told that Pilate raised a disturbance among the Jews by confiscating the money in the sacred treasury (*corban*) for the building of aqueducts to bring water to Jerusalem. The populace was enraged by this use of sacred funds and when Pilate came to Jerusalem a large crowd gathered and launched a stormy protest. However, the governor had been forewarned and had mixed his own soldiers in civilian clothes among the crowd, arming them with clubs and daggers. When he was unable to disperse the mob, he gave the signal and the soldiers fell on the crowd with such brutality that a good many Jews were killed. The people were quickly brought into submission and the resistance ceased.

The last incident described by Josephus is the episode of the Samaritans. Josephus states that a rebel leader took a group of his countrymen to Mount Gerizim, the sacred mountain of Samaria, promising to reveal a secret cache of sacred vessels which had been hidden there by Moses. The people brought arms and formed a large crowd at the foot of the mountain. At this point Pilate intervened and forcefully prevented their ascent. His horsemen and foot soldiers blocked the road and also attacked a nearby village. Some of the Samaritans were killed in the fighting; others were taken captive and then slain by Pilate's order. As a result of this affair, the Samaritan senate sent an embassy to Vitellius, the legate of Syria, accusing Pilate of murder and claiming that the gathering had been peaceful and nonpolitical. Vitellius appointed an emissary to take charge of the government in Judaea, then he ordered Pilate to Rome to answer charges before the emperor. This marked the end of Pilate's procuratorship.

This completes Josephus' record of Pilate, but an additional story and some specific descriptions of Pilate are supplied by Philo. The material comes from a letter, quoted by Philo, which was sent from Agrippa I (grandson of Herod the Great) to the Roman emperor Caligula.[7] According to Agrippa, Pilate had realized from the earlier difficulty over the Roman standards that the Jews detested the presence of any pagan symbols in Jerusalem. Nevertheless, at a later date he attempted to introduce votive shields into Herod's palace in the city. Agrippa claims that Pilate made this move not because of any desire to honor the emperor Tiberius, but only to anger the Jews. Although no pagan figures were represented on these shields, they did bear the emperor's name and the Jews reacted violently against them. In company with four sons of Herod who were then in Jerusalem for a feast, a Jewish delegation went to Pilate and insisted that the shields be removed. Pilate ignored all their demands. So the most distinguished citizens of the country petitioned the emperor and asked that he order the removal himself. Since Tiberius realized that Pilate's act was merely a needless display of power, he ordered Pilate to remove the shields at once and to return them to the temple of Augustus in Caesarea.

So much for the specific incidents recorded of Pilate's procuratorship. Despite his account of Pilate's excesses, Josephus does not condemn his rule generally. This is because Josephus was writing for a Gentile audience and he wanted to avoid displaying Roman justice in any more damaging light than necessary. But Agrippa's letter is far more explicit: it launches into a scathing description of Pilate and his administration. Agrippa describes Pilate as "unbending and recklessly hard." He portrays Pilate's rule as one of corruption, violence, robberies, ill-treatment of the people, grievances, continuous executions of native Jews without even the form of a trial, and other barbarisms against the people whom he had been sent to govern. In an empire which often suffered from the incompetence of provincial officials, Agrippa's description of Pilate is an unusually graphic description of continuous brutality and oppression.

The incidents and the testimony just reviewed obviously have direct relevance for the study of Jesus' trial. They unite in depicting a man who was *utterly unlike the governor described in the Gospels.*

All the evidence from Josephus and Philo shows that Pilate was determined to rule as he saw fit. He did not show the least concern, much less dread, over Jewish public opinion. It would be almost impossible to find any figure *less* likely to conduct himself at Jesus' trial in the manner described in the Gospels. Pilate apparently went out of his way to harass the Jews and then to crush their resistance violently. He repeatedly used force to obtain his ends and made no effort to reach even a reasonable compromise with the Jews and their officials.

In introducing the standards into Jerusalem Pilate evidently did what no procurator had ever attempted. This action was no innocent mistake; Pilate was undoubtedly familiar with the local customs and with the patterns established by his predecessors. Also, the aftermath dispels any suggestion of an accident. When confronted in Caesarea, Pilate stubbornly refused to change the orders and even threatened the lives of those who pleaded with him. He eventually removed the standards only because that course seemed preferable to a mass execution. Later he again introduced pagan symbols into Jerusalem, and this time—despite another outcry—he did not relent until he received direct orders from the emperor. In these instances Pilate was not in the least intimidated by the hostility of a crowd or by the insistence of the Jewish officials.

The same is true in the dispute over the aqueducts. In this case, a large mob confronted Pilate, calling out insults and threats against his person. Again this popular resistance had no effect on the governor, except to strengthen his resolve. He ordered his soldiers to attack the Jews and the disturbance was quickly ended. It must have been a common occurrence for a provincial governor to hear the jibes of an angry mob, particularly in a country like Judaea. In Pilate's case, such hostility seems to have produced the opposite of its desired effect. The incident of the Samaritans gives another illustration of the governor's determination to stamp out all resistance. It is noteworthy that this event occurred at the end of Pilate's rule; he never modified the iron-fisted policies which Agrippa described so well.[8]

Pilate's conduct in one incident is not final proof of what he might do in another. But when his actions in four instances of mob pressure and official resistance are almost identical, they provide a convincing picture of his character under such conditions. In Pilate's case, these actions reflect a consistent political policy. Agrippa's letter indicates that these incidents are only a few samples of Pilate's uncompromising methods. Interestingly, the only Gospel reference to Pilate's activities aside from Jesus' trial also describes his violent suppression of resistance. In Luke 13:1 some people in a crowd around Jesus inform him of ". . . the Galileans whose blood Pilate had mingled with their sacrifices." We have no other details, but the words undoubtedly refer to Pilate's slaughter of some Galilean Jews who had been engaged in a politically harmless activity. This is shown by the fact that Jesus discusses the incident as an example of the way in which innocent people often suffer as much as those who are guilty.

In the face of this persistent testimony, how can we account for Pilate's strange conduct in Jesus' trial? Why did this man who had consistently been arbitrary and heavy-handed suddenly become, in Jesus' prosecution, meekly submissive to the will of his subjects?

Two alternatives present themselves. We can argue that these contradictions in our sources reflect deep and unexplained contradictions in the man himself. Perhaps, just at the time of Jesus' trial, Pilate had undergone some temporary change of character which made him vulnerable to the Jewish demands. The other alternative is that one or the other of our two descriptions of Pilate is distorted. It is difficult to find any reason why the evidence supplied by Josephus or Philo should have been seriously inaccurate, but on the other hand, there is persuasive evidence that the Gospels have been influenced by the desire to create a new image of the governor. The differences between the two Pilates—the man described as "violent, unbending and recklessly hard," and the badgered figure we find in the Gospels—do not reflect differences within the man. They reflect the very special interests of the Gospel writers. In describing the trial and death of Jesus, the Gospel writers were motivated by both spiritual and practical aims. These aims required the description of a governor who was freely manipulated by the opponents of Jesus and who gave in to these opponents in spite of his convictions. What those aims were, and how they affected the Gospel representations of Pilate, will become clear when we reconstruct the trial events themselves.

3

THE EARLIEST RECORDS
OF JESUS' DEATH

". . . these are written that you may believe . . ."

John 20:31

When we lay out the available sources for the study of Jesus' death, we are confronted by an odd mixture of plenty and want.

In a sense we are unusually fortunate to have such full records on which to draw. We have not one but four separate and distinct accounts of Jesus' trial and execution, all written relatively soon after the events themselves. Very few ancient events of importance are recorded in as many primitive documents. From these four accounts we obtain a variety of details and several differing viewpoints which can enrich our grasp of what took place. Yet from another standpoint these records seem painfully scanty and inadequate. For one thing, our only records of Jesus' death are those provided us by the Christian Church. There is no testimony from the side of the Jewish authorities, none from the Romans, either in Judaea or elsewhere, and none from any "interested bystanders" who might have provided us a somewhat more objective account than we could reasonably expect from those whose faith was wrapped up in these events.

Also, although each of these four Gospels has its own particular outlook, they all reflect the common faith of the early Church. Their multiplicity is to some degree an illusion; all four are the "official" records of the early Christian community, and they have been shaped by the doctrinal beliefs and the practical needs of the first Christians. The value of having four records of these ancient events instead of one is also diluted by the fact that these four often disagree with one another even at critical points. For that reason, in using these sources we cannot simply combine their testimony to create one unified account. We often have to pick and choose, to compare and contrast them and to find solid reasons for preferring one record over another.

On what grounds are we to make such judgments? How are we to determine which account is superior to another at a given point? Further, how could these numerous and significant differences have developed in the first place? If the Gospels all reflect the beliefs of the early Christians, one might expect them to be identical or almost so. How was it possible for such varied interpretations of these crucial events to arise in the earliest days of the Church? These questions are fundamental to a serious appraisal of the trial and death of Jesus. It is impossible to understand the final days of Jesus without a thorough grasp of the origin and nature of our four Gospel stories. Our task in the present chapter is two-fold: to see how the earliest stories of Jesus' arrest, trial and crucifixion developed in the early Church, and to evaluate the reliability of these stories as historical records. We begin by describing the very special and distinctive nature of these climactic stories, which differ from all other portions of the Gospel narratives.

.   .   .   .   .

If we read the Gospels with care, we soon observe a fact which has had a tremendous impact on New Testament study in the twentieth century. We begin to notice that much of the Gospel material about Jesus is made up of short units of material which have no special connection to what goes just before or after them. These small units are somewhat like beads on a string and could be restrung in an entirely different order without adversely affecting their value or our picture of Jesus. In the Synoptic Gospels, particularly in Mark, this phenomenon is very noticeable, until we come to the record of Jesus' last days in Jerusalem.

It was this fact which, in the early years of this century, gave rise to a new method of New Testament study. This method is called "form criticism," or, more correctly, "form analysis" (German formgeschichte).[1] One goal of this study has been to explain why and how the Gospels came to be composed largely of these individual units of material, rather than more connected, sequential accounts of Jesus' career such as we might find in a modern biography.

To answer these questions, a small group of European critics began by emphasizing that the Gospel material had circulated for many years by word of mouth before it was set down in writing. Among both Jews and Gentiles in the first century A.D. there was a strong tradition of oral instruction, because of the inconvenience and expense of producing literary works. In Jesus' time religious beliefs, folk tales, and other traditions were commonly passed from one generation to another by speech rather than by the written word. This was also true of the early Christian message. It began as a spontaneous outburst of faith which was spread by face-to-face witnessing, not by the creation of lengthy written reports.

In proclaiming the good news about Jesus the earliest Christians did not, of course, give a full and connected account of his life, with complete details about his teachings, miracles and personal movements every time they talked about him. A systematic biography of Jesus was not one of the major needs of the early Church. Instead, Christians based their preaching on *individual incidents* from Jesus' career, in order to communicate specific information about his deity or his message. Therefore, as Christians scattered throughout the Mediterranean world, it was inevitable that their personal testimonials about Jesus easily became disconnected from any long chronological account of his ministry.

In the same way, the original *setting* of a parable or miracle or particular incident about Jesus was often quickly forgotten. For preaching purposes it made little difference whether a certain miraculous healing by Jesus had been performed in Capernaum or Bethsaida, or whether this act had occurred just before or just after a certain saying of Jesus in a nearby town. What mattered was *what* Jesus had said or done, not where or when. For this reason the stories of Jesus tended to become separated from their original context as well as from their original order. That is why we must not assume, when reading any Gospel, that it gives us a careful chronological or topographical account of Jesus' career.

It is also obvious that only a small percentage of Jesus' words and deeds throughout his career have been retained in our Gospels. Why are certain things included in these records and not others? What was the basis of selection? According to form critics the *needs* of the early Church determined which remembrances of Jesus were to survive in the Christian memory. Therefore, to understand the significance of any individual unit of Gospel material we must recover the life-situation in which it was used by the early disciples.

Further, according to form-critical theory, as these individual stories about Jesus were told and retold in the early Church they tended to harden into certain verbal patterns or "forms." Through constant repetition the oral remembrances of the first Christians began to assume characteristic verbal shapes. For example, it was natural for all stories about Jesus' miraculous works to be retold in the same general linguistic style. Form critics do not agree on the number or the types of verbal "forms" which can be discovered in our Gospels. But their common presumption is that most of the Gospel material had evolved into rather fixed patterns before it was set down in writing—patterns which made it easier for the early Christians to remember and relate this material.

These form-critical judgments have certainly not gained universal acceptance.[2] Form critics base their theories on questionable premises about the life and character of the early Church. But we have reviewed these theories because at one particular point form critics have had a decisive influence on New Testament study. They have shown beyond doubt that the stories of Jesus' last days, including his trial and death, provide *a marked contrast to the rest of the Gospel material*. Instead of being composed of individual, unrelated units, without careful reference to time and place, the narratives of Jesus' suffering and death present a connected chronological sequence.[3] In this story, commonly called the "passion (i.e., suffering) narrative," nearly all the units have a close and logical interrelation. As a result, we can follow Jesus' movements almost step-by-step in the events preceding the crucifixion and resurrection, unlike any other stage of his career.

The reason for the distinctive character of the passion narrative is obvious: *this was the one part of the Gospel material which was always related as a connected whole*. The passion story was normally told as one unit; it does not consist of individual "beads" which could be arranged in a different order. In Martin Dibelius' words, the passion story is ". . . the only piece of Gospel tradition which in early times gave events in their larger connection."[4]

Why was this so? It was because this continuous narrative represented the heart of the Christian message. The last supper, the arrest and trial, the crucifixion and resurrection were not viewed as isolated stories but as a unified drama which conveyed the message of redemption.[5] From its beginnings, Christianity was founded not on Jesus' teachings, nor on his miracles; it was founded on his death and resurrection. Whatever else Christians might tell about Jesus, the heart of their proclamation was the good news of salvation which had come through Jesus' death on the cross and his rising from the dead.[6] Therefore, the story of his suffering and death was related *in toto* as an explanation of God's divine plan.[7] In a slightly different sense, a connected passion story was needed in order to show that the otherwise tragic events of the arrest, trial and crucifixion were only part of a larger, victorious scheme of events.[8] The circumstances of Jesus' death offered an opportunity for opponents to heap scorn on the Church. In reply, the unified passion story depicted these events as the providential workings of God, rather than as a human tragedy.

This tendency had a profound effect: it caused the passion story to reach a relatively fixed form at an early date. Because of its centrality in the Christian message, this part of the tradition about Jesus attained a definite shape in the early Church before any other Gospel material. On matters of such importance it was inevitable that a substantial agreement should prevail among all Christians. The extent of this agreement is shown by the unusually close harmony among our Gospels when they come to the passion events. In describing the earlier stages of Jesus' ministry, our four Gospels give us accounts which often differ radically. John's story is particularly distinctive; only a small portion of the material found in the first three Gospels is present in John, and vice-versa. Even Matthew, Mark and Luke vary widely in many portions. But when we come to the last days of Jesus' life, we suddenly find much greater unanimity in our Gospels.[9] This, of course, is no accident: it is obvious that our Evangelists were dealing with a tradition which had coalesced into a fairly standard shape before it came into their hands.

The unusual harmony of our four Gospels in the passion events is clearly illustrated by their close similarity of length in this section. Matthew's narrative has 233 lines, Mark's 201, Luke's 199, and John's 224. Their average is 214 lines, and no Gospel varies over ten percent from this average.[10] Nothing approaching this equality can be found in any other portion of the Gospels. As we will see, this unusual harmony between the Gospels has profound implications for the study of Jesus' trial and death.

·   ·   ·   ·   ·

We are now at a point at which we can begin to understand the agreements and disagreements in our Gospel accounts of Jesus' trial and death.

As we have just seen, a coherent oral account of Jesus' passion developed in the early Church well before our Gospels were written. We can call this pre-Gospel period the "oral stage" of the passion narrative. As the Church spread rapidly throughout the Gentile world, variations began to appear in this oral story. Individual Christian communities did not share *identical* accounts of Jesus' suffering and death, because each Christian missionary cast the story in a somewhat different light, just as ministers do today when they relate these events. But all the early oral versions followed a common pattern which was known to Christians everywhere.

For this reason, when the first written accounts of the passion were produced, their authors were in large measure *editors*. These authors accumulated and wove together the stories which were circulating orally in the Church. But each writer also made his distinctive contributions to his account. Our Evangelists were not simply clerks who recorded the preaching of others; each played a personal creative role in the composition of his Gospel. He picked and chose his material; he linked the various traditions by editorial insertions; and, equally important, he often added his personal insights and interpretation to the material with which he worked. As a result, each Gospel presents the passion narrative in the light of the Evangelist's personal convictions and ideals.

The following illustration will help to make this historical process clear.

Let us suppose that for some ten years—about A.D. 30–40—the early Church was concentrated primarily in Palestine. Then in the next ten years—A.D. 40–50—strong Christian communities developed at Antioch in Syria, Ephesus in Asia Minor, Athens in Greece, Alexandria in Egypt, and Rome. Let us suppose also that these cities were the pivotal points from which the Gospel spread among Gentiles.

These cities would have shared the common early account of Jesus' suffering and death which had circulated in Palestine, which we can label PN (passion narrative). The Church in each city would also have had its own *special* traditions or interpretations concerning Jesus' last days, traditions which the Church had received from its founding preacher or some visiting apostle. These individual local traditions could be designated by the first letter of each city (in the order listed above): A_1, E, A_2, A_3 and R. Thus, by about A.D. 50, five slightly varying versions of the passion events would be in circulation in these areas. The Antiochene narrative would consist of PN + A_1; the Ephesian would be PN + E, and so on.

We can feel confident that Mark was the earliest of our four

Gospels to be written.[11] If we accept the common view that the Gospel according to Mark was composed in Rome about A.D. 70, our presumption would be that Mark's passion story gives us principally PN + R: the common early narrative plus the special traditions known in Rome. Further, an early Christian tradition says that Mark's Gospel was based largely on the preaching of Simon Peter.[12] If so, Peter's personal reminiscences would certainly be reflected in Mark's passion story, and we gain the formula, Mark = PN + R + P.[13] Finally, Mark undoubtedly added his own editorial links and interpretations, which we can call Mk. So the complete "formula" for Mark's account of the passion narrative would be Mark = PN + R + P + Mk.

Obviously, the Gospels were not composed as mechanistically as this. But this is a useful example of how our earliest Gospel account of Jesus' passion might have been put together about A.D. 70 in Rome. The central point is that Mark's passion narrative, like our other three, is made up of the primitive elements in the passion story, plus certain traditions and insights which developed at a later date, plus Mark's own literary work.[14]

This fact raises a tantalizing question. Is it possible, by analyzing the Gospels carefully, to recover the primitive passion narrative *as it was told in its earliest oral stage before it was shaped by later traditions and by the editorial work of our Evangelists?*

For the study of Jesus' trial, this recovery would naturally have great importance. Despite their general similarity, our four accounts of the trial differ significantly; that is the main reason why our grasp of the events has always been so confused. We must assume that these differences result from the divergent *later traditions* which developed gradually, and from the personal contributions of each Gospel writer. Therefore, it would be of tremendous value if we could reconstruct the trial as it was described in the earliest oral narrative, before these later additions developed around it. Almost certainly the earliest oral stage of the passion story represents a more authentic and unadulterated account of the events than that which we find in our written Gospels. We know that as the years passed the Christian traditions about Jesus' death were greatly influenced by certain doctrinal and apologetic interests, which will be discussed in a later chapter. Therefore, the closer we can get to uncovering the early *oral* reports about Jesus' trial and execution, the closer we would seem to be to the true historical facts, before those facts became overladen with less trustworthy traditions.

For these reasons, form critics have shown great interest in attempting to reconstruct the early oral passion narrative on which our four Gospels are based. In order to understand the problems involved in this attempt, it will be very helpful to the reader if he goes to one of the Gospels—preferably Mark (14:1–15:47)—and reads the passion narrative in full. For convenience Mark's passion narrative is printed in Appendix I at the end of the book; it should be read at this point and referred to in the succeeding discussion. Below is an outline of the passion events as they are presented in our first three Gospels. (Incidents with direct bearing on Jesus' trial have been capitalized.)

The Passion Narrative in Matthew, Mark and Luke:

1. THE PLOT AGAINST JESUS' LIFE
2. Jesus' anointing by a woman in nearby Bethany[a]
3. THE BETRAYAL BY JUDAS ISCARIOT
4. The preparation and eating of the last supper
5. The brief scene at the Mount of Olives[b]
6. Jesus' anxiety in the Garden of Gethsemane
7. JESUS' ARREST
8. THE JEWISH PROCEEDINGS AGAINST JESUS
9. Peter's denial of Jesus
10. THE ROMAN PROCEEDINGS AGAINST JESUS
11. The scourging by the soldiers[c]
12. The crucifixion[d]

[a] Omitted by Luke.
[b] Omitted by Luke, although he includes some of this material in his description of the last supper.
[c] In Luke this brief incident is placed in the midst of the Roman proceedings, when Jesus is questioned by Herod Antipas.
[d] Whether the resurrection is also included in the passion narrative is only a question of terminology. It is certain that the telling of the passion events was always climaxed by the story of the resurrection.

The narrative in John is very similar. After a lengthy account of the last meal—which is described in very different terms in this Gospel—John relates the same sequence of events given in the other Gospels: the arrest, the Jewish proceedings, Peter's denial, the Roman proceedings, the scourging and the crucifixion. Compared with all the earlier sections of the Gospels, the agreement in the passion story between John and the other Gospels is extremely close.

According to form critics, which elements in this narrative are the more primitive and authentic, and which resulted from later traditions? [15] It will be very instructive, particularly for those who are unfamiliar with New Testament research, to note briefly the conclusions of some of the major form critics concerning the evolution of this narrative.

The most famous name in New Testament study in this century is that of Rudolf Bultmann. Bultmann has exerted a powerful influence not only on the analysis of the New Testament, particularly the Gospels, but on Christian theology as well. His was one of the key voices in the development of form criticism as a method of Gospel study. According to Bultmann,[16] the early oral passion narrative was a quite brief account which presented only the bare essentials of Jesus' suffering and death. This account began with the arrest of Jesus, then told of a meeting before the Jewish officials, the condemnation by Pilate, Jesus' removal to Golgotha, and the crucifixion. In Bultmann's view, the following elements were added in later years: the stories connected with Simon Peter, the Lord's supper, Jesus' anointing at Bethany, the Gethsemane scene, the formal trial of Jesus before the Sanhedrin, the mockings to which Jesus was subjected, the women at the cross, and the burial.

Another major spokesman for the form-critical method was Martin Dibelius. Dibelius' analysis of the early passion story was closely similar to Bultmann's, except that Dibelius allowed for the inclusion of more units in the early oral stage. Dibelius argued that Mark's most important additions to the earliest narrative were: the anointing at Bethany, the preparation of the last meal, some elements in the Gethsemane story, the trial of Jesus before the Sanhedrin, and the story about the empty tomb.[17] In the same year that Dibelius' major work appeared, K. L. Schmidt also produced one of the most influential of the early form–critical studies, which, however, did not include a detailed analysis of the passion narrative; Schmidt was content to observe that Mark's account represented an expansion of the earlier oral story.[18]

Although it was German scholars who pioneered form–critical study, English and American scholars have made important contributions as well. A leading interpreter of form criticism in England, Vincent Taylor, has given special attention to the passion narrative and to the additions which our earliest written Gospel made to it. Taylor agrees that Mark's account is based on a shorter, simpler story to which Mark added various units of later tradition. In Taylor's opinion, these later additions include: Jesus' anointing at Bethany, the Gethsemane scene, the trial before the Jewish Sanhedrin, Peter's denial, and the soldiers' mockery of Jesus. Unlike most critics who distinguish between the earlier and later stages of the passion story, Taylor defends the historical value of some of the later insertions.[19]

Among American scholars, the name of F. C. Grant is most prominent in form–critical research. According to Grant, the very earliest narrative consisted of the following: the plot against Jesus, Judas' betrayal, parts of the last supper story, the arrest, the trial before Pilate, and the crucifixion. The later additions include the Passover preparation, the Gethsemane scene, Peter's denial of Jesus, Jesus' trial before the Sanhedrin, and the mocking by the soldiers.[20]

These examples illustrate the attempt to recreate the story of Jesus' last days as it was told before its elaboration and expansion in our Gospels. No one today can adequately evaluate the Gospels without taking into account these judgments of the form critics. But what specific value do their conclusions have for our problem of interpreting Jesus' trial and execution?

.   .   .   .   .

Three significant results emerge from form–critical study for the study of Jesus' trial.

First, as we have already indicated, a coherent verbal record of the trial was one of the first portions of the Gospel to take shape. For this reason, we can feel confident that the Gospel stories of Jesus' trial and death are based on a reliable historical tradition which goes back to the very earliest recollections of the Church. Much of the Gospel material has been under critical bombardment in the last century. In fact, some critics have argued that we can now recover only the barest outlines of Jesus' career, because of the influence of Christian doctrine on the Gospel records of his life. If this negative opinion applied also to the stories of Jesus' last days, it would raise serious doubts about our hopes of recovering the truth about those days. But while form critics are often considered nihilistic in their evaluation of the Gospel material, their work actually tends to *increase* our faith in our Gospel records of Jesus' trial and death. It is highly probable that there is a more reliable fund of information here than in any other part of the Gospels. While most Christians will continue to regard all the Gospel material as completely trustworthy, the open-minded student of today is bound to have reservations about large portions of this material. To do otherwise is simply to close one's eyes to the literary and historical problems which exist in our Gospels. But when we come to the passion narrative, we can have a strong conviction that this narrative rests on solid historical ground. Hardly any conclusion could be more important for the study of Jesus' execution.

Second, however, modern analysis of the passion story makes it clear that we cannot simply take the reliability of our Gospel records for granted. Our Gospels give us this narrative in a highly developed and secondary form. Although they are based on a primitive historical core, extensive later material has been added, either from developing traditions or from the Evangelists' own hands. Therefore, *each part of the Gospel narratives must be evaluated on its own merits*. We must subject the four Gospels to the most careful comparisons, to determine which elements in them reflect later, secondary traditions and which seem to reflect the most primitive stage of development. No matter how deep our respect for the Gospels, we cannot simply decide to accept them at face value.

Such an approach is shattered by the records themselves. Our Gospels contain irreconcilable differences in reporting Jesus' trial and they cannot simply be woven together without doing violence to one or more of them. Our problem is to decide, by literary and historical analysis, which parts of the story are the most accurate and reliable and which parts are most suspect. Only then can we proceed to firm judgments about what actually happened in Jerusalem.

The third important point from our brief survey of form–critical analysis is even more concrete. In the representative form–critical works cited above, there is unanimous agreement that the story of Jesus' trial before the Sanhedrin is a secondary addition which was not part of the primitive passion story. We shall return in the succeeding chapters to the significance of this judgment.

. . . . .

Despite these useful results we ought to observe some cautions about the form–critical attempts to recover the oral, pre-Markan stories of Jesus' trial.

Too many commentators assume that if we can remove Mark's own editorial additions we will automatically uncover a much more reliable account of the trial than Mark gives us. This judgment is based on a faulty conception of the oral stage of the passion tradition. This oral stage covered four decades before the Gospel of Mark appeared. During this time the passion narrative was in a constant state of development. Even if we could separate Mark's personal editorial additions from the earlier sources which he used—a very delicate task—we would still be faced with material which had undergone a lengthy evolution before Mark made use of it.[21] In short, "pre-Markan" does not automatically mean "reliable and accurate." [22]

Second, no matter how great our ingenuity we cannot distinguish confidently between (1) the earliest Palestinian version of Jesus' trial and death (2) the later *oral* traditions which grew up around this version and (3) the editorial changes made by Mark and the other Evangelists.[23] If we could divide all our Gospel material into those neat categories, most of our problems would be solved; unfortunately, this is impossible. The best we can hope for is to explain generally why certain units in the Gospels seem to go back to the more primitive stages of the passion narrative and why others seem to reflect later and less reliable traditions. That is what we shall try to do in the coming chapters. Wherever we can draw this thin line we are one step closer to reconstructing what actually happened to Jesus.

In summary, we should visualize the following historical process when evaluating our Gospel records of Jesus' trial and death:

(1) A rather simple connected account of Jesus' last days, including a brief description of his arrest and trial, took shape rapidly in the early Palestinian Church. However, even in these earliest days the narrative was in a continual state of development; there was never an inflexible Christian record of Jesus' death. The passion story was perpetually evolving as an expression of the Church's faith.

(2) Therefore, as the Church spread into the Gentile world Christian missionaries proclaimed slightly differing versions of the passion events. The basic outline remained constant, but the individual units varied. By the latter half of the first century, there was substantial diversity here and there in describing the trial and death of Jesus. This diversity is clearly reflected in our four written Gospels. The development of the passion stories was deeply influenced by the theological and apologetic needs of the early Church.

(3) The first written accounts of the trial probably appeared sometime after A.D. 50. It is possible that Mark was the first literary record of this story, but this seems unlikely since some forty years had passed between Jesus' death and the writing of this Gospel. We have recovered no versions of the passion story earlier than Mark's account, so the question cannot be answered.[24]

(4) The oral development of the passion narrative did not end when Mark's Gospel was written; it contains one version of the events, but other traditions—oral and probably written—continued to circulate in the Church. In fact, the oral interpretation of the passion events continued long after all four of our Gospels had appeared. What our Gospels provide us is four versions of Jesus'

death as it was described in different areas of the Church between about A.D. 70 and A.D. 100.

Our task is now one of the most interesting and challenging in the whole field of New Testament study: to analyze these four varied descriptions and to piece together a single authentic account of Jesus' arrest, trial and death.

4

THE TRIAL IN MARK AND
MATTHEW

". . . and they all condemned him . . ."
Mark 14:64

If we were forced to rely on only one Gospel, our chances of reconstructing the circumstances of the death of Jesus would be greatly diminished; with four, our prospects are considerably improved. But this multiplicity of sources is a mixed blessing. As we noted in the previous chapter, these accounts disagree with one another repeatedly, and at every step of the way we have to establish sound reasons for preferring one version over another.

The beginning point in making these judgments is to understand the literary relationship between these four books. Why are these writings so similar and yet so different? Why do they sometimes use almost identical language, and at other times vary widely in their basic outlook? Over the past two hundred years a tremendous expenditure of scholarly energy has been invested in answering these questions. The results of this exhaustive inquiry, which is still being conducted today, cannot be recounted here in detail. But a few fundamental conclusions, which represent a consensus of modern Biblical scholarship, must be kept in mind if we want to understand both the similarities and the differences in our four versions of Jesus' last days. The following points will serve as a brief guideline to the literary relationship of our four Gospels.

1) The first three Gospels show considerable similarity in their material, in their arrangement, and even in their wording, much of which is almost identical. By comparison, the fourth Gospel is quite distinctive and its portrait of Jesus is notably different from the others. For this reason, the first three Gospels are commonly grouped together and are called the *Synoptic* Gospels—from a Greek word meaning "from the same viewpoint."

2) The similarities between the Synoptic Gospels are much closer than can be explained by their common subject matter. It is obvious that there is some close literary relationship between them. By careful analyses, we can assert with confidence that the earliest of these Gospels was Mark, and that both Matthew and Luke used Mark as a source in composing their Gospels.[1] This fact explains the fundamental similarity between these three Gospels. Mark may cautiously be dated about A.D. 70 and, again as we have seen, many scholars believe it was written in Rome. Matthew and Luke were probably written about A.D. 80–90; their place of origin is less certain.

3) Although both Matthew and Luke used Mark in composing their Gospels, they used it in very different ways. For Matthew, Mark was obviously the major source; Matthew could even be called an expanded edition of Mark. Matthew's expansions consist mainly of additional examples of Jesus' teachings which are inserted in large blocks throughout this Gospel. On the other hand, Luke is much more independent of Mark. In Luke there is much less of Mark's material and this material has been freely rearranged. Some scholars believe that Luke already existed as a complete Gospel *before* the Markan material was inserted into it. Although most scholars reject this belief,[2] this theory does point up Luke's considerable independence of Mark in outline and content.

4) Matthew and Luke also share much material in common

which is not found in Mark. This means either that one of these Gospels borrowed this material from the other, or that both Gospels drew from *another* source just as they had drawn from Mark. The latter alternative is probably correct. This other source has never been recovered, but for convenience it is labelled "*Q*," from the German word *Quelle*, meaning "source." Until such a document is actually recovered its existence is only problematical. If it did exist it was composed primarily of Jesus' teachings and therefore is sometimes called the "Sayings Source." It is possible *Q* was not a single document at all but simply a group of early traditions which were used by both Matthew and Luke. But whatever form *Q* took, its existence must be affirmed until some better explanation can be found for the close parallels in Matthew and Luke which are not from Mark.[3] Therefore, we can theorize that two major sources, Mark and *Q*, are the chief documents which went into the make-up of our first three Gospels. This theory is called the "two-document hypothesis" of Synoptic relations, and it is accepted by the majority of New Testament scholars today, although sometimes with reservations.

5) However, Matthew and Luke individually contain a good bit of material which is not found in any other Gospel. This "private" material includes some of the most important sections in each of these Gospels. For that reason, it is a mistake to think of Mark and *Q* as the only sources of the Synoptic Gospels. It is obvious that Matthew and Luke drew on other traditions as well—traditions which may well have been just as valuable and authentic as those found in Mark and *Q*.

6) The Gospel of John shows several points of similarity with the first three Gospels, just enough to raise the question whether there is any literary relationship between John and these Gospels. We will return to this subject when we come to John's account of the execution of Jesus in Chapter 6.

These judgments of Biblical scholarship have a direct bearing on our investigation into the death of Jesus. For example, we will find that Mark and Matthew are strikingly similar in their accounts of Jesus' trial and execution, while Luke contains important differences. As we would expect, John gives the most distinctive version of all.

Regrettably, many interpretations of Jesus' death fail because they do not deal seriously with the disagreements in our four sources. This error is common among the most conservative scholars, who hold that all four accounts must be equally correct since all are equally inspired. By this view, the supposed disagreements between the Gospels are only the result of our faulty human understanding. But however deep our reverence for these books, we cannot solve the problems of Jesus' execution by ignoring the obvious and important conflicts between them. We must take seriously the fact that they are disjointed and somewhat unharmonious accounts of Jesus' death. Our problem is to draw from these four accounts a single, trustworthy record of the events. We begin this effort with the story of Jesus' death as it is told in our earliest Gospel, Mark.

.   .   .   .   .

According to Mark (and the other Synoptics), Jesus did not bring his ministry to Jerusalem until the last few days of his life. He had concentrated his work in his homeland of Galilee and came to the capital only at the climax of his brief public career. In Chapter 9 we will survey his activities during these final days and their bearing on his death. For the present we are concerned only with Mark's version of Jesus' arrest and trial.

In Mark's account the final drama of Jesus' career begins two days before the annual Passover celebration. The chief priests and scribes gather together and make plans to arrest Jesus secretly and to kill him. No explanation is given of their motives; they merely agree not to carry out their plan during the feast, because they fear a reaction from the crowds gathered for this occasion (14:1–2).

Mark here describes Jesus' anointing by a woman in nearby Bethany while he and his disciples shared a meal at the home of Simon the Leper. Then he resumes his story of the passion events by relating the betrayal by Judas Iscariot. Mark's description of this dark episode is brief and clear: Judas, one of the inner circle of

twelve disciples, seeks out the chief priests for the purpose of helping them in their plot to dispose of Jesus. The priests readily take
advantage of this unexpected aid, and promise to give Judas money
in return. So Judas begins to look for an opportunity when he can
deliver Jesus into their hands. Mark then relates the series of events
leading up to Jesus' arrest: the preparation of the last supper (14:12–
26a), the brief scene on the Mount of Olives (14:26b–31) and the
prayer in Gethsemane (14:32–34).

Immediately after Jesus' prayer in Gethsemane, Judas Iscariot
appears in the garden, leading an armed crowd sent by the chief
priests, scribes, and elders. He singles out Jesus by means of a kiss
of greeting and the crowd seizes Jesus. A brief resistance ensues
when one of Jesus' followers cuts off the ear of the slave of the
high priest; but we hear of no further struggle. Then Jesus addresses his captors: Why have they come out armed, as if facing a
"robber" (Greek, λῃστής), since he had been teaching openly in the
temple?—but he adds, "Let the scriptures be fulfilled." At this
point his followers all flee, including an unknown young man.[4]

Jesus is then taken from the garden and led away to the high
priest. Here begins the crucial section in Mark's account. Although
it is the middle of the night, Mark claims that the whole Sanhedrin
is assembled—chief priests, scribes and elders. Peter follows Jesus
and the crowd at a distance into the court. The Jewish Council then
initiates formal legal proceedings against Jesus; they seek to find
some testimony by which to condemn him to death. But this proves
unsuccessful, for the witnesses who speak against him give false and
conflicting testimony. Then others arise and declare—falsely—that
Jesus had said he would destroy the Jewish temple and in three days
build another temple not made with hands. Again the testimony is
contradictory and proves to be of no value.

So the high priest takes personal command of the proceedings.
Despite the fact that the witnesses have lied and contradicted one
another, the high priest requires Jesus to answer their testimony.
But Jesus remains silent. So the high priest asks him, "Are you the
Christ (Messiah), the Son of the Blessed?" To this question Jesus
gives a direct and dramatic reply: "I am, and you shall see the Son

of Man sitting at the right hand of Power, and coming with the clouds of heaven." When he hears this declaration the high priest tears his mantle and cries to the assembly, "Why do we need any further witnesses? You have heard his blasphemy." The high priest then calls for their decision, and they all condemn Jesus and declare that he deserves death. Then some of the Sanhedrin members begin to spit on Jesus and to hit him and yell taunts at him.

At this point, Mark interjects the story of Peter's three-fold denial of Jesus. Then he picks up the trial narrative again. It is morning and the whole Council meets again for a "consultation." Unfortunately, Mark does not give us any information about the purpose or the events of this morning meeting. He simply states that afterward the Jewish officials bind Jesus and lead him away to Pontius Pilate.

Mark's description of the proceedings before the Roman governor leaves a great deal to be desired from a judicial point of view. Here, as with the Jewish proceedings, we want so much more from the narrative than it gives us. Obviously Mark's account is greatly condensed. We must remember that it was of no interest to any Gospel writer to elaborate in detail the legal processes of the trial. Mark says nothing whatever of any formal opening of the proceedings or of the nature of the charges brought against Jesus: the account launches abruptly into Pilate's questioning of the accused. As soon as Jesus is delivered to the governor, Pilate asks him, "Are you the king of the Jews?" Jesus gives an enigmatic reply, "You have said so." Then the chief priests begin to accuse Jesus of various crimes, which again are unspecified by Mark. Pilate asks Jesus to reply to the charges but this time Jesus gives no answer at all. The silence of Jesus throughout the trial proceedings is a prominent note in Mark's account.

Up to this point, the trial is apparently at a stalemate: the officials have brought charges and Jesus has given no rebuttal. Then comes an incident which, according to Mark, turned the proceedings against Jesus and led to his execution. It was a custom at the Passover feast, Mark says, for Pilate to release one prisoner at the request of the Jewish people. For this reason, a crowd gathers outside the place where Pilate is interrogating Jesus. Mark's language is somewhat vague, but the crowd's purpose is evidently to seek the release of *any* prisoner, in accordance with the custom. Since Pilate can see that the charges are based only on the high priests' "envy," he asks the crowd if it is Jesus whom they want released. But the chief priests encourage the crowd to seek the release of a man named Barabbas, an insurrectionist and murderer who was then in prison. Pilate then asks the crowd what should be done with Jesus, and they reply, "Crucify him." He inquires what evil Jesus has done, but they merely repeat their demand that Jesus be killed. So Pilate, to satisfy the crowd's wishes, releases Barabbas to them and delivers Jesus to be crucified. There is no formal condemnation of Jesus; Pilate simply turns him over to the soldiers who will take him to the place of execution.

So runs our earliest surviving account of Jesus' arrest and trial.

.   .   .   .   .

When we turn to Matthew's account, one fact stands out vividly: this Gospel presents a version of the events which is amazingly similar to Mark's. There is no extended passage anywhere in the Synoptics in which two Gospels agree more closely. True, Matthew has introduced a few minor changes and additions, but it is obvious that he followed Mark ". . . with a faithfulness that amounts almost to piety." [5] Matthew uses a great many of Mark's very words. Sir John Hawkins has shown that fifty-one percent of the words in Matthew's passion narrative are taken directly from Mark.[6] This is almost twice the percentage borrowed from Mark by Luke. More important, in the trial itself Matthew's pattern of events is almost identical to Mark's, whereas Luke often gives a quite different picture. Therefore, when evaluating Matthew's record we should think of it as a close copy of Mark, with only occasional minor variations. There is no reason to suppose that Matthew used any other extensive source in writing his narrative of the passion.[7]

However, the very fact that Matthew is following Mark so closely makes these minor changes all the more interesting. They are excellent illustrations of the way in which an Evangelist could reshape even a fixed, written tradition to suit his special aims. Matthew's innovations show that he had two distinct interests in his story of Jesus' prosecution: he wanted to put more emphasis on the deity of Jesus than Mark had done, and he wanted to fix the blame for Jesus' death squarely on the Jewish people and their leaders, even more than Mark. Because Matthew's account of the events is so similar to Mark's we will limit our summary of Matthew to those points where he has pointedly revised Mark's narrative.

Mark had launched his passion story by referring to the plot of the Jewish officials against Jesus. Matthew makes this notice more vivid: he dramatizes the actual scene in the court of Caiaphas in which the officials lay their plans.[8] He then follows Mark very closely in describing Judas' betrayal, the anointing at Bethany, the last supper, and the events in Gethsemane. His first significant revisions come in the arrest scene, where he considerably expands Mark's brief account: he increases the size of the mob which arrests Jesus, and he points out that Jesus actually encouraged Judas to carry out the betrayal. Mark had described the sword-play very simply; Matthew elaborates by adding a three-fold saying of Jesus. Jesus first rebukes the follower who had struck the blow, then assures him that he could call on twelve legions of angels if he wished to resist. He concludes by noting that the arrest must take place in order to fulfill the scriptures. The purpose of this addition is obvious: Matthew wants to emphasize that Jesus submitted willingly to his enemies because his arrest and crucifixion were a part of God's plan. The early Christians were anxious to show that Jesus' death was not a sign of impotence but of self-sacrifice.

Jesus is then led away from the garden. As in Mark's version, the entire Sanhedrin is assembled in the midst of the night. Matthew's story of the Sanhedrin proceedings follows the general pattern given by Mark, but Matthew is not content merely to follow Mark verbatim. In this section he suddenly assumes much more editorial freedom, although he stays within Mark's format. First, he provides a different account of the witnesses against Jesus. He states once, as does Mark, that their testimony concerning Jesus' threat to destroy the temple was false, but twice he avoids Mark's statements that the witnesses did not agree. The reason for this change is not completely clear. Matthew may have felt that these comments were unnecessary, since he had already stated that the witnesses' testimony was false; however, it is probable that Matthew omitted this statement in order to account for the continuation of the proceedings. If the testimony of the witnesses was obviously perjured and contradictory, it is hard to see how even a hostile court could have relied on it. Matthew's revision makes it easier to understand why the high priest, at the end of the witnesses' testimony, demands that Jesus answer the charges.[9] Matthew also alters the charges centering around Jesus' remarks about the temple. In Matthew's Gospel, Jesus is charged with saying "I am *able* to destroy the temple," not "I *will*" as in that of Mark. Matthew apparently wanted to avoid any suggestion that Jesus had actually issued a *threat* against the temple; he changes Jesus' words into an affirmation of his divine power.

Matthew makes several other minor but interesting changes in the exact words spoken during the Jewish proceedings.[10] However, his most important alteration comes at the end of the Sanhedrin proceedings, when he pointedly avoids saying that Jesus was "condemned" [11] by the Council. According to Matthew, Jesus is declared "worthy of death," [12] but there is no formal condemnation. There can be no doubt that Matthew's revision has some purpose. He uses Mark's exact words both before and after, but skips over this conclusion to the proceedings. Finally, Matthew makes *all* the Sanhedrin members share in the abuse heaped on Jesus, where Mark had assigned this act only to the attending guards. This is in line with Matthew's desire to intensify the guilt of the Jewish officials.

In the trial before Pilate Matthew follows Mark's story faithfully[13] but inserts two particularly significant items. Matthew reports that, in the very midst of Pilate's examination of Jesus, Pilate's wife sent word that the governor should have nothing to do with "that righteous man," because she had been deeply troubled by a dream about him that very day. This brief reference is certainly one of the most unusual in the Gospel narratives. A few verses later Matthew adds his second insertion:

> So when Pilate saw that he was gaining nothing, but rather that a riot was beginning, he took water and washed his hands before the crowd, saying, "I am innocent of this man's blood, see to it yourselves." And all the people answered, "His blood be on us and on our children!" (27:24-25)

What is the origin of these two references, which so vividly portray Pilate's belief in Jesus' innocence while at the same time magnifying the guilt of the Jews? Did they come from some special tradition known only to Matthew, or did he create these episodes himself in order to make his case more convincing? It is impossible to tell, but in either case these additions show how easily the details of the passion story could be influenced by the particular aims of the early Church and the Gospel writers. In Chapter 7 we will return to these and similar additions and to the specific Christian interests which generated them.

In summary, Mark and Matthew combine to give us one fairly consistent account of Jesus' prosecution. These are its essential features: After his arrest Jesus is taken before the Sanhedrin, which is assembled during the night. Here he is subjected to a formal trial, complete with charges, testifying witnesses and—at least in Mark's account—a formal death sentence. The exact charges against Jesus are not specified but the testimony centers about Jesus' intent to destroy the temple, and he is questioned directly about being the Messiah. When Jesus affirms his Messiahship the high priest accuses him of blasphemy and the whole Sanhedrin agrees that he is guilty. In the morning the Sanhedrin conducts another meeting of some sort, after which Jesus is led away to Pilate. Again the charges are not stated but the governor questions Jesus about being King of the Jews. Finally, because of pressure from an assembled crowd, Pilate delivers Jesus to be crucified, even though he realizes that Jesus is innocent.

The central point to be noted here is that, in both Mark and

Matthew, Jesus seems to be subjected to *two separate and distinct trials*. Strangely, these Gospels make no effort whatever to explain the relationship between these two trials. The only connecting link between them is the *morning* meeting of the Sanhedrin, about which we are told nothing. What was the purpose of this morning meeting? Many scholars think the answer is obvious: they believe that, having convicted Jesus of religious charges, the Jewish authorities had to prepare a case against him to present to Pilate so that Pilate would execute him. But if so, what was this case? Did the officials ask Pilate to execute Jesus because he was guilty of religious crimes? Did they deceitfully *alter* the charges against Jesus, so that Pilate would be misled into believing that he was guilty of offenses against the Roman government? These two Gospels give no answer; they simply state that Pilate interrogated Jesus about being "King of the Jews," a title which could have had either religious or political significance. In order to understand the relation between the Jewish proceedings and the Roman proceedings against Jesus, we have to turn to the evidence supplied in our other two Gospels.

5

THE TRIAL IN LUKE

"He stirs up the people . . ."
Luke 23:5

When one reads the passion narrative in Luke's Gospel, he suddenly realizes how serious are the historical problems surrounding Jesus' execution. Luke's story is no carbon copy of Mark and Matthew. In fact, Luke describes Jesus' trial in terms which make us rethink some of the central conclusions we have reached from the first two Gospels.

This should not really surprise us if we recall the nature of Luke's Gospel as a whole: it might be called the least synoptic of the Synoptics. As noted in the preceding chapter, it is clear that Mark was one of Luke's major sources and that Luke also has a special literary tie to Matthew. Generally, Luke's portrait of Jesus fits comfortably alongside those painted by these two, in contrast to the picture in John. Yet compared to the other two Synoptics Luke shows unusual independence in material and outline. The situation is much as if the three Synoptics were members of the same family, two of the members showing very close resemblance while the third combines the family traits with very distinctive qualities of his own.

The same mixture of similarity and difference characterizes Luke's story of Jesus' trial and execution. Luke follows the broad pattern of Mark and Matthew, but introduces material which contradicts some of the main emphases of these Gospels. In fact, Luke's differences with the first two Gospels raise more difficulties than John's differences with the Synoptics as a group. The reason is that we can often explain John's uniqueness by reference to his very compelling editorial aims, so that when his account disagrees with the Synoptics there is usually a strong preference for their record over his; but Luke's differences with Mark and Matthew cannot be accounted for so easily. There is no discernible reason, generally speaking, why Luke's version of the events should not be given as much weight as Mark's and Matthew's. In fact, there are often persuasive reasons for *preferring* Luke's account, with its important innovations in relating the events of Jesus' death.[1]

First, Luke has nothing new to bring to the story of the plot against Jesus; he simply abbreviates Mark's account by omitting the priests' intention to seize Jesus secretly before the feast begins. Since Jesus' death eventually occurred at the height of the feast-time, Luke may have considered this reference confusing. However, he agrees that the officials exercised caution because of their desire to avoid any outbreak among the people.[2]

Luke omits the anointing at Bethany, since he has already told this story in an earlier section (7:36–50). After the plot he proceeds directly to the story of Judas' betrayal, which he describes in terms very similar to Mark and Matthew. His only important nuance is the addition of "captains" to the group of priests with whom Judas holds his clandestine meeting. These captains are apparently the leaders of the official temple police[3] who might naturally have joined in the conspiracy against Jesus.

In his description of the last supper Luke introduces an item which has special interest for the study of Jesus' arrest and trial. In the midst of the conversation at the table Jesus instructs the disciples to sell their mantles and buy swords. He explains this command by adding that, in fulfillment of the scripture, he will be regarded by some as a transgressor of the law. The meaning is clear: since Jesus will soon be treated as a criminal, the disciples should arm themselves in preparation. This interpretation of Jesus' words is confirmed by the fact that the disciples reply, "Look, Lord, here are two swords," and Jesus answers, "It is enough." It seems surprising that some of Jesus' disciples were armed at the meal, but it is even more remarkable that Jesus himself should have encouraged and confirmed their action. We will return shortly to the significance of this reference in Luke.

As in the accounts of Mark and Matthew, Jesus and the disciples proceed from the site of their last meal to the Mount of Olives and the Garden of Gethsemane. In describing the arrest Luke makes further changes in the Mark/Matthew account. When Jesus' captors appear in the garden Luke again calls attention to the swords carried by Jesus' followers: the disciples ask Jesus if they should use these swords to resist the seizure. Luke also explains that it was the slave's *right* ear which was cut off by a disciple, and he alone tells us that Jesus healed the ear. Luke also omits the fact that the disciples deserted Jesus and fled. Most important, Luke claims that the chief priests, temple captains and elders were present themselves and *personally* took Jesus into custody. In Mark's and Matthew's versions only the hirelings of these important officials are involved in the arrest.[4]

It is after Jesus is taken from the garden that Luke's version veers most sharply from that of Mark and Matthew. According to Luke, Jesus is led away to the house of the high priest; here Simon Peter's denial of Jesus takes place. Then Luke reports that Jesus was mocked, beaten and ridiculed by those who had arrested him. *Nothing more takes place during the night.* Then in the morning the Jewish officials gather and lead Jesus away to a meeting of their Council. They launch directly into questions: they ask Jesus if he is the Christ and he gives an ambiguous reply. They press for a more direct answer, asking if he is the Son of God. He replies, "You say that I am," and they apparently interpret this answer affirmatively, for they say, "What further testimony do we need? We have heard it ourselves from his own lips." With this comment the meeting abruptly ends and the Council members then take Jesus to Pilate.

The remarkable difference between this story and the record of Mark and Matthew is obvious if we lay them side by side and review them carefully. In Luke's account there is no judicial process whatever during the night; Jesus is simply held in custody and is taunted and beaten by his captors. But much more important, there is no Jewish *trial* at any time. The entire Markan picture of testifying witnesses, questions about the temple, accusations of blasphemy and a formal pronouncement of condemnation against Jesus is missing. Instead, we read only of a brief *inquiry* at which Jesus is questioned about his personal claims. Then when the officials are satisfied that they have an incriminating answer from Jesus, they take him before Pilate, where they level specific charges against him. The heart of Mark's story—the Jewish prosecution and condemnation of Jesus for blasphemy—is deleted or at least sharply revised by Luke. A brief battery of questions has replaced an elaborate trial sequence.

To understand the significance of Luke's account, we must first dispense with the notion that the only major difference between Luke and the first two Gospels is the *hour* at which the Jewish trial took place. Unfortunately, this is the most common interpretation of their differences.[5] But the exact hour is relatively insignificant; *what matters is that Luke's interpretation of the nature of the proceedings is directly at odds with Mark's and Matthew's*. There is no doubt that in composing his account Luke had Mark's record of the nighttime Sanhedrin trial before him, but he substituted an entirely different explanation of the proceedings. In Luke, Jesus is not declared guilty of anything and is not even said to deserve death; he is simply questioned until the officials are satisfied that they have all the information they need. No effort at *combining* Luke's account with Mark's can be successful, because these Gospels are irreconcilable not only as to the time but as to the purpose and outcome of the Jewish action against Jesus. Luke's version is not a revision of Mark's but a rebuttal of it. As we will see, Luke's story is by no means the only grounds for challenging Mark's record of the Sanhedrin trial.

At the conclusion of the Sanhedrin inquiry, Jesus is taken directly to Pilate. The high priests and a Jewish crowd [6] immediately begin to accuse Jesus before the governor. At this point Luke makes a contribution of major significance: he states the exact charges which the Jewish officials presented to the governor. They consist of three specific accusations against Jesus: that he has perverted the nation, has forbidden the Jews to pay tribute to Caesar and has called himself a king. This three-fold indictment makes it clear that Jesus is on trial before Pilate for alleged political crimes, not for violations of any Jewish religious laws. Regrettably, Luke tells us nothing of any interrogation on the first two charges; he reports Pilate's questioning of Jesus in terms very similar to those of Mark and Matthew. Pilate asks Jesus, "Are you the King of the Jews?" Jesus gives the same noncommittal answer, "You have said so," and Pilate tells the chief priests and the crowd that he finds no crime in Jesus. As with the other Gospels, Luke's narrative obviously has serious gaps. Pilate could hardly have determined from this one brief answer that Jesus was innocent of all the accusations brought against him. But Luke's point is only that after *all* his questions Pilate considered Jesus guiltless of any wrongdoing.

Then Luke's story takes a new and unexpected turn. Pilate learns that Jesus is from Galilee and he decides to send him to Herod Antipas, the ruler of Galilee who was then in Jerusalem, evidently for the celebration of the feast. Luke's explanation of Pilate's act is that Jesus "belonged to Herod's jurisdiction." This sudden shift of scene is unknown in any other Gospel. According to Luke, Antipas was pleased at seeing Jesus, since he had heard about him and had wanted to see him perform a "sign." He questions Jesus at length, but Jesus again makes no answer. The Sanhedrin officials (this time without the crowd) are present and they accuse Jesus bitterly. Luke tells us nothing of Antipas' opinion of Jesus, but he implies that Antipas waived judgment, since he simply returned Jesus to Pilate. Luke states that this incident became the basis of a friendship between the two previously antagonistic rulers.

Also, while the other three Gospels describe the abuse heaped on Jesus by Pilate's soldiers, Luke transfers this cruelty to Antipas' men, who mock and taunt Jesus.

After Jesus has been returned to Pilate, the governor assembles the Jews and affirms even more forcefully his belief that Jesus is innocent. He announces his intention to release Jesus, but now the crowd calls for Barabbas to be freed instead. A second and third time Pilate tries to persuade the Jews that Jesus should be released; he even suggests that Jesus be punished by scourging in order to satisfy their demands. Pilate's desire to free Jesus is much more pronounced in Luke than in Mark and Matthew. But the Jews are urgent and unrelenting: with loud cries they demand that Jesus be killed. Pilate finally gives in to their wishes.

.   .   .   .   .

How are Luke's major variations from Mark and Matthew to be accounted for?

The answer we give to that question will have a profound effect on our interpretation of Jesus' trial and death. We are almost certain to misconstrue the legal processes of the trial if we fail to grasp the origin and significance of Luke's differences with the first two Gospels, particularly at the point of the Sanhedrin's activity. This failure is one of the recurrent shortcomings in most popular discussions of the trial. There is no doubt that Luke made use of Mark's account of the passion; about 27 percent of Luke's words in this narrative seem to have been borrowed directly from Mark.[7] But did Luke employ another source in addition to Mark? Are his disagreements with Mark to be explained by his preference for this other source? If so, does this other source give a more reliable picture of the events than the record given by Mark and Matthew?

This subject poses one of the most complex problems in the literary analysis of the Gospels. The question at stake can be easily defined. Is Luke's account of the passion events, and particularly his record of the trial, simply a free revision of Mark? Did Luke merely adapt Mark's material as he borrowed it? Or is Luke's story based on entirely different and perhaps more authentic sources? To answer, we have to have a clear grasp of the nature of Luke's material. For convenience, we can describe the literary characteristics of Luke's passion narrative under four headings:[8]

1) *Revisions in Mark's order of events.* Throughout his Gospel, Luke has a strong tendency to preserve the order of Mark's material whenever he borrows from Mark. In the chapters prior to Jesus' climactic journey to Jerusalem (Luke 1:1–18:14), Luke makes only three changes in the order of his Markan material, none of which affect the basic sequence of events. But in the passion story Luke's use of Mark is suddenly very different: he transposes four large sections of Markan material, seven smaller sections, and fourteen verses or part-verses. Further, these transpositions have a much more pronounced effect on the narrative than the changes made in earlier sections. Because the shape of the passion story was relatively stable throughout the early Church, we would expect Luke's order of material to more closely agree with Mark's in this section, but just the opposite is the case. Although these two Gospels naturally agree as to the general pattern of events, Luke revises Mark more frequently and more seriously in this section than in any other. It is hard to see why Luke would suddenly begin to make such fundamental revisions in Mark's account unless he was relying on another source which he preferred to Mark.

2) *Changes and additions to the Markan material.* In the passion narrative, Luke not only changes the order of his Markan material, he suddenly starts to deal more freely with the *substance* of this material. In the earlier sections of his Gospel, Luke has 199 verses dealing with the ministry of Jesus which contain material borrowed from Mark, to which he made only six slight additions totalling six verses. But in the passion story, where Luke has only 176 verses in which there is Markan material, he makes 15 additions (two and a half times as many), totalling $39\frac{1}{2}$ verses (five times as many). Further, at 16 points in the passion story Luke specifically corrects a point in Mark's account. Finally, in his earlier portions Luke tends to follow Mark most closely when borrowing dialogue, as opposed to narrative. In the Jewish and Roman trial proceedings, which are primarily dialogue, Luke is especially independent of

Mark and, if he uses Mark's material at all, makes serious changes in its language and its impact.

3) *Use of non-Markan material throughout the passion narrative.* In Luke's passion narrative there are 28 units of material which have no parallel in Mark, even though these two Gospels are tracing the same general events. These non-Markan units total 127½ verses (if we include all the material after Jesus' arrival in Jerusalem in Luke 19:28). Within these verses only 11.75 percent of Luke's words are in common with Mark, so it is obvious that he has not used Mark at all in these portions; the limited verbal agreements are only coincidental. Even if we restrict ourselves to the material from the last supper to the announcement of the resurrection (Luke 22:14–24:11), only 32.3 percent of Luke's words agree with Mark's. This is only 60 percent of the ratio of agreement found in the portions of Luke prior to the passion. Further, when all these non-Markan words are extracted from Luke's narrative and read as a unit, *they seem to form a coherent account of the passion events,* and also reflect a unity of style, language and thought which is unlike the Markan material. By contrast, the Markan material which remains when the non-Markan words are removed form a less continuous and coherent narrative than the non-Markan sections. From this, it appears not only that Luke used another source but that he used it more extensively than he used Mark.

4) *Use of non-Markan material in the Jewish and Roman proceedings.* Luke's use of non-Markan material is especially obvious in his description of the Jewish and Roman trial proceedings. As we have seen, Luke gives an entirely different meaning to the Jewish action and seems to be completely independent of Mark in this section. Only 33 of Luke's 94 words are paralleled in Mark, and most of these are too general in nature to reflect any literary dependence. It is doubtful that a single verse in Luke's account of the Jewish proceedings is dependent on Mark.[9] Luke also makes serious changes in Mark's description of the Roman trial; only 13.7 percent of Luke's words in this section are identical with Mark's. Again, over one half of these are minor words which do not indicate a literary relationship, and 16 of the words in common occur within

a single verse (23:3). Twelve of Luke's 24 verses in the Roman trial are completely non-Markan and 11 of the remaining 12 show major expansions or changes in Mark's material.

These statistical data are of great importance; they are strong evidence for the view that Luke relied primarily on non-Markan material and that he merely inserted portions of Mark into his account. W. E. Bundy's summary is correct: "It is obvious, even to the uncritical reader, that Luke is not using Mark as his basic source . . . If Luke uses Mark at all in this section, it is only incidentally and at only a few particular points." [10] Paul Winter, who has made a special study of Luke's account, says concerning Luke's non-Markan material in the trial story:

> This matter owes its presence in the Third Gospel not to the imagination or free composition of the Evangelist who "re-wrote Mark." Its source was a literary record with qualities and characteristics of its own, and the editor of Luke merely combined it with matter excerpted from Mark.[11]

This judgment that Luke relied on a special source in writing his passion narrative is by no means unanimous. Many scholars believe that Luke merely exercised a very free editorial hand in revising Mark's story. But the evidence overwhelmingly suggests that Mark was only one of Luke's sources in this section of his Gospel, and probably not even his main source.[12] But what was this special source?

Unfortunately, no answer can be given. All the inquiry into this subject over the years has proved fruitless. Some scholars believe that Luke's distinctive passion material stems from Q, the same non-Markan source which Matthew and Luke shared in the main body of their Gospels.[13] Others think it is drawn from the same "private" material which Luke used in his earlier sections.[14] In truth, we have no idea where it came from; we can only feel sure that Luke put great faith in it in composing his account of Jesus' trial and execution, and that he showed preference for it over Mark's version, particularly in describing the Jewish and Roman proceedings. In fact, in these sections he seems to have rejected Mark's explanation altogether.[15] Whatever his reasons for doing so, his account gives an entirely new cast to the judicial processes by which Jesus met his death. This fact creates some of our major problems in deciphering the trial events.

6

THE TRIAL IN JOHN

"Are you the King of the Jews?"
John 18:33

Few literary works can properly be called unique. The Gospel of John is one of those few. In both form and content it stands apart not only from all non-Christian literature, ancient and modern, but even from its sister Gospels of the New Testament.

The differences between John and the Synoptics cannot be summarized in a few words, but a suitable comparison was supplied by a prominent Christian writer of the third century A.D. He noted that John is a "spiritual" Gospel, in contrast to the more human Synoptics.[1] In John we meet Jesus on a somewhat different plane than in Matthew, Mark and Luke. The glimpses of humanity which frequently shine through in the Synoptics are almost totally absent in John. In this Gospel Jesus' every word and deed bear the full stamp of divinity. The purpose of John's Gospel is clear: it is to present Jesus as one whose eternal home is with God but who has dwelt temporarily among men in order to bring them redemption.

Though Jesus was in the world he was not *of* the world, and his message in this Gospel centers on his close relation to the Father from whom he is momentarily separated.

This emphasis on the divine majesty of Jesus permeates the Gospel from its prologue to its climactic presentation of the risen Christ. It has had a pronounced effect on John's interpretation of Jesus' trial and death. The most noticeable feature of John's passion story is that it is not a record of things happening *to* Jesus, in which he is a victim, but a series of events directed *by* Jesus himself, in which he is the hero. All other figures in the drama—Judas Iscariot, the arresting party, the Jewish leaders and Pontius Pilate—are able to act their parts only because they help to fulfill God's plan and because they are encouraged by Jesus to do so.[2]

To dramatize this theme, John has obviously exercised considerable freedom in his description of Jesus' arrest and trial. As we saw in Chapter 3, he has to fit his version into the traditional Christian outline because the general course of events was well established long before he wrote. But he is able to bring the deity of Jesus into sharp focus by both what he adds to and what he omits from this common framework.

John's description of the plot is in much different and more dramatic terms than the Synoptics. John has repeatedly emphasized the hostility of the Jews and their leaders to Jesus; finally this opposition becomes (shortly before Passover week, earlier than in Synoptics) a concerted effort to get rid of Jesus (11:46–50). The whole Council meets and agrees to seize Jesus before the country falls into difficulty with the Romans. No explanation is given for the view that Jesus' increasing popularity with the people might lead to a national political calamity. Whereas in the Synoptics the priestly leaders plot stealthily to do away with Jesus without alerting the people, in John the Council launches a public search for Jesus and orders the populace to inform on his whereabouts. To escape arrest Jesus temporarily flees outside Jerusalem with his disciples (11:54), but soon re-enters the city in triumph, shortly before being taken into custody.

John's treatment of the betrayal by Judas Iscariot is equally interesting. He does not describe Judas' secret meeting with the priests, because this meeting might suggest that the passion events were outside the personal control of Jesus. Instead, he weaves the mention of Judas' treachery into the story of the last meal, where he can point out that Jesus not only had divine foreknowledge of Judas' intent but even ordered him to carry out his treacherous mission. At the meal Jesus calls attention to the fact that one of the disciples will betray him, and he indicates Judas indirectly. He then instructs him to go and do his work quickly. Because of this reconstruction, John is forced to explain why the disciples did not stop Judas at the time: he points out that they had simply misunderstood Jesus' words and thought that Judas was being sent on a special mission. After Judas has gone Jesus again shows his supernatural understanding of what is to come by informing the remaining disciples that the end is near. The entire thrust of this scene is Jesus' own direction of the events which will culminate in his death.

Following the meal, which John relates in very different terms than do the Synoptics,[3] Jesus crosses the brook Kidron and enters the garden with his disciples. Here again John omits part of the Synoptic record because it conflicts with his dominant emphasis. He deletes the dramatic scene in Gethsemane in which Jesus agonizes in prayer while the disciples show their frailty and incomprehension by falling asleep. This tradition was unacceptable to him because it revealed the normal human anguish which swept over Jesus as he faced the final moments of his life. According to John, Jesus must show no such hesitancy to go to the cross. He cannot ask, as he does in the Synoptics, that if possible the cup of death be withheld from him.[4]

The first incident in John's account of the passion which parallels the Synoptics is the appearance of Judas in the garden at the head of an armed arresting party. But in this Gospel Judas has no real function to perform. He does not need to single out Jesus, because Jesus himself takes command of the events by stepping forward and identifying himself. He asks his captors, "Whom do you seek?" and when they answer he says openly, "I am he." At these words the entire arresting party falls back help-lessly to the ground. This is perhaps the most forceful example in John's passion story of the majesty and power of Jesus. John has demonstrated earlier that all attempts to arrest Jesus before the divinely appointed time were useless (7:30,32,44–46; 8:20; 10:39). Even now, when the final moment has come, Jesus' enemies are helpless before him. Jesus must ask a second time whom they seek, and he is forced to encourage them to make the arrest. Further, although the Synoptics declare that the disciples deserted Jesus, in this Gospel Jesus is directly responsible for their escape; he asks of his captors that his followers be allowed to go free. John has al-ready presented Jesus as the Good Shepherd (10:1–18); Jesus fulfills this role in the garden by protecting his disciples even at the mo-ment when he faces death. John also mentions the brief sword-play in the garden and he alone names Simon Peter as the disciple who inflicts the wound on the slave of the high priest. Jesus restrains Simon with the reminder that nothing must stand in the way of the task which the Father has given him. Most important, John tells us that a cohort of (Roman) soldiers and their captain also par-ticipated in the arrest. This reference is John's most significant contribution to the arrest scene. The Synoptics assign the seizure of Jesus solely to the Jewish officials or their representatives, but John includes the Roman government itself in the opposition to Jesus.

So Jesus is led from the garden in the custody of the Jewish and Roman officials. The Synoptics have already disagreed about the Jewish proceedings against Jesus; John now adds to our confusion. He states that, between his arrest and the Roman trial, Jesus was taken successively before only *two* of the leading Jewish officials, Annas and the∴ Caiaphas. John tells us nothing that happened be-tween Jesus and Caiaphas, but he states that before Annas Jesus was interrogated "about his disciples and his teaching." Jesus re-plies by reminding Annas that he had taught openly; why did Annas not ask all those who had heard him speak? Because of this answer, which was interpreted as an insult to Annas, Jesus is struck by one of the attending officers. The scene then ends abruptly. Here, as in Luke, there is no formal trial of Jesus by the Jews. We hear of no charges, no witnesses, and no conviction or sentencing; there is only a brief inquiry.[5]

In the account of the trial before Pilate, John continues to introduce novel material. He has ample opportunity to do so, since his description of the Roman proceedings is much longer than in any other Gospel and is over two and a half times as long as Mark's account (38 verses to 14). It is obvious that John saw little importance in the Jewish proceedings, to which he devotes only five verses, as compared to the Roman. From this one would suppose that we gain extensive additional information from John about the Roman proceedings, but most of this Gospel's extra material, even if historical, does not substantially advance our understanding. Much of it consists of dialogue between Jesus, Pilate and the Jewish officials on the same themes already mentioned in the Synoptics. For example, Pilate discusses the subject of kingship with Jesus at some length, and Jesus explains that his kingship is spiritual, not physical. John again develops his theme that Jesus' death is a part of God's plan; Jesus is not a helpless victim of circumstances. When Pilate threatens Jesus near the end of the proceedings, Jesus replies, "You would have no power over me unless it had been given you from above."

One element in John's account is of special interest. John provides a very clear statement of the charges brought against Jesus, just as Luke had done. But in contrast to Luke, John emphasized that the Jews presented Jesus to Pilate as a violator of *their own religious laws*.[6] Even before the proceedings begin, Pilate tells the Jews to take Jesus and judge him by their own law; but the Jews remind Pilate that they cannot put any man to death. Later, in pressing for Jesus' execution, the Jews state, "We have a law, and by that law he ought to die, because he has made himself the Son of God." Thus Jesus is clearly on trial because of alleged religious crimes. This directly contradicts Luke's account and brings us full circle: Mark and Matthew give no explanation of the charges, Luke indicates that they are political and John explains that they are religious. What John does not do is to explain why Pilate should have been called on to judge Jesus for violating the Jewish religious code. Although this riddle is not specifically answered by John, the implication is strong that the Jews simply want Pilate to execute Jesus *on their behalf*. They are unable legally to carry out an execution, so they demand that Pilate perform the act for them. This explanation of the proceedings is further complicated by the fact that Pilate, instead of ordering Jesus' execution, gives Jesus back to the Jews so that they may crucify him!

Finally, John places even greater emphasis than the Synoptics on Pilate's desire to release Jesus. It is Pilate himself who reminds the Jews of the custom of releasing a prisoner at Passover and suggests that Jesus be set free. Later, when the Jews will not agree to releasing Jesus, Pilate invites them to crucify him—anything to keep from having to condemn Jesus himself. The Jews, in turn, use various devices to convince the governor to kill Jesus. Eventually, it is a clever psychological threat by the Jews which leads Pilate to pass sentence against Jesus. The Jews remind Pilate that he is not Caesar's friend if he releases Jesus, since anyone who calls himself a king is obviously an opponent of the emperor. Not wishing to be vulnerable to the charge of protecting an enemy of Caesar, Pilate capitulates to the wishes of the Jews and allows them to execute Jesus.

.   .   .   .   .

The central problem raised by John's trial narrative is similar to that encountered in Luke. Are its distinctive features primarily the result of the author's personal creative work, or do they show that he had access to special—and perhaps very valuable—non-Synoptic traditions? [7]

Obviously, the answer to these questions goes a long way toward settling the value of this Gospel's account. If the unique elements in John's story are only the result of his theological and apologetic imagination, we can safely conclude that they have little historical value, and can discount them in reconstructing the trial. We have already seen that John's doctrinal aims have had a serious influence on his record of the events; that is why the reliability of his entire account is under grave suspicion. But are *all* the distinctive episodes in John to be explained as the author's imaginative additions, or are some of them based on earlier traditions much like the traditions which lie behind the Synoptics? If so, then the variations found in the fourth Gospel must be weighed with great care, and we cannot assume in advance that they are any less reliable than the Synoptic records.

The starting point in evaluating John's account is to determine its literary relationship with the Synoptic accounts. This problem is part of a larger issue: did John know and use the Synoptics in writing his Gospel as a whole? For a great many years an affirmative answer was taken for granted by scholars. Although there are few direct parallels between John and the other Gospels before the passion events, there seemed to be just enough points of harmony to indicate a literary relationship. This judgment was natural since it was presumed that John was written several years after the Synoptics. It seemed only logical that the author of this Gospel should have been familiar with these earlier and influential Christian writings.

However, in recent years a very healthy skepticism has arisen on this issue. Today there is no longer any assurance that John had the slightest acquaintance with our other Gospels.[8] The supposed points of contact are very doubtful evidence of a direct relationship, and we are no longer even sure that John appeared at a later date than our other Gospels.[9] But the central fact is that, even if John was acquainted with the Synoptics, they obviously had little effect on the nature of his Gospel. This is what matters. It is somewhat idle to debate whether John "knew" the Synoptics, since from all indications he did not draw on them extensively as a source or, if he did, he revised their material so radically that almost no evidence of this literary dependence is now visible.

So we cannot assume that John made use of the Synoptics in composing his Gospel as a whole. But what of the trial narrative in particular? There is no doubt that John's account of the passion events is much closer to the Synoptics than any other portion of his Gospel. Prior to Chapter 18 in John, the close parallels between this Gospel and the Synoptics can be numbered on the fingers of one hand. But in the next two chapters—the passion events—there are continuous points of comparison. But as we saw in Chapter 3, this sudden harmony is explained by the fact that a relatively stable passion story developed in the Church well before our Gospels were written. It would have been impossible for John or any other Christian author to record a version of the passion story which ignored the basic elements of this story as it was told throughout the Church. The broad similarities between John and the other Gospels in the trial narratives are no proof of a literary relationship.[10] In fact, considering the universality of the passion narrative, it is the *distinctiveness* of John's version which attracts our attention. The surprise is not that John's account is so similar to the Synoptics, but that it is so different. We must recall that in this Gospel there is a new description of the plot against Jesus, no scene in which Judas conspires with the priests, no last supper of the type described by the Synoptics, no Gethsemane scene, and a completely new description of the Jewish proceedings. Prior to the crucifixion there are only three units in which John shows fairly close similarity to the Synoptics in the passion events: the plot, the arrest and the Roman proceedings. Even in these John introduces unique ingredients which seriously revise the Synoptic stories. These facts give strong support to the view that John's account of the passion is fully independent of the Synoptic records.

If John did use any Synoptic Gospel in writing his account, that Gospel was apparently Luke.[11] Three points of comparison are often cited as evidence that John borrowed from Luke or that they shared a common tradition not known to Mark and Matthew. (1) Both Luke and John specify that Jesus' disciple cut off the *right* ear of the slave of the high priest when Jesus was arrested. (2) Both Gospels make the Jewish proceedings against Jesus only an inquiry, not a formal trial. (3) Both quote *three* declarations by Pilate, in the Roman trial, that Jesus was innocent.[12] Chiefly for these reasons, B. W. Bacon speaks of John's account of the passion as "the Lucan form of the Synoptic tradition," which John follows "without wide divergence." [13]

But this judgment is unjustified. The points of contact between these two Gospels are much too weak to indicate that John was using Luke or Luke's special source. In comparing these Gospels we must not lose sight of the fact that the major dissimilarities between Luke and John greatly outweigh the minor similarities. Considering the number of distinctive points found in each of these Gospels individually, the actual agreement between them on particular points is extremely small. If John had used Luke as a source, we would expect to find a much higher incidence of harmony between these two accounts.

Further, even the three supposed agreements listed above are very questionable. The first amounts to only one word; it is impossible to base any literary judgments on such a parallel. Next, although Luke and John both describe the Jewish action against Jesus as an investigation, not a trial, they portray this investigation in entirely different ways. There is no substantial harmony between Luke and John in this section *aside from the fact that they deny the claim of Mark and Matthew that there was a full-scale prosecution of Jesus by the Jews between his arrest and the Roman trial.* Their broad agreement on this point is no evidence of interdependence. If the Jewish proceedings against Jesus were commonly described as only a hearing in the earliest oral passion story, then the joint testimony of Luke and John to this effect merely indicates that they are independent variations of this primitive oral story. In short, the best corrective to the suggestion of a literary tie between Luke and John on this issue is a correct understanding of the nature of the pre-Gospel passion narrative itself. Finally, there is no significant similarity between these Gospels in their descriptions of the Roman trial. Luke's version has two major differences from Mark and Matthew: he lists the specific charges against Jesus which the Jews presented to Pilate and he interjects Jesus' trial before Herod Antipas into the midst of the proceedings. Both these elements are much more significant than the exact number of times in which Pilate declares Jesus' innocence; yet both are missing in John.[14] If John made use of Luke's account, he seems to have borrowed only the least important of Luke's distinctive material, and if they shared a common source they evidently drew very different information from it.[15] Most important, as we have just seen, Luke and John are directly contradictory in their interpretation of the *basis* of the Roman trial. In Luke's account the charges are political and Pilate is quite naturally the judge of the case. According to John the charges are religious and Pilate seeks to avoid adjudicating the dispute for that very reason.[16] When we read these two accounts of the Roman trial side by side, it is hard to believe that there is any close tie between them.[17]

We return then to our original question: are John's unique features the result of his own editorial work or are they evidence that he made use of special non-Synoptic material? What additional sources, if any, did John use in composing his trial narrative?

A few years ago Vincent Taylor could say that the question whether John had relied on an early non-Synoptic source in writing his passion story had not received due attention.[18] Today that comment is no longer true, yet, despite the protracted inquiry into this subject in recent years, no substantial agreement has been reached. Unfortunately, this applies to the study of John's sources throughout all his Gospel. Even the reader who is unfamiliar with Biblical study can understand the perplexities of this subject. If an author obviously exercises great freedom in composing a historical work, how can we decide when he is relying only on his fertile imagination and when he is using earlier source-material—especially if we have no idea what that source-material contained?

However, we can safely take refuge in the following judgment of John's narrative: the burden of proof is on anyone who believes that John had access to any extensive non-Synoptic information.[19] The bulk of John's unique material is easily accounted for by reference to his special theological and apologetic interests, rather than by reference to some unknown source. The vast majority of John's distinctive additions are clearly contributions which he has made personally to the narrative. A typical example is John's description of the helplessness of the arresting party: this dramatic addition is certainly a product of John's own hand, not a survival of some primitive source. It is one of the brush strokes by which John has highlighted the divine majesty of Jesus in the passion events.

Only two points in John's story are specific enough and unusual enough to suggest that he might have drawn them from an earlier oral or written tradition. These are the presence of Roman soldiers at the arrest and the introduction of Annas into the Jewish proceedings against Jesus. In the coming chapters we will return to both these references and will discuss their origin and their historical value. For the present we can affirm that these units are clearly insufficient to support the view that John employed a connected, non-Synoptic source in recording the passion. At most they are two isolated bits of tradition which John included because they helped dramatize a point of special importance for his story. Indeed, the fact that these two items fit so ideally into John's interpretation of the passion events increases the likelihood that they stemmed from his own hand. There is no doubt that John was resourceful enough to have authored both of these references himself in order to establish his interpretation of Jesus' death.

In summary, we can safely conclude that in composing his account of Jesus' death John simply took the traditional events known throughout the early Church and elaborated them richly in accordance with his particular aims. He may also have incorporated a small number of earlier, isolated traditions which had not been recorded by the Synoptists. But in John we should not suppose that even the most distinctive material must be explained by reference to a special source. Our initial presumption in dealing with such matter in the fourth Gospel should be that its origin lies within the Evangelist himself.

7

THE JEWS, THE ROMANS AND
THE GOSPEL RECORDS

"Let his blood be upon us . . ."
Matthew 27:25

One point emerges clearly from our survey of the four Gospels: these records of Jesus' trial and execution are not historical documents in the usual sense. They were not written merely to record certain events, but to convey the faith of the Church. To the early Christians these climactic events were manifestations of God's divine purpose. Therefore, it should not surprise us that these stories have been seriously conditioned by the religious beliefs of the Christian community. To understand how this conditioning affected the description of Jesus' trial, we need to recall some facts about the development of early Christian thought.

As the Christian message spread through Palestine and beyond during the first century, the belief arose gradually that Jesus' death had been a great victory. Christians soon came to regard the cross as a necessary stage in God's redemptive plan: Jesus' death had paid the debt for man's sins so that man could be reunited with God.

But in the first days of the Church, Christians had a quite different attitude toward Jesus' crucifixion: they regarded it as an unparalleled tragedy. Jesus' death was initially considered a bitter, although temporary, defeat of God's purposes. God had sent his Messiah into the world, but the Messiah had been persecuted and killed at the hands of evil men. From the first, Christians associated this treachery with the Jewish people as a whole, because of the blindness and wickedness of the Jews in refusing to accept Jesus. To grasp the intensity of this feeling we must imagine how the first disciples felt as they witnessed Jesus' suffering and death. How thunderstruck they must have been that this man of God, whom they were sure had brought the good news of the kingdom, could have been scorned by his own people and subjected to a torturous death on a cross. The grief of these early Christians inevitably turned to deep bitterness, especially when they themselves began to suffer for their devotion to Jesus.[1]

Of course, it was the Jewish officials who had actually initiated Jesus' crucifixion. But in turning their backs on Jesus' mission the whole nation shared in the blame. Even when Christians came to view Jesus' death in a redemptive and victorious light, the guilt of the Jews was not diminished: they had been the sinful agents by which God's purposes had been accomplished. This ambivalent viewpoint has continued throughout the life of the Church. Today Christians continue to rejoice in Jesus' death as a means of their redemption while at the same time condemning those who were humanly responsible.

Because they regarded their fellow Jews as ultimately to blame for Jesus' death, it did not occur to the early Christians to consider Pilate *morally* guilty. The governor was merely the instrument through which the Jews had disposed of Jesus. This exoneration of Pilate and the Roman government is all the more surprising when we recall that Roman soldiers had actually carried out the execution and Pilate had ordered Jesus crucified when he had full power to free him.

This theme—the Jewish national guilt and the relative innocence of Pilate—is vividly illustrated in the book of Acts, our chief source for the study of early Christianity. When we remember the

role played by the Roman governor and his soldiers in the crucifixion, the descriptions of Jesus' death in Acts are remarkable.

In Acts 2:23 Simon Peter addresses an assembled Jewish crowd
and refers to Jesus as one whom the Jews themselves (as a group)
had "crucified at the hands of lawless men." In 2:36 Peter again
speaks of "this Jesus whom you (that is, all the Jews within hearing)
crucified." Later, Peter says to the Jewish authorities, "The God of
our fathers raised Jesus whom you killed by hanging on a tree"
(5:30). He also declares that the healing of a certain cripple was
made possible through the name "of Jesus Christ of Nazareth, whom
you crucified" (4:10). In the same way Stephen, in a speech to the
Jewish authorities just before his martyrdom, refers to Jesus as the
one "whom you have now betrayed and murdered" (7:54).

In all these references it is emphasized that "the Jews," either
as a people or through their native officials, had murdered Jesus.
If we had no other information we would presume that a large
segment of the Jewish populace had actually shared physically in
executing Jesus—in fact, lynching him—and that Pilate had played
no role whatsoever. In Acts 3:13b–15 Peter does refer to Pilate, and
he undoubtedly provides the customary Christian interpretation of
the Roman involvement. Peter speaks to the Jews of "Jesus, whom
you delivered up and denied in the presence of Pilate, when he
had decided to release him . . . and (you) killed the Author of
life. . . ." So even when Pilate's participation is acknowledged it
can still be said that the Jews had killed Jesus and that the governor
bore no responsibility. This same conviction is expressed by the
Apostle Paul in one of his few references to the human circumstances of Jesus' death. In I Thessalonians 2:14–15 Paul writes of
"the Jews, who killed both the Lord Jesus and the prophets." [2]

In the Christian literature of the second century the emphasis
on the Jewish guilt is vividly increased. In these post-New Testament
writings almost every reference to the human causes of Jesus' death
focuses attention on the malicious hostility of the Jews as a whole
toward Jesus and their common guilt for his crucifixion.

A good example is found in *The Preaching of Peter,* a work
supposedly authored by Simon Peter but actually written long after

him. The author claims that the Old Testament prophets had predicted Jesus' coming and his death on the cross "and all the other
torments which the Jews inflicted on him." Justin Martyr, a leading
Christian writer of the second century, says that Jesus "endured all
things which the devils instigated the senseless Jews to inflict upon
him." [3] This is certainly one of the most bitter and reckless indict-
ments of the Jewish nation found anywhere in Christian literature.
In the *Dialogue with Trypho* Justin states specifically that the Jews
had crucified Jesus,[4] and in another passage he adds that Jesus was
not crucified *by* Pilate but in the *time* of Pilate *by the Jewish nation*.[5] Tertullian, another influential Christian writer, states that "the
Jews were so exasperated by his (Jesus') teaching . . . that at last
they brought him before Pontius Pilate, at that time Roman governor of Syria (*sic*); and by the violence of their outcries against
him, extorted a sentence giving him up *to them* to be crucified." [6]
It was apparently common for the second-century Church to declare without qualification that the Jews actually carried out the
act of execution themselves. Perhaps the most interesting example
in all the non-Gospel literature is found in the so-called *Gospel of
Peter*. This work apparently dates from the middle of the second
century[7] and is the earliest existing account of Jesus' trial outside
the Gospels. In this work the trial events are described with an
extremely anti-Jewish bias. In an effort to dramatize the common
Jewish guilt, this writing points out, after describing the handwashing by Pilate, that "of the Jews no man washed his hands." [8]
The Jewish ruler Herod Antipas (not Pilate) is said to have sentenced Jesus, and the Jews themselves lead Jesus away and crucify
him. It would be hard to find a more illuminating example of the
extent to which history can be rewritten by religious conviction.[9]

.   .   .   .   .

So the early Christian interpretation of Jesus' death was based
on the conviction that the Jewish people were morally guilty because they had rejected Jesus' Messiahship. But two other Christian
concerns also affected our Gospel records of the trial. To understand

these concerns we need to recall certain facts about the struggles of
the early Christians.

The primitive Church encountered a special difficulty in establishing itself in the Gentile world because of the fact that its founder,
Jesus of Nazareth, had been crucified by a Roman governor as a
lawbreaker. Christians gloried in the cross as a symbol of God's
divine sacrifice for man, but the cross also created a problem in
proclaiming Jesus in the Roman world. Many Gentiles interpreted
Jesus' crucifixion as proof that he had been condemned and executed
by the state as a political rebel. For citizens of the Roman Empire,
no crime seemed more heinous than sedition; it struck at the very
foundation of society. How then could Gentiles seriously be expected
to regard a convicted insurrectionist as a God-man able to redeem
them?

Further, if Jesus was regarded as a political criminal the whole
Christian movement itself came under suspicion as a subversive sect,
one whose interests were adverse to the empire's. Such suspicion
was extremely damaging, because the spread of the Christian message depended largely on the tolerance of the empire and its officials.
As W. D. Niven says, the basic charge which confronted the Church
in the Gentile world was anarchy;[10] this charge arose because the
Christian founder had been executed by a Roman governor on a
political charge.[11] We know that unbelievers taunted Christians with
this fact in the early years. Tacitus dismissed the Christian faith by
speaking of Jesus as follows: "Chrestus, the founder of the sect, was
put to death as a criminal by the procurator Pontius Pilate, in the
reign of Tiberius." [12] Another Latin writer, Celsus, charged that
Jesus was an instigator of rebellion.[13] These were, undoubtedly, typical pagan statements in describing Christianity and they reflect a
difficulty which plagued Christianity in its early days beyond
Palestine.

For these reasons, the Church was anxious to give assurance
that Jesus was not an enemy of the state and that his trial and crucifixion had resulted from entirely nonpolitical opposition.[14] Christians were forced to an extraordinary effort to show that there were

extenuating circumstances surrounding Jesus' execution. They emphasized that Jesus had not really been a criminal at all. They claimed that Pilate himself had realized this; Pilate had acted only because his hand was forced by the Jewish officials. Jesus had died because the Jews rejected his spiritual mission, not because the governor convicted him of any crime.[15]

So, three closely related motives combined to affect the early Christian interpretation of Jesus' trial and death. They united with unusual force to lay the responsibility for Jesus' death squarely at the feet of the Jewish people, while the Romans were absolved of any guilt. Any suggestion that the Roman governor had been responsible for Jesus' execution violated both the Church's moral convictions and its practical needs. But the primary factor was the Church's belief that Jesus' death had resulted from the malicious refusal of the Jews to accept him as the Messiah. The Church's desire to free itself of political liabilities would never have affected its memory of the crucifixion so radically without the prior certainty that the Jewish nation was actually to blame.[16]

.   .   .   .   .

It is no surprise that these Christian convictions have had a major influence on our Gospels and on their descriptions of Jesus' trial. In the years when the passion narrative was forming in the early Church, the trial stories became the means for demonstrating the manner in which the Jews had been *legally* responsible for Jesus' death, just as they had been *morally* responsible.[17] To Christians this was the central fact about Jesus' prosecution. To see how this interpretation has shaped our trial narratives, we can begin by looking at the Gospel descriptions of the proceedings before Pilate.

In the Gospel of Mark these proceedings are described rather simply. Pilate examines Jesus on charges brought by the Jewish officials; then, wishing to satisfy them, he orders Jesus' execution. Mark elaborates on this bare description only slightly: he states that Pilate knew that the Jewish officials were acting only from envy, and he makes Pilate imply Jesus' innocence by asking what evil he had done to deserve death. But Mark goes no further in illustrating the Jewish hostility or Pilate's doubts about Jesus' guilt.

But for Matthew this is not enough. As we saw in reviewing his account, he intensifies Pilate's belief in Jesus' innocence by inserting two items: the dream of Pilate's wife and the handwashing. In the former, Pilate is made to realize by means of a divine vision that the Jewish charges against Jesus are unfounded. Therefore, in the latter, he absolves himself of all responsibility for Jesus' death. When he washes his hands of the case, *all* the Jews cry out, "Let his blood be upon us and upon our children." Matthew's words were to become a macabre prophecy: the blame for Jesus' crucifixion continued to fall on Jewish generations through the years, partly because of just such verses as this. C. G. Montefiore rightly describes this as ". . . a terrible verse; a horrible invention . . . one of those phrases which have been responsible for oceans of human blood, and a ceaseless stream of misery and desolation." [18] There is no doubt that this tradition is completely fictitious. [19] These words are not a statement by the Jews at the trial, but a chilling summation of the Christian insistence on the Jewish national guilt.

In Luke's account the emphasis on the Jewish responsibility is carried still further. The most vivid evidence of Luke's aim is the manner in which he alters the role of the Jewish crowd. In Mark and Matthew a crowd intrudes itself into Jesus' trial somewhat by chance. Mark specifically explains that this group appears *during* the proceedings after Pilate has already questioned Jesus. The crowd has obviously come to Pilate only for the purpose of insisting that he observe the custom of releasing a prisoner. Their aim is that someone be released, not that Jesus be crucified. They later cry, "Crucify him!" simply because they are indifferent to Jesus; they say, in effect, "Let *him* be killed, but release Barabbas."

But Luke, by making a minor editorial change, creates an entirely new effect. He draws the Jewish crowd into the proceedings from the beginning and actually includes them in the group which first turns Jesus over to Pilate. The Jewish multitude has become a part of the official prosecuting group; they are present with the high priests *inside* the trial chambers and they join in pressing the charges against Jesus.[20] The point of this revision is obvious: the Jewish people as a whole are drawn symbolically into the passion events. No longer is it merely the Jewish officials who want to do away with Jesus because of envy; now a representative group from the populace as a whole seeks Jesus' death because they are hostile to him and his spiritual purposes.

In Luke's account this Jewish desire for Jesus' death has become an obsession: the Jews are urgent, vehement, crying out repeatedly for Jesus to be executed. Conversely, Pilate is all the more eager to release Jesus. Whereas in Mark he had once implied Jesus' innocence, he here declares it directly three times. Three times more he announces his intention to release Jesus. Luke is even unwilling to admit that Pilate ordered the crucifixion. Instead, the governor merely turns Jesus over to the Jewish officials so that *they* can crucify him. So the second-century notices to this effect have their roots in the Gospels themselves. As W. E. Bundy says, Luke's account of the Roman trial ". . . amounts to full-grown Christian propaganda." [21] In Acts, his second volume, Luke shows the same interests: he emphasizes that Christianity was not a subversive sect. S. Maclean Gilmour notes,

> Having demonstrated in his gospel volume that the crucifixion of Jesus had been due to the virulent animosity of the Jews and not to the intervention of the Roman authorities, Luke proceeds in his Acts volume to show that the church, in its relationships with the state, could be absolved from any suspicion of anti-Roman bias.[22]

In the Gospel of John these same motives are vividly in evidence. Throughout his account of the Roman proceedings John grasps every opportunity to magnify the guilt of the Jews. In addressing Jesus, Pilate emphasizes that "Your own *nation* and the chief priests have handed you over to me . . ."; according to the governor, the whole population is implicated in Jesus' seizure and trial. The accusers of Jesus have become simply "the Jews," not a designated group of officials.[23] The Christian conviction about the responsibility for Jesus' death is placed on the lips of Jesus himself. In 19:11 Jesus asserts that the guilt of the Jews—his own people—is greater than the guilt of Pilate. As we have seen, John agrees with Luke that Pilate repeatedly insisted on Jesus' innocence.[24] John goes a step further: he claims that Jesus' trial before Pilate had nothing whatever to do with political charges, even false charges. In John's version the issues at stake are solely religious; both Pilate and the Jews emphasize this fact. Their discussion of this point constitutes the opening scene of the trial. Pilate even seeks to avoid conducting a trial at all, because Jesus' crimes are religious, not civil or political. John's point is not merely that the Jews were responsible, but that there was no conflict whatever between Jesus and Pilate—nor, by extension, between Jesus' followers and the Roman state. At the conclusion of the proceedings John states (with Luke) that Pilate handed Jesus over to the Jews so that they might crucify him; the Roman soldiers have nothing to do with the execution.[25]

All these elaborations arose in our four Gospels for the reasons we have described; they are uniformly without historical validity. The Evangelists have recast the events to show that the blame for Jesus' death lay wholly on the Jews and that the Roman governor was convinced of Jesus' innocence. Fortunately, from Mark's fairly straightforward account we are able to measure the extent to which these later interpretations have distorted the picture of the Roman trial.

What of the Jewish proceedings? Ironically, it is in Mark's Gospel that the emphasis on the Jewish guilt has most seriously conditioned the narrative. The other Gospels concentrate most of their polemic in the Roman trial, but Mark created a scene which even more forcefully illustrated the Jewish responsibility. As we saw in our review of Mark's story, its author declares that after Jesus' arrest the whole Sanhedrin assembled and conducted a formal trial of Jesus on religious grounds. Jesus was charged with breaking the Jewish law against blasphemy and was convicted and sentenced to death. This trial was illegal and prejudiced; the witnesses against Jesus lied and contradicted each other. Yet the court persisted, and after their unjust condemnation of Jesus the

Council members even subjected him to the most perverse abuse and insult.

We will shortly return to this important section, in which Mark has sought to lay the legal blame for Jesus' death squarely on the Jewish authorities. Regrettably, Mark achieved his goal too well. He cast responsibility on the Jews so convincingly that this single unit of tradition has done more to influence the interpretation of the trial than any other in the Gospels.

8

JESUS AND THE POLITICAL CRISIS

". . . these men sowed the seed
of every kind of misery . . ."
Josephus, *Antiquities of the Jews,* XVIII,i,l

Whenever we set out to interpret the life and death of
Jesus, we must take special care to visualize him within the context
of contemporary Jewish life. It is a constant temptation to us to
draw Jesus away from his own age and into our own; to isolate him
from his native environment. But he was a Jew, deeply involved in
the national life of his people, and the evidence of this fact leaps
vividly to us from the Gospels once we are alert to it.

Because the Gospels say so little about it directly, we are especially inclined to overlook one important backdrop to the story of
Jesus: the political crisis which prevailed in Judea during Jesus'
lifetime.

Throughout the first century A.D. the Roman occupation was
the most vivid of Jewish concerns. No problem had more daily and
deep-seated relevance for the Jews than the presence of a foreign

conqueror. We can recapture this feeling if we imagine our own country under foreign domination as a result of military conquest. Like the ancient Jews, we would feel constantly restive, often desperate, under this bondage. Every popular leader would have to address himself to this central issue and we would look hopefully for some group or individual to lead us back to freedom. As for our conquerors, they would have to remain constantly alert to potential rebellion.

Such was the state of the country in which Jesus lived and died.

Yet the Jews were not all of one mind in their reaction to the Roman occupation. One group, the Sadducean leaders, was quite sympathetic to the presence of a Roman governor in Judaea. This clique, which centered about the high priest, cemented its position of authority by an unwritten league with the procurators. For the governors this was a convenient alliance, and they made good use of the Sadducees in controlling the country. On the other hand, the Pharisees reflected the temper of the populace as a whole. They ardently wished the Romans gone but there seemed little to do about the problem. During Jesus' lifetime neither the Pharisees nor most of the common people engaged in active revolt, undoubtedly because such action seemed futile. It was not until some forty years after Jesus' time that this caution was finally overridden by patriotism, hatred and religious fervor in the war of A.D. 66–72.

However, one group worked throughout the procuratorial period for the immediate overthrow of the Romans. These were the Zealots—small, unorganized bands which sprang up here and there offering scattered, fanatical resistance to the Romans.[1] These nationalists crystallized the hostility felt by the majority of the people, and the common folk were largely sympathetic to this resistance movement.[2] It was because of these groups that the Romans were forced to constant concern over the threat of uprisings.

We can hardly overestimate the relevance of this political climate and this Zealotist resistance for the career of Jesus. As Oscar Cullmann comments, "For the understanding of the New Testament and of the events which led up to the death of Jesus, the Zealot movement is of extraordinary significance."[3] The truth of this statement becomes clear when we review the widespread resistance to the procurators and its effect on daily Jewish life in Jesus' time.[4]

．　　．　　．　　．　　．

Armed resistance to Roman control had begun as early as the days of Herod the Great.[5] Josephus cites the agitation raised by a certain Hezekias, whose bands of "robbers" (The Greek word is $\lambda\eta\sigma\tau\eta s$; English transliteration, *lestes*; plural, *lestai*) warred against Herod. These men were undoubtedly political rebels.[6] During Archelaus' reign the country was further overrun by marauding bands. But it was when Archelaus was banished and the procurators arrived that the rebel movement began in earnest. In fact, Josephus' history of the procurators is to a large extent merely a record of their struggle with rebellious elements in the country. There is no doubt that, in his histories, Josephus was strongly biased against these first-century resistance leaders and against all acts of violence by which the Jews sought to overthrow the Romans.[7] Although himself a Jew, Josephus was writing for a Roman audience. It was his aim to demonstrate that the Jews *as a people* were not opposed to Rome and that there need be no strife between the two peoples. He was anxious to show that the Jewish war of A.D. 66 had developed only because certain hotheads had led the people into rebellion. He never dignifies these leaders with the name of patriots. One would never know from him that religious zeal or even simple nationalism played any part in their activity. However, although there were probably some who were mere opportunists, these insurrectionists (*lestai*) were in the main patriots. Many were undoubtedly motivated primarily by religious convictions.[8] When we hear from Josephus of the many *lestai* roaming the country, engaging in guerrilla actions against the Romans, we must recognize that these men were resistance leaders, not simply thieves and cutthroats.[9] This meaning of the word *lestes* (*lestai*) must also be kept in view when we come to the trial of Jesus.

Josephus describes the effect of Zealotism in the years after A.D. 6 as follows:

. . . these men sowed the seed of every kind of misery, which so afflicted the nation that words are inadequate . . . wars (were) set afoot that (were) bound to rage beyond control . . . friends (were) done away with who might have alleviated the suffering . . . raids (were made) by great hordes of brigands, and men of the highest standing (were) assassinated. . . . They sowed the seeds whence sprang strife between factions and the slaughter of fellow citizens. Some were slain in civil strife . . . others were slain by the enemy in war. Then came famine . . . followed by the storming and razing of cities until at last the very temple of God was ravaged by the enemy's fire through this revolt.[10]

It was under Pontius Pilate, whose rule the Jews considered an utter barbarity,[11] that this Jewish resistance first became a continual problem. Josephus cites three particular instances of trouble, which we noted in our earlier discussion of Pilate: the mob violence stirred by the introduction of military standards and later the votive shields; the trouble over the aqueducts; and the slaughter of the Samaritans who gathered in force on Mount Gerizim. The last case is an especially useful example of the Roman fear of mass rebellion. We are also told that Pilate crucified a great many other Jews;[12] these executions were almost certainly due to seditious activity.[13] It is of great importance that the crucifixion of Jesus alongside two criminals occurred during just this period of increased unrest and executions.

Insurrection and Zealotist activity were intensified in the years after Pilate. Conditions worsened still further when the province was restored to procuratorial rule after the brief reign of Herod Agrippa I in A.D. 41–44. The return of the procurators seemed to most Jews like a return to slavery, and a deluge of violence followed. Fadus (A.D. 44–48), the first of these later procurators, suppressed a movement led by Theudas, who gathered a multitude, went with them to the Jordan River, and promised to part its waters miraculously. Apparently this was not a political movement, but Fadus imagined the worst and his cavalry slew most of Theudas' followers. This is another evidence of the degree to which even religious enthusiasm was regarded with suspicion by the procurators. Fadus was also forced to repress numerous bands of Zealots who had begun stirring up trouble in Perea. His successor, the apostate Jew Tiberius Alexander, also resorted to crucifixions in order to control at least one revolt.

Then under Ventidius Cumanus (A.D. 48–52), "the people were in a constant state of insurrection." [14] As many as thirty thousand Jews died as a result of an uprising precipitated by the indecent act of a Roman soldier at Passover. Shortly afterward a large-scale revolt by the Jews was barely averted when a Roman soldier tore to shreds a copy of the *Torah,* the heart of the Jewish Scriptures. Later, Cumanus had to quell a Jewish attack on the neighboring Samaritans, and those who were captured were crucified by Quadratus, the Syrian governor who intervened as arbiter.[15]

Under the last four procurators rebellious activities became almost too numerous to describe. Felix (A.D. 52–60) crucified a great many Zealots and had to repel a large army of Jews who marched under arms against Jerusalem itself.[16] Even after this defeat the Zealots stirred up the people and set fire to those villages which would not support the rebellion. During the brief rule of Festus (A.D. 60–62) the country was again in the grip of Zealots who plundered and burned villages. Josephus tells us that the *Sicarii*—"men of the knife"—who were political assassins, spread violence throughout the country during this period.[17] Under the last two procurators these Sicarii and other Zealots operated almost unchecked across Judaea.[18]

Eventually in A.D. 66 this perennial hostility erupted into full-scale war. After six years of hopeless resistance the struggle ended in a crushing defeat for the Jews. Their temple, the focal point of the Jewish national and religious life, was destroyed. The nation never recovered from this tragic war. Some seventy years later, in A.D. 130, Bar Cochba was to lead a final revolt against the Romans. The result was again defeat and the Romans, tired of trying to control the Jews in their homeland, scattered them outside Judaea and even changed the country's name. From that time forward the Jews became a dispossessed people; they were not to reclaim Palestine as their national home until the United Nations partition in 1948.

In summary, it would be hard to imagine a more intense record of political strife than that set down by Josephus, especially within the ordered structure of the Roman Empire. Yet there are, undoubtedly, a great many other acts of resistance which were crowded from Josephus' pages. He has merely elaborated some of the more spectacular incidents, but his survey is enough to illustrate vividly the impact of Roman rule on all first-century Jews. The occupation was of course the central public issue. In these years, thousands gave their lives in battle or were crucified, either because of open sedition or simply because their actions seemed to threaten the civil order. Before we come to the trial of Jesus it is most important to remember not only the number of people crucified on political charges, but also those who seem to have been politically innocuous yet lost their lives because of the nervous apprehensions of the procurators. The list of those accused of political crimes and sent to their deaths is long. It was particularly long during the reign of Pilate, who not only crucified "countless" Jews but who also executed Jesus of Nazareth alongside two men designated in the Gospels as *lestai*.

.   .   .   .   .

In recent years, increasing attention has been focused on the relation of this revolutionary background to the ministry and death of Jesus.[19] This awareness has been impeded by the fact that the Gospels themselves divorce Jesus almost completely from the national crisis and from all interest in political affairs. There are two reasons for this divorce; both are important for the study of Jesus' death.

The first is that described in Chapter 7: the apologetic desire of the Gospel writers to show that Jesus was not a political criminal and that he had not even been concerned with political affairs.[20] We have already seen the effect of this interest on the trial accounts; but during Jesus' ministry also, the Gospels dissociate him from all political concerns, *except when emphasizing that he was directly opposed to violent political resistance to Rome and that his program was pacifistic.* Needless to say, the Evangelists did not have to invent this interpretation. It is certainly true that Jesus rejected the Zealotist cause. But this fact has been preserved and amplified in the Gospels largely because of apologetic necessity.

Secondly, the Gospel writers themselves simply were not concerned about these political issues. The Gospels are not records of Jewish life in Jesus' day; they are documents designed to persuade men that Jesus of Nazareth was the spiritual Messiah and Son of God. The Gospels include only the material which was useful to the Church in illustrating his divine mission. There was no reason to describe the political scene amidst which Jesus had worked; that issue had no relevance for the Church's faith at the time when the Gospels were composed. Therefore, the Evangelists have virtually no interest in the political problems of Jewish national life. H. B. Sharman expresses the circumstances well:

> To the men who produced the Synoptic Gospels, it did not seem important to sketch the political background. They were not influenced by a purpose to make the acts and words of Jesus more vivid and vital by a portrayal of the events and movements of his day . . . it did not become a concern of the evangelists to set forth in an adequate way the trend of Roman rule in Palestine, and its far-reaching effect upon Jewish political and religious life, its effect upon the policy of Jesus himself, and upon many phases of the attitude of the leaders among his people toward Jesus.[21]

This is precisely why, in the Gospels, Jesus' career seems so remote from the prevailing political turbulence. The Evangelists have succeeded so well that any number of commentators have stressed Jesus' total disinterest in political matters.[22] But it is clear that the political life of Judaea had direct bearing on his career and that he faced the political test-question wherever he went. This was especially true in Galilee, where Zealots were particularly active. Whenever he attracted a crowd it must have been necessary for him to set forth clearly the nature of his mission. John's record that on one occasion a crowd sought to make him king[23] reflects how easily the people could misunderstand his intent. There were undoubtedly many listeners who were eager to interpret his career in terms of the national crisis.

Despite the Evangelists' strong inclination to ignore political issues entirely, several interesting hints of the contemporary conditions have made their way into our Gospels. First, it is certain that Jesus had at least one Zealot and possibly more among his own intimate followers. In Luke 6:15 and Acts 1:13, Simon "the Zealot" is named among the twelve disciples.[24] It is extraordinary that one of Jesus' own disciples should have been active in the resistance movement. It is possible that other disciples had Zealotist connections. As Oscar Cullmann suggests, the name Judas "Iscariot" may represent a Semitic transcription of the Latin *sicarius,* which would identify Judas with the Sicarii described in Josephus.[25] Simon "bar Jonah" may erroneously translate a Hebrew word meaning "terrorist." [26] However, except for Simon the Zealot these assumptions cannot be verified. The argument regarding "bar Jonah" has found little support,[27] and although the meaning of "Iscariot" is in doubt the attempt to trace it through Aramaic (the common language of Palestinian Jews in Jesus' day) back to Latin is no more persuasive than simply translating it "a man of Kerioth."

Several of Jesus' sayings reflect the current political tension and attest his attitude toward resistance and sedition. The problem of submission to Rome is in view when Jesus is asked whether the Roman tax should be paid.[28] Although his answer ("Render to Caesar the things that are Caesar's, and to God the things that are God's") seems equivocal, the question is an example of the pressure which Jesus encountered to declare himself on the central public question.

Other Gospel references are equally interesting when set within this framework. Jesus' enigmatic saying concerning the attempt to establish the Kingdom of God by violence is best explained as a direct condemnation of the Zealotist cause.[29] In John 10:8 Jesus declares, "All who came before me are thieves and robbers (*lestai*) . . ." It is not clear whom Jesus (or the Evangelist) has in mind, but the reference best fits those who had appeared in recent years, claiming divine guidance and leading the Jews in their struggle with Rome. The reference to false Messiahs and false prophets in Matthew 24:24 probably denotes such leaders. C. J. Cadoux has suggested plausibly that all those passages, especially in Luke's account, in which Jesus warns of the coming destruction or urges a turn from a disastrous course[30] constitute Jesus' appeal to the people to reject the Zealot resistance which will bring the nation's downfall.[31] The so-called eschatalogical discourses of Jesus contain this same warning.[32] Finally, several sayings in the Sermon on the Mount may have special relevance for the political situation.[33] "Do not resist one who is evil . . ."; "Love your enemies and pray for those who persecute you . . ."; and "Blessed are the peacemakers . . ." are probably rejections of political as well as personal violence.

But it is not among Jesus' disciples, nor in his teachings, that we come into closest contact with the political crisis. We encounter this problem most directly when we come to the climactic events of his life—his arrival in Jerusalem, his activity in the city, and his trial and crucifixion.

9

THE CLIMACTIC DAYS
IN JERUSALEM

"Have you come out as against a *lestes?*"
Mark 14:48

It is quite possible that Jesus' ministry had been conducted wholly outside of Jerusalem. John's account places Jesus frequently in Jerusalem during his career, but the Synoptics indicate that he had not come to the city until a few days before his death. The reasons for Jesus' decision to carry his work to the capital city are uncertain and do not concern us here. The fact is that after an undetermined period of work in Galilee he journeyed with a group of followers to Jerusalem at the time of the Passover feast. From the time Jesus enters the city until he is crucified, the political significance of these last few days emerges in a rather clear light.

At the time of the annual Passover feast the ancient city of Jerusalem was mobbed with people. Jews from all over the Mediterranean world made pilgrimages to their native homeland to observe this sacred season. Passover was the supreme Jewish holy day and, more than at any other time, nationalistic feelings were at a fever pitch. This feast commemorated the divine act by which God had helped the primitive Hebrews attain their freedom from oppression some 1,300 years before. The remembrance of that act was very much alive among the thousands who mingled together in Jerusalem. It is no wonder that the governors were particularly apprehensive at this time. Each year the Roman garrison made special preparations to quell any Passover disturbances.[1] The authorities must have been especially concerned in the year of Jesus' visit, for there had recently been an insurrection; its leader was at that moment imprisoned in the city, awaiting execution.[2] Because of the conditions then prevailing in Jerusalem, Jesus could hardly have made his appearance at a less opportune time.

The Romans were not the only potentially hostile force with which Jesus had to reckon in the city. As H. T. F. Duckworth points out, it was a Roman practice in the provinces to make the important native offices available "only to men who stood to lose most heavily by wars or revolutions, and whose position in the community was analogous to that of the *nobiles* in Roman society." [3] In Judaea these men were the Sadducean priests. As we have seen, these leaders controlled the temple worship and held the chief positions in the supreme Sanhedrin of Jerusalem. There had been an unusually successful *rapprochement* between this group and Pontius Pilate. This harmony is evidenced by the fact that Caiaphas, the high priest, held his office throughout the ten-year rule of Pilate, in marked contrast to the number of high priests deposed by other governors.[4] The Sadducees had everything to gain by helping to maintain order. In tracing Jesus' activity in Jerusalem it is important to keep in view the aims of these Jewish leaders.

This threatening situation in Jerusalem is revealed quite clearly in our sources. Why then is it hard for us to grasp the significance of these conditions for Jesus' last days? Our problem is the same as that of the Gospel writers: we know that Jesus' mission was not political and that he should not have met troubles of a civil or political nature. That is why it is extremely difficult for us to associate Jesus' death with the political conditions prevailing in Judaea. Yet from the moment of his arrival in the city until his crucifixion, every major development in the story is directly explained by the political tension. This would be obvious to us if the Gospel writers had not focused so much attention in their earlier sections on the *religious* opposition of the Pharisees to Jesus. But the Gospels themselves show that Jesus' arrest and trial did not result from such opposition. On careful inspection they show that an entirely different animosity lies at the root of Jesus' death. We see that animosity clearly in focus when we analyze Jesus' entry into Jerusalem and his "cleansing" of the temple.

According to the Gospels, Jesus' entry into Jerusalem was accompanied by an excited outburst of popular acclaim.[5] A large crowd lined the roadside, shouting greetings and praise at the Galilean prophet. Jesus was heralded as a potential Messiah in language which reflected the Jewish nationalistic hopes. Even the palm branches laid before him were symbolic of the Messianic expectancy.[6] We are also told that Jesus arranged to enter the city on the back of a donkey, apparently as a fulfillment of an ancient prophecy.[7] Undoubtedly the Gospel accounts have been influenced to some extent by later Christian belief in Jesus' divine mission, but the substance of their report is probably true. It would be unimaginative not to see why Jesus' appearance might well have set off a demonstration in Jerusalem. Jesus had attracted large crowds in Galilee— proclaiming the Kingdom of God, teaching with authority and performing remarkable acts of healing. He would naturally have been welcomed with enthusiasm by many of those gathered in Jerusalem, some of whom were from Galilee and knew him firsthand. It can hardly be doubted that to the ears of the Roman and Jewish authorities the acclaim given to Jesus reflected the intense patriotic feelings of the Jews.[8]

Yet however dramatic Jesus' arrival, it was soon overshadowed by another event: his challenge to the Sadducean authority in the temple.

Shortly after he appeared in the city, Jesus made his way to the temple. This central sanctuary of Jewish religious life, a building of remarkable beauty, had been built by Herod the Great, and despite their attitude toward Herod the Jews took justifiable pride in its magnificence. It is possible that Jesus himself had not previously seen the temple, at least not at the time of the Passover feast. When he passed through one of the gates into the temple courtyard, he was shocked by the sight which greeted him. This outer court surrounded a small inner courtyard, within which stood the temple itself. Activity within the temple building proper was carefully regulated, and only specified religious practices were permitted. But in the outer courtyard, where Gentiles were permitted and Jews mingled about freely, the standards of conduct were less rigid. In the absence of severe restrictions certain common practices had developed, as a concession to convenience, which seriously compromised the religious purity of the temple.[9] These practices included the commercial enterprises of the temple priests.

The offering of sacrifices and the payment of the half-shekel temple tax were central to the celebration of the Passover. In paying this annual *per capita* tax, it was not permissible for Jews to use the coins of everyday commerce; worshippers were required to obtain Tyrian half-shekel coins for this purpose.[10] In the time of Jesus, the temple priesthood set up tables in the courtyard, or perhaps on the pillared porch which bordered it,[11] where worshippers could exchange their own money for the needed coins. Since it was also inconvenient for the worshippers to carry sacrificial animals a great distance to the temple, the priests apparently established booths in the courtyard where animals—oxen, sheep and pigeons, according to John[12]—could be bought for sacrifice.[13] Both practices were useful and well-intended, but the effect was to make of the temple grounds more a market-place than a site for reverence. It is also possible that inflated prices were being required of the Passover crowds, since Jesus is said to have called the money-changers "robbers." [14]

Another practice contributed to this undesirable atmosphere. When walking from one area of the city to another, the people sometimes used the outer courtyard as a shortcut, particularly when carrying some burden. The number of people who hurried back and forth through the courtyard undoubtedly swelled during the feast season.

It was into this atmosphere that Jesus walked on his first or second day in the city.[15] Viewing his reaction in human terms, it is reasonable to suppose that his Galilean piety was deeply offended by practices which seemed to him callous and irreligious. He was incensed by the barter and haggling within the shadow of the holy place. The Gospels agree that his response was bold and decisive. By violent means he began to overthrow the commercial activity in the temple courtyard. He overturned the tables of the "money-changers" and the seats of those selling animals, and Mark states that he drove out of the temple grounds not only those who sold but even those who were buying animals. It was not permissible to bring weapons into the temple grounds, but John claims that Jesus used a whip of cords, which he perhaps fashioned hurriedly within the grounds, to disperse those engaged in the traffic of coins and animals.

Our familiarity with this story often dulls our appreciation of its importance and its relevance for the study of Jesus' trial and execution. Jesus' action was not simply a symbolic gesture nor a momentary show of temper, quickly subsided. It was a frontal assault, perhaps planned in advance,[16] on a major activity in the temple, and was accomplished by a remarkable show of force. The Gospels clearly reveal the violence of Jesus' actions.[17] Certainly nothing less would have been sufficient to clear the temple of this commercial activity. It is natural to suppose that Jesus' disciples aided him; it would hardly have been possible for him to have accomplished as much alone.[18] This supposition is furthered by a comment in Mark. He reports that Jesus was in such command of the temple grounds that he effectively prevented any use of the court as a thoroughfare by those carrying burdens.[19] This control would certainly have required the support of his followers. Even if Mark has exaggerated in suggesting that Jesus eliminated such traffic entirely, and even if Jesus' control was of brief duration, the scope of his actions is striking. It is interesting that Matthew, copying Mark almost word-for-word, skips over this reference to the suspension of all trespassing through the courtyard, and Luke also omits it. Their reason is clear enough. It was one thing to show how Jesus defied the Jewish priests and their questionable practices, but quite another to admit that Jesus went so far as to seize control of the grounds and to prohibit all human traffic. There is every reason to believe that Mark's report goes back to the primitive record, and that Matthew and Luke found this record uncomfortable, particularly since they were anxious to show Jesus' political innocence. Although Matthew and Luke edited the record, all the Gospels agree in substance about the nature and significance of Jesus' action.[20] There are few incidents outside the passion narrative on which the Gospels agree so closely. John has relocated the incident to an early stage in Jesus' career, for stylistic reasons,[21] but his description is quite similar to that of the Synoptics.

There is no doubt that Jesus' action was one of the most important and perilous events of the Passover. This surprising assault must have had a great impact on the people and officials alike. The event was undoubtedly witnessed by the Roman soldiers who were posted on the temple wall during the Passover.[22] It is natural to suppose that word of the uproar reached the commanding officer in the Tower of Antonia, at the corner of the temple grounds, where the main body of the Roman garrison was barracked.[23] It would not be surprising if the Romans had intervened directly, because of the potential menace of Jesus' action. However, the Romans would have exercised great restraint, since their intrusion into the sacred grounds would have created a far more serious incident than that created by Jesus himself. As long as the disturbance was contained within the walls of the temple, and as long as there was little or no bloodshed nor violent involvement of large crowds, it is understandable that the soldiers did not intervene directly.

But why did the Jewish authorities themselves not seize Jesus? Even in a less dangerous time, such force and defiance at the temple would have excited the worst fears of those in authority. Why was Jesus not apprehended at once?

The Gospels give a convincing explanation of the delay. They agree that the officials would have arrested Jesus immediately, but they feared to do so because of his popularity with the people.[24] It should be remembered that the Jewish populace evidently gave at least passive support to Jesus' actions. Had his acts been construed as blasphemy or as an affront to the temple, the Jews would have fallen on him themselves. Instead, they apparently reacted sympathetically to Jesus' deed. They may well have interpreted it as a prophetic act which brought honor to him.[25] As a result, any attempt by the Sadducean authorities to arrest Jesus would certainly have been met with an outburst of opposition. The officials were naturally hesitant in this dilemma. They challenged Jesus' authority and joined in heated arguments with him, but they avoided a more forceful confrontation. Within a few days, however, circumstances developed in which Jesus could safely be arrested, tried and convicted with a minimum of public outcry.

.   .   .   .   .

The Gospels agree that Jesus' arrest and trial were the result of a carefully laid plot. The actual details of this conspiracy, as supplied by the Synoptics, are only speculation. The early Christians had no way of knowing exactly what had taken place in the authorities' private chambers. They only knew, from what followed, that some of the officials had made up their minds to get Jesus out of the way.[26] What matters most is not the details of the conspiracy but the motives which inspired the officials in Jerusalem to act against Jesus.

The Gospel writers call special attention to the opposition directed against Jesus throughout his career by the Pharisees. In Mark's account the Pharisees appear in the very first chapter as enemies of Jesus, lurking in the background, finding fault with his words and deeds. Their continual opposition is directed, of course, at his religious message.[27] Even in the last days in Jerusalem the verbal controversies described by the Evangelists relate almost entirely to spiritual topics.[28]

Thus, when we come to the records of the conspiracy, arrest and so on we naturally suppose that these events are explained by the religious opposition of the Pharisees. But this supposition is in error: the Synoptic Gospels themselves make it plain that it was the *temple authorities,* not the Pharisees, who sought Jesus' life, and that religious disputes were not at the root of their actions. In the Gospel accounts of Jesus' death the earlier opposition to his novel religious ideas, his violation of the Sabbath laws, and so on is not in view.[29]

An entirely new set of conditions is now present. We would expect the Evangelists to point the finger of blame directly at the Jewish religious leaders because of their rejection of Jesus' Messiahship; that is the view found in the later Christian writings. But the Gospels admit that the Jewish opposition in the conspiracy and trial was different from that described earlier. The Pharisees are prominent by their absence, except in John, where *all* the forces around Jesus share in seeking his death. It is the Sadducean priests who dominate the scene. This can be documented easily from the Synoptic Gospels.

In the descriptions of the plot the conspirators are said to be the chief priests and scribes (and in Matthew 26:3 the "elders"), and the plot is laid in the court of the high priest. Of all the prominent Jewish leaders, the Pharisees alone are not named.[30] This should not surprise us; nothing would be more incredible than that the Pharisees should have joined their arch-rivals, the Sadducees, in a clandestine plot laid in the very backyard of the high priest. But the other allusions in the Gospels make it even clearer that the Jewish plot resulted from the *political* concerns of the Sadducean authorities. After Jesus had "cleansed" the temple the *chief priests and scribes* sought a way to destroy him.[31] Later, Jesus is accosted by the *chief priests, scribes and elders* who challenge his authority for his action at the temple.[32] Next, it is to these temple authorities that Judas goes to betray Jesus, not to the Pharisees. When we come to the arrest and trial we will see that the Pharisees as a group, and the religious opposition which they represent, again play no part in the proceedings.

In short, it was the small coterie headed by the high priest who instituted the prosecution of Jesus. What caused this group to move against Jesus? It was certainly not their religious objections to the teachings of Jesus which spurred these officials. The creed of the Sadducees was at odds with that of the entire Pharisaic movement; indeed, the vast majority of the people held religious views opposed by the priestly circle. The Sadducees hardly resorted to violent measures in the heart of the Passover celebration simply because Jesus had voiced distinctive religious ideas. Rather, it was their personal political interests which were at stake: this is what led to their decision. Mark specifically tells us that the plot was laid *because the authorities feared the possible consequences of Jesus' activity,* namely, an outbreak of public disturbances.[33] John gives an even more explicit statement of their motives and it is almost certain that he describes the circumstances correctly.

> So the chief priests and the Pharisees gathered the council, and said, "What are we to do? For this man performs many signs. If we let him go on thus, every one will believe in him, and the Romans will come and destroy both our (holy) place and our nation." But one of them, Caiaphas, who was high priest that year, said to them, "You know nothing at all; you do not understand that it is expedient for you that one man should die for the people, and that the whole nation should not perish." (John 11:47-50)

In this account the Jewish leaders fear that Jesus will initiate a disturbance which will bring a disastrous retaliation by the Romans. The means to avoid this calamity is for the officials to do away with Jesus before the whole nation suffers.

Did any Pharisees share in these crucial events? It is virtually certain they did not, despite John's claim to the contrary. If any Pharisees participated, it was undoubtedly their own national loyalties which motivated them also. Some of the leading Pharisees in Jerusalem, perhaps some who sat in the Sanhedrin, may well have shared the fears of the Sadducees and the Romans. It is conceivable that they have thought it necessary to restrain Jesus before serious consequences resulted. But this is only speculation. The point is that the Pharisaic animosity to Jesus' *religious* messages does not explain the events of the passion.

In summary, we cannot know the precise details agreed on by the authorities for disposing of Jesus, but their motives are clear. They considered him a threat to the delicate balance of political order in the city and did not want him to become the spark which might ignite an insurrection.[34] All that restrained the Sadducees was their fear of the public reaction. The people's resentment of the pro-Roman temple officials might easily have become violent if a popular religious figure had been publicly seized and condemned. The arrest of Jesus had to await a suitable time and place when he could be taken quietly with a minimum of disturbance.

.   .   .   .   .

The name of the man who supplied that time and place has become one of the most famous and tragic in history. Yet, at first glance, the most significant feature of Judas Iscariot's betrayal of Jesus is that it seems to have little actual importance for what follows. What attracts our attention is the ignominious character of the betrayal, rather than its historical relevance. Partly for this reason the exact nature of Judas' role has been widely disputed. To some it seems hard to locate an adequate use which Judas served for the authorities, and a few inventive commentators have allowed their imagination to fill in the gaps in the Gospel records.

Two questions have stirred the curiosity of critics: why did Judas betray Jesus, and what information did he supply to the authorities? For reconstructing Jesus' trial and execution, the first question is irrelevant. In tracing these events it does not really matter what impulses moved Judas to seek out the temple officials. This is fortunate, for there is no possibility of answering this popular question, unless we are willing to accept the simple but unlikely explanation in the Gospels that Judas was motivated by greed: he betrayed Jesus for the 30 pieces of silver.[35]

As for the information Judas provided, there are only two likely possibilities. The first is suggested directly by the Gospels—that Judas supplied the authorities with a suitable time and place for the arrest and then identified Jesus personally to the captors. The alternate possibility was put forward by Albert Schweitzer[36] and has since been adopted by a few other commentators: that Judas supplied not the physical opportunity for the arrest, but certain esoteric information about Jesus' mission which proved useful to the authorities in convicting him. In Schweitzer's view, this testimony concerned Jesus' claim to Messiahship, which the Jewish officials then used to condemn Jesus in the trial. This view is based

partly on the argument that Jesus could easily have been apprehended without the treachery of a disciple, since he was seen constantly in the city during the feast. Also, why would an insider's
cooperation be needed to identify a man who was known on sight to
hundreds, including the temple authorities themselves? Judas must
have betrayed something more important, something which could
have been used by the officials in prosecuting Jesus.

One thing which makes this suggestion appealing is that it
endows Judas' betrayal with greater significance; it makes his
crime equal to his guilt, so to speak. But despite its appeal there is
nothing to justify this farfetched theory. Such a conjecture should
at least have some indirect evidence to support it, but in this case
sheer intuition seems to suffice. Nothing in the later course of the
trial requires more of the betrayal than the Gospels describe. Are
we to suppose that the Church remembered Judas' betrayal so well
but completely missed the point of what he betrayed?[37] The Church
could easily have claimed that Judas betrayed Jesus by revealing to
the authorities his claim to be the Messiah. This would have ideally
suited the Church's theology and would also have cast even more
blame on the Jews. But instead the Gospels provide a simple, logical
explanation of Judas' act. It is obvious that the Jewish leaders were
not waiting for some evidence on which to arrest Jesus; of this there
was already more than enough. They sought only a suitable *occasion* at which Jesus might be arrested while not in the public eye.
This was what Judas supplied. Through the perfidy of one of
Jesus' close followers the officials gained a time and place at which
to arrest Jesus without popular interference. Seen in this light, the
Gospels' description of Judas' offer is very interesting. When he
first approaches the priests he has no definite occasion to suggest
for the arrest; he must look for a good opportunity.[38] Shortly thereafter Jesus schedules a private gathering with the disciples at night
in the Garden of Gethsemane, outside the city proper. Judas then
informs the officials, who grasp this opportunity to take Jesus in
secret before any resistance can be mounted by the people.

Finally, it is not unreasonable that Judas should have identified
Jesus personally to his captors. Jesus may have been unknown to

those in the arresting party and a sure identification would be particularly important at night in an out-of-the-way place. There is no reason to suppose that Judas' role was any larger than this. He delivered Jesus into the hands of his adversaries and then pointed him out so there could be no mistake. It is no wonder that the Church remembered him with such bitterness.

.   .   .   .   .

Jesus' brief days in Jerusalem were filled with activity. He had apparently come to the city in order to bring his message to the nation's heart; the Gospels indicate that his wish was amply fulfilled. After the temple incident he engaged in intensive religious discussion with the Pharisees, Sadducees and common folk who were in the city (see Mark 11:27–13:37).

It was evidently on Thursday evening that Jesus sat down with his disciples for what was to be their last meal together.[39] There is good reason to believe the Gospel reports that Jesus knew, at this supper, that the end was near. Even if we leave aside the Gospels' conviction that he had divine foreknowledge of what was to come, it is logical that Jesus should have been fully aware of the serious threat to his safety. The hostility of the officials could hardly have been a secret, and during the meal the small group probably occupied itself with questions about what lay ahead.

Following the supper, Jesus and his followers journeyed outside the city to the Mount of Olives. Luke tells us that this was his custom during his days in Jerusalem. The Mount stood just east of the city and was separated from it by the valley of the brook Kidron. We are not told of anything which took place at the Mount, only that the group moved shortly to the Garden of Gethsemane which lay near its base. Here the Synoptics recount the moving story of Jesus' struggle with himself over his full commitment to God's will. Faced with the imminent danger of losing his life, Jesus agonizes in prayer to God while his followers show their incomprehension by falling asleep. It is into this scene that Judas and the arresting party thrust themselves, armed with weapons and, according to John, with torches and lanterns to light their way.

Who was it who actually came to the garden to seize Jesus? The answer to this question tells us important things about the nature of the opposition which led to his death.

First, it is clear that the Pharisees were not present. It is also obvious that the arresting party did not come to the garden to make an arrest simply because a Galilean rabbi had been expressing radical religious ideas. Mark and Matthew state that a crowd came out "from" [40] the temple authorities. This language apparently refers to certain hired agents. But Luke claims that the temple officials were actually present themselves; in fact, that the chief priests and captains of the temple actually laid hold of Jesus and carried him away. Luke has certainly exaggerated; it is clear that the Sanhedrin had its own police force which was employed in making arrests. [41] Moreover, it is unthinkable that the highest officials of Jerusalem, who could easily have sent armed representatives to the garden, came out during the night bearing clubs and swords to take Jesus captive personally. But all three Synoptics agree in pointing the finger of responsibility at the chief public officials, not at the common folk of Jerusalem nor at the Pharisees who had objected to Jesus' religious views.

As we saw in Chapter 6, the Gospel of John puts a unique interpretation on the arrest. John claims that the arresting party was made up not only of the temple officials themselves, but a cohort of Roman soldiers and their captain [42] as well. If John's account is accurate, it provides dramatic evidence of the political nature of the proceedings against Jesus. It is obvious that the Romans would not have dispatched an armed detachment of troops to the garden to arrest Jesus simply because his religious opinions were unacceptable to some of the Jewish religious leaders. Roman troops could only have been acting on a matter which concerned the civil order.

Is John's claim true? The accuracy of this report has been defended by several commentators. [43] Their chief argument is that no Gospel writer would have *invented* a story involving the Romans, since all the Gospels were intent on placing blame on the Jews and absolving the Romans of all guilt. Since this theme is especially prominent in John, some writers consider it impossible that this

Evangelist could have arbitrarily created a reference to the soldiers. As Maurice Goguel states, ". . . the philo-Roman tendency being still stronger in the Fourth Gospel than in the Synoptic Gospels, it is impossible to suppose that the cohort and the centurion have been introduced into the narrative by John." [44]

It is true enough that the most common argument against John's account has little merit. It is often said that if Roman soldiers had been present they would surely have taken Jesus directly to Pilate, not to the Jewish authorities. [45] But when we remember the close cooperation of the Sadducean priests with Pilate, it seems quite possible that the soldiers could have conducted Jesus first to the Jewish officials so that preparatory charges could be formulated against him prior to the Roman trial.

But John's record must be rejected for other reasons. Our certainty about the political basis of Jesus' arrest must not tempt us into credulously accepting John's statement. He has arbitrarily added the Roman soldiers to the arrest scene, and his reason is obvious if we recall the central emphasis of his account of Jesus' trial and death: John's main concern in the passion narrative is to show that no powers of any kind can prevail against Jesus until he submits voluntarily. This motif is particularly prominent in the arrest scene, where John graphically demonstrates that *all* the forces in Jesus' environment, although united against him, were helpless before his power. The scene is a dramatic tableau, such as an artist might construct to portray the majesty of Jesus. According to John, the garden is filled not only with high priestly officials (not merely their servants), but with a whole cohort of Roman troops—six hundred men! [46]—and in addition, *Jesus' religious opponents, the Pharisees.* All these are deployed about Jesus and his small band of followers. Yet this entire assemblage falls helplessly to the ground when Jesus steps forward and addresses them. Indeed, Jesus is forced to insist that his captors take him into custody; they are unable to act until he instructs them about their role in the divine drama. This scene is obviously a symbolic representation of Jesus' divinity, not a literal description of what took place in the garden. [47]

The symbolism is underlined by John's inclusion of the Pharisees. Although missing in the Synoptic accounts, this group is added by John because they also have been Jesus' enemies and it must be shown that they, like the Jewish and Roman officials, are impotent before him. It is interesting that the Roman cohort and their captain and the Jewish officials all share physically in seizing and binding Jesus. No more than two or three captors were needed to remove Jesus, and, again, it is incredible to suppose that the noblest members of the Jewish aristocracy and of the Pharisees were in the garden and personally assisted in taking Jesus by violence. Such details are merely the product of John's imaginative pen, designed to heighten the impact of the moment when the Son of God falls victim to evil men.

Thus, John's usual apologetic interest—to blame the Jews and absolve the Romans—has been overcome in this instance by his emphasis on Jesus' deity. Further, it was not difficult for John to introduce the Roman troops into the garden. In Mark a full cohort of troops is present at the Roman trial; John simply revises this tradition and advances the participation of the soldiers to the arrest scene. The supposition that John would not have arbitrarily added the Romans fails to take into account the important dogmatic significance of this section. John would not have hesitated to omit the soldiers if he had found their presence embarrassing. Rather, he has interjected them into the story because they served his particular purpose. We can feel confident that the group which seized Jesus in Gethsemane was composed simply of the paid servants of the temple priests.

The Gospels agree that the men who follow Judas into the garden are armed with clubs and swords, prepared for violent resistance. Jesus is not being arrested as one who had voiced unorthodox religious teachings, but as one thought to be—literally—a dangerous man. Some of the disciples themselves were armed with swords. It is surprising to find any Jews bearing arms, considering the prevailing conditions, and this act seems especially foreign to the aims of Jesus and his disciples. As we have seen, Luke states that the group had made definite plans at their last meal together to have these arms ready for just such an emergency. This reference is one of the most thought-provoking in the entire New Testament; it is remarkable that so little attention has been paid to it. Many commentators have sought to avoid the meaning of Jesus' words by searching for some hidden spiritual meaning in them.[48] But the scene which follows proves that Jesus' words and those of the disciples must be taken literally. In the garden the disciples actually use their swords in a brief resistance to the arrest. Here again we are surprised *only if Jesus' apprehension as a political criminal is not kept in view*. Jesus' disciples were not prepared for bloodshed because Jesus' message was adversely received in Jerusalem. Rather they recognized that his actions in routing the temple officials and in "stirring up the people" (Luke 23:5) had brought him under the eye of the city's officials, who were responsible for keeping the peace. For this reason they were armed, expecting the worst. But their defense of Jesus in the garden disintegrated quickly and they all fled.

Finally, Jesus' own words to the captors emphasize specifically the political character of the arrest. Jesus' objection to the arrest party is not so much to his being arrested, but to his being arrested *as an insurrectionist* (*lestes*). This word *lestes* can only refer, here and throughout the New Testament, to a political criminal, particularly an insurrectionist.[49] In this saying Jesus rebukes the temple agents for treating him as if he were a rebel engaged in secret sedition, since he has been teaching openly at the temple. This saying alone should dispense with one of the most common interpretations of the trial, namely, that Jesus was arrested and tried by the Jews on religious grounds, and that only later was a political charge trumped up, in order to get Pilate to pass sentence against Jesus. The arrest scene shows that civil issues are already at the root of the problem. This reasoning holds true even if Jesus' words to his captors are only the later creation of the Church. In that case, the Church has indicated, through this tradition, that Jesus was seized and put on trial because the authorities regarded him as another Zealot trouble-maker. There is some doubt about the authenticity of Jesus' words, because he concludes by saying (in Mark and Matthew) that his arrest merely fulfills the scriptures. The early Christians put great stress on Jesus' fulfillment of scripture, particularly in the passion events, and there are obviously several passages in our Gospels which arose later in the Church because of this desire to show how Jesus' suffering and death had fulfilled the ancient prophecies. Therefore, all references by Jesus to his fulfillment of scripture are considered suspect by many critics. But any doubts should apply only to the last clause in Mark and Matthew. The remark concerning *lestes* is independent in thought and construction, and there is no reason to suppose that this tradition was developed simply as a fulfillment of prophecy. This is emphasized by the fact that Luke relates the same saying by Jesus about *lestes* but without any reference to the fulfillment of the scriptures. This very apt and pointed remark by Jesus at the crucial moment of his arrest would probably have been well remembered by the disciples. It was, in fact, probably the last words they heard from his lips before he was raised onto the cross. The fact that it is found in all three Synoptic Gospels, and in similar form in John, adds to our assurance. There can be little doubt that Jesus objected to his seizure as a teacher of violence and rebellion.

But despite his objections, Jesus was taken in hand and dragged from the garden. To their later humiliation, the disciples deserted him and ran away into the night. They were not in the crowd when Jesus was taken to the house of the high priest, where formal charges were to be preferred against him.

10

THE JEWISH PROCEEDINGS
AGAINST JESUS

"What further testimony do we need?"

Luke 22:71

After Jesus is taken at night from the Garden of Gethsemane, the events suddenly slip into darkness, both literally and
figuratively. The hours between Jesus' nocturnal arrest and his
presentation the next morning before Pilate present us our chief
problem in unravelling his trial and execution. The heart of this
problem is deciphering the Jewish proceedings against Jesus.

So serious are the difficulties that we have to ask whether there
is any hope of determining what actually took place behind the closed
doors of the Jewish chambers. A good many critics have answered
negatively.[1] This doubt arises from four factors. First, it is here in
the Jewish proceedings that our Gospels seem to be most divergent
and confused. After the arrest, our four accounts immediately begin
to disagree with one another much more dramatically than before.
Second, it is also at this point that the Christian doctrinal and
apologetic interests seem to have taken their biggest toll on the

113

reliability of the accounts. Since it was an irresistible tendency of the early Christians to overemphasize the guilt of the Jews, the Church's records of the Jewish legal proceedings were especially susceptible to distortion. There is strong evidence that the early Church has completely rewritten the role played by the Jewish people and their officials in the events surrounding Jesus' death, particularly in the story of the "Jewish trial." Also, how could the early Christians have known what had taken place in the secret sessions of the Jewish authorities? There were no Christian eyewitnesses. Nor is there any likely way in which the small handful of early Christians could have obtained a careful, objective summary of what had been said and done. Finally, the earliest Christians were primarily peasant-folk who were not trained in court procedures. They were not then concerned (as we are now) with the technical processes of the trial.[2] These dedicated followers, who were not ashamed to be labelled "unlearned" people,[3] had little interest in the legal subtleties which had resulted in Jesus' death. We attempt the impossible when we try to transform these first Christians into modern-day court reporters who can satisfy our curiosity on every legal point.

All this is why Montefiore's sentiment is a frequent one: "We shall never be able to tell or decide with any certainty what took place in the high priest's house . . ."[4]

But such extreme skepticism is unjustified. It is true that we cannot recover the precise details—the actual words spoken by the authorities and by Jesus between his arrest and his presentation to Pilate. These are irrevocably lost. But they are of little consequence for understanding the *overall purpose and nature* of the Jewish action. There are excellent reasons for believing that we can recover the main course followed by the temple officials, if we make a careful study of our sources and of the historical circumstances and outcome of the trial.[5]

There is one key which unlocks the correct understanding of the Jewish proceedings against Jesus. That is the realization that the nighttime "Jewish trial" described by Mark (and copied by Matthew) is completely unhistorical. Discrediting this tradition is the most important single step in analyzing Jesus' trial correctly. This supposed Jewish trial represents a grave and lamentable distortion of the events of that night. More than all other factors combined it has created the confusion over the causes of Jesus' death and the legal procedures by which it occurred. We have already touched briefly on this fact; it is now time to present the full case against this unfortunate unit of tradition.[6]

·   ·   ·   ·   ·

By the proper reckoning, the story that Jesus was formally tried by the Jewish authorities on religious charges—*at night or at any other time*—is a minority report in our sources. It contradicts the clear statement of the majority of our accounts. It is essential to deal with this tradition in that perspective, rather than as a consensus of all the Gospels.

This Jewish trial is related first by Mark. Matthew then copies it almost verbatim from him. It is clear that Matthew does not bring us any independent information, any second source, concerning the trial. Almost no scholar has ever suggested that Matthew had any special material whatever to contribute to the trial narrative.[7] The case is much as if a modern scholar were to analyze Jesus' trial, then a second person were simply to copy his study. The numerical addition of this second study would not lend the theory any greater weight; we would still have only one analysis. That is just our situation with regard to Mark and Matthew. These two Gospels together give us *one* early Christian record of the trial—a record which tells of a formal Jewish prosecution of Jesus by the whole Sanhedrin shortly after his arrest.

But Luke gives us a very different story. As we have seen, although Luke obviously makes some use of Mark, he rejects Mark's story of a Jewish trial. In fact, he indicates that there were *no judicial proceedings whatever at night*. In the morning there was only an inquiry, at which Jesus was subjected to questions. In Luke there are no blasphemy charges, no disagreeing witnesses, no formal condemnation, no announcement that Jesus must suffer death. Were we to rely on Luke alone, it would be clear that the Jewish proceedings were only of a grand-jury nature, and were a preparation for the Roman trial. I have already argued that Luke is using an independent source in the passion narrative. But Luke's version is equally significant if it is only the author's own editorial revision of Mark. In the latter case Luke has consciously rejected Mark's account and replaced it with one which he considers more authentic. Whatever the source of Luke's material, he supplies us a second, independent account of the trial, one which contains no reference to any Jewish prosecution.

Third, we have John. Like Luke, John also rejects the Markan story of a Jewish trial and gives an entirely different version of what happened. As noted, it is very difficult to tell when John is relying on special sources and when he is merely creating his own material. But whichever view we take in this case, John gives us a detailed record of the trial events which specifically omits any mention of a Jewish trial. Again there are no formal religious charges, no condemnation, no sentence. In fact, in John we do not even hear of a Jewish assembly of any kind. Jesus is interrogated by two individuals, Annas and Caiaphas, and then taken directly to Pilate. Here also, if we were judging Jesus' trial by this Gospel alone, it would not occur to us to believe that Jesus had been subjected to a Jewish trial in which he was formally convicted of any religious offense.

Thus we have three primary sources for studying the events, two of which reject the notion of a Jewish trial. But even Matthew seems reluctant to follow Mark's version without qualification. Matthew pointedly avoids the statement that the Jewish proceedings ended in a formal condemnation of Jesus. Although his passion narrative puts even greater emphasis than Mark's on the hostility of the Jews toward Jesus, Matthew balks at the claim that there was a formal judicial condemnation by the Jews. In fact, it is possible to argue that in Matthew, as in Luke and John, there is only a Jewish *inquiry*. If we read Matthew's account on its own terms, without reference to Mark, we find a nocturnal Council meeting at which the Jewish leaders agree that Jesus must die, but they do not convict him of any religious charges.[8] As we saw earlier, Matthew also refuses to repeat Mark's claim that the witnesses against Jesus could not agree. This is further evidence of his hesitancy to blame the Jews for an illegal and unjust prosecution.

All this is why we must avoid the notion that the nighttime trial is a central part of the tradition by which all other parts of the narrative must be interpreted. This Markan section has long been the cornerstone of most trial interpretation, but it should never have carried this weight. It is only a rather frail strand of tradition which is not only refuted by our other sources but which can be shown to be unhistorical on still other grounds.

A final factor must be considered in evaluating our three sources. Whenever we are assessing the historicity of any Gospel material it is helpful to ask: why might this unit have found its way into the record if it is not actually true? If we can find no obvious answer, that fact tends to affirm the historical reliability of the section. Conversely, when some passage which is prominent in one Gospel is missing in another, we can ask: why would this Evangelist have omitted this section, if it is obvious that he must have been familiar with it? The answer often gives us another good insight into the historical value of the passage.

These two questions are extremely useful in the case of the Jewish trial in Mark's account. A strong argument against this section is the fact that it is so easy to see why Mark would have added this tradition to his account of the trial, even if it were not true; but it is virtually impossible to see why Luke and John would have omitted this story if they had considered it an authentic part of the trial events. This Markan unit was profoundly useful to the Church in presenting its views about Jesus' death. This tradition cast the blame upon the Jews; it depicted the Jewish leaders as perverse and irresponsible opponents of Jesus; it showed that religious rather than political disputes lay at the root of Jesus' death; and it shifted the blame for the crucifixion away from Pilate and the Romans, which was an urgent Christian concern! There is hardly any passage in the Gospels which could have had more *usefulness* in the developing Church's struggles on Gentile soil. Furthermore, these same apologetic interests were just as important to Luke and John as to Mark. Luke was especially anxious to fix the blame upon the

Jews. In his account of the Roman trial he vividly intensifies the Jewish animosity toward Jesus. The Jewish officials are almost beside themselves in their desire for Jesus' death, and Pilate is all the more convinced of Jesus' innocence. Yet Luke, working with Mark's account as he composed his own trial story, stopped short of resorting to Mark's account of a Jewish trial, although it would have clinched his argument. As the early Church's chief historian, Luke apparently found it possible to exaggerate, but he was not willing to rewrite history entirely in order to make his point.

The same is true of John. John is also intent on emphasizing the Jewish guilt. In this Gospel the entire nation is depicted as Jesus' enemy, even during his earlier ministry; yet John does not resort to Mark's device in order to underline his argument.

Considering the value of this section for the Church, it is striking that both these later Gospels reject it and that even Matthew qualifies it. Here was just the material the Church needed: how tempting to pin the guilt squarely on the Jews by means of this tradition! Yet our other Gospels avoid this Markan claim and give an account of the trial which fits the historical circumstances much more closely. Although Luke and John do not agree in detail, they both affirm that the Jewish officials merely conducted an inquiry, which served as a preparation for the trial before Pilate. This interpretation of the trial should be regarded as the majority opinion in our sources, against which Mark's account cannot prevail.

.   .   .   .   .

How then could this distorted tradition of a Jewish trial have arisen?

We can dismiss any suggestion of a conscious historical fraud. It misses the point to imagine that certain early Christians concocted this fictitious record with the expressed purpose of casting blame on an innocent people. Rather, this story was an almost inevitable outgrowth of the basic Christian conviction about the Jewish guilt. Considering the bitter hostility which developed between Christians and Jews in the early years of the Church, it would have been virtually impossible for some such tradition not to develop in some Christian quarters.

This becomes clear if we recall the historical setting of the trial events. At the moment when Jesus was seized and taken from the garden, *all of his disciples fled*. Up to this point in the narrative the Gospels have given a rather lucid account of the events in Jerusalem, because their records are based on the remembrances of Jesus' followers. But after the arrest, the disciples deserted Jesus and ran away in fear.[9] This is almost a certain historical fact. It was only Jesus' adversaries who were present at the ensuing proceedings. There were no Christian eye-witnesses; no followers who could later give even a rough accounting of what had taken place.

Therefore, the earliest Christians had to evaluate the trial events from what they actually knew: that the Jewish authorities had arrested Jesus, had held him in custody, and had conducted some sort of proceedings before taking him to Pilate. The Christians did not know the exact nature of these proceedings, but they knew their cause—the animosity of the Jewish leaders—and their result—Jesus' arraignment before Pilate and his execution. It was only a brief step to interpret the Jewish activity as a formal prosecution of Jesus, based on the same sort of *religious* opposition which he had encountered during his career. Since the first Christians knew that some Jewish officials had arrested Jesus and had instituted proceedings against him, they needed only the slightest nudge to believe that these officials had actually tried and condemned Jesus themselves.

In addition, it hardly occurred to the early Christians to assign "political" motivations to the Jewish leaders. The Christians' own interests were wholly religious, as Jesus' had been. To these early Palestinian disciples, who had little interest in political affairs, the Romans were a remote enemy. For them Jesus was the Anointed One from God, not a political pretender. Although the Jewish officials had acted because they considered Jesus a civil threat, not a religious blasphemer, this fact would have been quickly blurred in the Christian memory. It was inevitable that the entire sequence of events would be viewed by these Christians in a religious light.

Also, in the months after Jesus' death there was never any

calm dialogue between these two camps which might have altered these judgments. The Sadducean priests had acted by stealth for their own interests; they certainly would not have wished to discuss their actions openly and frankly with Jesus' followers. We should not imagine that the full facts of the case were ever laid bare before the Christians. The deep rift between the two groups soon reached such proportions that the Christians were excluded from the synagogues, physically intimidated, and ultimately cut off from the Jewish nation.[10] Under these conditions it would have been amazing if the early Christians had developed a measured, "objective" account of the Jewish involvement in Jesus' death.

The development of this Jewish-trial tradition is further clarified when we recall that our written records of the trial were not set down until long after the events. Even if our accounts had been produced within a year or so after Jesus' death, we would expect them to be richly colored by the Christian sentiments. But some forty years elapsed between the events of that day and the writing of Mark's Gospel. During that long period the story had been retold countless times all the way from Jerusalem to Rome. Although the main outline of the passion events was determined quite early, there was room for inventive elaboration, as our Gospels show. It was no problem for this altered tradition to intrude itself here or there into the record.

It is particularly instructive to see how Mark made use of this later tradition. He inserted it into his record with little effort to make it compatible with the rest of his account; it is almost as if he inserted it as an afterthought between the lines of his existing story, without making any logical place for it. If we remove this section (14:55–65), the narrative reads smoothly without any editorial adjustment whatever. Our story then states that Jesus was taken from the garden, that Peter followed at a distance, and that the officials gathered after daybreak in a consultation of some sort. This revised account fits the Lukan version almost exactly and also approximates John's description.

Because of this nighttime trial, Mark's reference to the morning meeting of the Sanhedrin has now become redundant and pointless.

Mark can assign no meaning whatever to this morning assembly of the Jewish officials; he leaves it in the record only because it was a fixed part of the trial narrative.[11] It is usually supposed that this second meeting was held for the purpose of preparing false political charges to be used before Pilate, since the Jews either could not or would not execute Jesus for his alleged religious crimes. But this view is unfounded: there is nothing in Mark's narrative to suggest this explanation of the morning meeting. If Mark intended this interpretation of the two meetings, he missed an excellent opportunity to say so. Such an explanation would have fit perfectly with the Christian effort to show that the political charges were only a fraudulent device of the Jewish leaders. But Mark was not as sophisticated as many modern interpreters; it did not occur to him to rewrite the trial story entirely. Fortunately for us, he merely placed this fictional trial in his record without adapting the rest of his material to it.

It is especially regrettable that Mark placed this Jewish trial in the middle of the night. The nocturnal hour is often cited as evidence of the treachery of the officials, who hastily moved against Jesus and hid their actions from public view. But of course this completely misses the point. Mark *had* to locate the trial during the night, simply because there could have been no other time for it. By force of circumstance, this unit had to be inserted between the arrest and the Council meeting at daybreak. The nighttime hour has no greater significance than that. Yet because of it, even greater abuse has been heaped upon the Jewish officials through the centuries. This is an example of how profoundly Mark's story has affected our understanding of the proceedings.

Perhaps the clearest refutation of this section is simply its incredibility, taken as a whole. This unit would strain our belief even if there were no special evidence against it. In order to accept Mark's account, we must believe that the supreme Sanhedrin of Jerusalem —the nation's leading religious and judicial body—gathered furtively during the night and conducted hasty and prejudicial proceedings against Jesus; and that they did so in the very season when its members would have been especially preoccupied with the most careful observance of religious and civil regulations, namely, the Passover season.

The Synoptic Gospels agree that Jesus was arrested and tried on the day of the Passover feast.[12] From the standpoint of probabilities, there was no day in the year when the Sanhedrin would have been less likely to engage in such clandestine and illegal activity. The Passover was observed according to the strictest rules; it called for the most careful exercises of piety. Yet the Sanhedrin's members are found violating every rule of moral and judicial ethics under the cover of darkness. Even the logistics of such a meeting raise serious doubts: were all the Sanhedrin's members available on a moment's notice to gather in the night in order to place Jesus on trial?

Further, there can be no doubt that the Sanhedrin's proceedings, as described by Mark, would have been flagrantly illegal. It is often noted that the Jewish trial in Mark violates fourteen points in the Jewish judicial regulations described in the *Mishnah*. Many commentators discount Mark's story on that basis alone. We have already shown why it cannot be assumed that all these Mishnaic regulations were in force during Jesus' lifetime, particularly those which relate to the handling of capital cases,[13] but it is highly probable that at least *some* of these rules were applicable during the first century,[14] and one could say that if the Sanhedrin was bound by any rules whatever, this "trial" would surely have violated them.[15] We must assume either that this trial was illegal or that Mark's account of it is unhistorical. The available evidence overwhelmingly substantiates the latter view.

The incredibility of Mark's account is heightened by his description of the conduct of the Sanhedrin members. Luke tells us that some of the arresting party manhandled and taunted Jesus after seizing him. But Mark and Matthew assign this severe personal abuse to the Council members themselves. One must have considerable contempt for the quality of the nation's leaders in order to accept such a tradition. Their treatment of Jesus—spitting on him, striking him, yelling insults—is such as we would expect from the worst rabble of Jerusalem. As B. W. Bacon notes, it is surely beyond reason to imagine such conduct from a Sanhedrin composed of men like Gamaliel and Nicodemus.[16]

In summary, there can be little doubt that this "Jewish trial" was not part of the earliest passion narrative. It is unlikely that Mark created this unit himself, but it is quite possible that he was the first to set this later tradition down in writing. It is very interesting that Mark's Gospel is usually believed to have been produced in Rome. This would put it farther from the scene of the passion events than any of our other Gospels, and thus more remote from the facts. Rome is also the one city in which it would have been most urgent to assign the blame wholly to the Jews and to show that Jesus' death resulted from religious rather than political opposition. It is probably no coincidence that this "Roman" Gospel, Mark, contains this tradition which would have been so useful in that city.

.   .   .   .   .

Once the Mark/Matthew account of a formal Jewish trial has been removed from our records, most of the haze enveloping the events begins to clear away. The most obvious effect of this removal is to render all discussion of the blasphemy charges against Jesus irrelevant.

For years there has been an extensive debate of the exact nature of the charge on which Jesus was convicted at the Jewish trial. Most of this discussion has presumed that Jesus was condemned for his personal blasphemy, since Mark specifically gives that explanation.[17] But exactly what was blasphemous in Jesus' words? Was it the total weight of his answer to the high priest (Mark 14:62)? Was it his remarks concerning the destruction of the temple?[18] Was it the claim to be the Messiah or the Son of the Blessed, or his reference to sitting at the right hand of God? What were the Jewish laws governing blasphemy in Jesus' day? The answer to these questions has usually been sought through a minute examination of both Mark's record and the Jewish literature of this period.[19]

But such efforts pursue a useless course. The explanation of Jesus' death is not found in any religious claims he made before the assembled Sanhedrin after he was arrested. There was no formal trial, on religious charges or any other. Even if we were to accept this nocturnal trial as historical, we could not regard Mark's account as a verbatim transcript of the very words spoken. In fact, there are few places in the Gospels where we would have less right to expect an exact and detailed account. Not only were there no Christian witnesses, but the words supplied by Mark are a reflection of the early Church's beliefs about Jesus, rather than his own self-testimony. It is clear that these are the Church's words, and in this tradition the early Christians are affirming that Jesus is the Messiah, the Son of the Blessed, who will soon return in power from his throne at the side of God. This scene before the Sanhedrin must not be read as a precise explanation of Jesus' conviction, but as a dramatic declaration of the faith of the early Christian community.

Removing the Jewish trial story also brings a second major result. At one stroke we are able to dispense with the long-standing view that the Jews first convicted Jesus of a religious charge and then switched the charge to a political one in order to secure a conviction before Pilate. This has been the most popular interpretation of the trial, somewhat more often among popular authors than among serious students of the trial.

Faced with the dilemma of a full-scale Jewish trial on religious grounds, and a subsequent trial before Pilate, many readers have naturally settled on this solution. After all, what purpose could have been served by a separate trial before the Roman governor, once the Jews had already convicted Jesus? There obviously could have been no further *religious* trial before Pilate. We can feel certain that the Roman governor would not have put a native Jew on trial for his life because he had violated a certain Jewish religious regulation. The proceedings before Pilate were clearly based on civil or political questions. By deduction, then, the Jewish officials must have changed the charges against Jesus after they had convicted him of blasphemy.[20]

But why should they have done so? As we saw in Chapter 1, three answers have commonly been supplied. First, the Jews were forced to this subterfuge because they lacked the authority to execute Jesus. They had to get Pilate to execute him, and for this they needed political charges. Second, the authorities switched the charges because they did not want to assume the public blame for Jesus' death; they wanted Pilate to appear the culprit. Therefore, they duped him into believing that Jesus was a political offender. Third, the Jews did not take Jesus to Pilate for a trial at all. They only sought for Pilate to ratify their own conviction of Jesus, and to grant them the right to execute him—or even to perform this act for them.

But such tortuous speculation is eliminated once the night trial disappears.[21] The exhaustive debate over these solutions shows how impossible it is to solve the riddles of the trial if we accept Mark's account. By accepting Mark's version, we not only lose sight of the political character of the trial, we also multiply our problems, literally. We have to wrestle with *two* trials on *two* entirely different charges in *two* courts before *two* sets of magistrates. The removal of this single strand of tradition immediately reduces the trial to its proper dimensions.

. . . . .

We thus arrive at the question: if there was no formal Jewish trial, what action did the temple officials take against Jesus between the time of his arrest and his trial before Pilate?

We can feel sure that these authorities simply conducted an informal inquiry. This inquiry was for the purpose of indicting Jesus as a threat to the civil order and perhaps as an insurrectionist. The evidence for this view comes from three strands of evidence: the political character of the opposition which led to Jesus' arrest, the ensuing trial before Pilate on political charges, and the testimony of Luke and John.

We have already explored the first of these three. Jesus' arrest resulted from the fear of some Jewish officials that he would ignite a political uprising during the Passover season. After they had arrested Jesus, we would naturally expect them to cement their concerns by conducting a firsthand investigation, after which they would take Jesus to Pilate. We would not anticipate any formal Jewish trial, for it was not their responsibility to prosecute political crimes. That was the province of the Roman government. The officials could only prepare the indictment to be presented to the governor.

This supposition is substantiated by what takes place at the Roman trial. The Jewish officials present Jesus as a troublemaker who has stirred up the people and who has kingly pretensions. This indictment bears out the suggestion that the Jewish officials simply built a case against Jesus for use before the governor.

But we are not dependent only on these deductions. Both Luke and John specifically present the actions of the Jewish officials as a questioning of Jesus, without any conviction or condemnation. Interestingly, John merely states that "the high priest questioned Jesus about his disciples and his teaching." This is a good summary, for it is all that was known with accuracy. Luke supplies some of the actual interrogation, but his description is only a reflection of the Christian belief that Jesus openly affirmed his divine Sonship before these hostile officials. As in the case of Mark, Luke's dialogue is based on the early Church's faith rather than on an actual remembrance of Jesus' words.

Yet there is one point of special significance about this inquiry. All the Synoptics make the subject of Messiahship central to this investigation. It is likely that this report is correct, even though the Evangelists have misconstrued its meaning. It is clear that the issue of "kingship" was central when Jesus was accused before Pontius Pilate; therefore, it is reasonable to suppose that the Jewish proceedings against Jesus dwelt on his claim to be the Messiah, *because of the political implications which this word would have conveyed to Pilate*. To Romans, the equivalent of "Messiah" (*Christos*) would have been "king" (*Basileus*). Further, the political overtones of Jewish Messianism could not have been unknown to the governor. Since the issue of Jesus' kingship was central at the Roman trial, the temple officials must have examined Jesus closely on this point. That is just what the Gospels indicate, although they naturally direct their attention to the spiritual, not the political, significance of the investigation.

What was Jesus' reply to these questions about Messiahship? A verbatim record would be of tremendous interest to us here. It would give us insight into one of our most perplexing questions: what concept did Jesus have of his own ministry? While most Christians would consider this a strange question, it has long been one of the most celebrated issues of New Testament study. We can only conjecture, but the evidence of the Roman trial suggests that Jesus did voice a Messianic claim of some sort during the Jewish investigation. Before Pilate, Jesus is charged with the *claim* to kingship, and he is examined directly by Pilate on this point. If Jesus had denied any such self-designation at the Jewish inquiry, it seems unlikely that this issue would have been so central in the Roman trial. However, all this is speculation, for our records of the Roman trial have also been seriously affected by the Church's theology, and we cannot put confidence in their exact phraseology. What matters for our purposes is that, at their inquiry, the Jewish officials satisfied themselves that Jesus should be taken before Pilate as an enemy of the Roman government. That was all which their investigation was intended to accomplish.[22]

Who was involved in this inquiry? The reasons for believing that only a small handful of temple officials was active in the effort to remove Jesus have already been traced. It was probably later Christian tradition which involved the entire Sanhedrin.[23] The Mark/Matthew report that the whole Council participated is based on the tradition of a formal trial; it has no historical value. Luke mentions only the chief priests and scribes; there is no reference to the Pharisaic members whom he certainly would have designated if they had taken part. The conspiracy and arrest had been conducted by the temple officials centered about the high priest; it was undoubtedly this same group which conducted the inquiry. John agrees with Luke that the whole Sanhedrin was not involved.

Was Annas among those who made the investigation, as John claims? This suggestion is one of those tantalizing historical references which are so difficult to evaluate. Fortunately, Annas' presence or absence does not materially affect the course of events. The best attitude toward John's claim is a mild skepticism, based on the absence of Annas' name in the Synoptics and the fact that John shows a very strong interest in making Jesus' opposition as powerful as possible in the arrest and trial. He alone has added the Roman soldiers and the Pharisees; how fitting that he alone should add the most prominent member of the Jewish hierarchy.[24] On the other hand, Annas may well have been present: because of his leadership in the Sanhedrin, it is reasonable that he should have played some role in the seizure and investigation of Jesus. Although he was no longer the high priest, he would certainly have been granted the right of interrogating Jesus, perhaps even before the other officials gathered at daybreak.

We can summarize the Jewish proceedings as follows: after Jesus was removed from the garden he was held in custody and probably subjected to some abuse by the temple servants who had taken him into custody;[25] he may have been taken to the house of Annas and questioned briefly. In the morning, a group of the temple officials gathered and conducted an investigation into his activities. They asked him about his teachings, his followers, and particularly his personal claims and ambitions. We do not know whether any witnesses were called to testify, nor the exact course of the discussion. Since no Christian witnesses were present, the accounts in Luke and John are simply summations based on the later course of events. However, there is good reason to believe that special attention was directed toward Jesus' claim to be the Messiah, and it seems probable that Jesus affirmed such a claim. When the officials were satisfied that they had adequate information for an indictment, they dismissed the hearing and prepared to take Jesus before the governor. The preliminary stage of Jesus' prosecution was ended.

11

THE ROMAN CONDEMNATION

". . . perverting our nation . . ."
Luke 23:2

It was about mid-morning on Friday when a small group of Jewish officials presented Jesus to Pontius Pilate as an accused criminal.

This was undoubtedly the first encounter between the two men. Pilate had probably arrived in Jerusalem only shortly before the day of Jesus' trial. The governor's residence was in the coastal city of Caesarea and, like the other procurators, he had made the special journey to the city at the Passover season, accompanied by a detachment of troops, because of the importance of the celebration and the threat of uprisings. It is unlikely that Pilate had heard of this itinerant Galilean rabbi prior to his trip to Jerusalem. In fact, Jesus may have been unknown to Pilate up until the moment when he was ushered into the governor's presence at the praetorium.

If we could transport ourselves back into the original scene we would undoubtedly be struck by the casualness of the proceedings which were to take place. Jesus' trial was almost surely conducted very informally, quite unlike the processes which we associate with courtroom activity today. Judicial administration in the provinces was much less precise and technical than that which was required in Rome itself.[1] Pilate's investigation of the charges was probably brief and to the point, much as Mark's account suggests. Further, we must not exaggerate the importance which this meeting had for Pilate. Only in retrospect was this encounter to appear as a decisive moment in history. For the governor it was nothing new to face accused criminals from among the Jewish populace or to pronounce sentences of death.

In analyzing what took place before Pilate we meet problems which are much different from those encountered in the Jewish proceedings. Fortunately, despite their interest and complexity, they do not obscure the main course of events nearly so much as in the case of the priests' investigation of Jesus. The chief difficulty is not in understanding the general purpose or the outcome of these Roman proceedings. It is clear that Jesus was on trial before the governor as a threat to the peace of a Roman province and perhaps specifically as an insurrectionist. He was interrogated, witnesses spoke against him, and he was pronounced guilty and sentenced to death. It is strange that it has been necessary to insist on this basic reconstruction.[2] As we have seen, Pilate certainly would not have condemned Jesus for any transgression of the Jewish religious code.[3] Nor is there the slightest suggestion in the Synoptics that the Jews were merely seeking for Pilate to approve their own conviction of Jesus. Jesus was on trial for his life before the Roman governor and the basis of the prosecution was his danger to the Roman state. The very means of execution shows that Jesus died as an offender against Rome, not against the Jewish nation. As already emphasized, crucifixion was exclusively a Roman means of execution, never a Jewish one.[4] This extremely cruel and protracted punishment was employed by the Romans especially in cases of treason.[5]

So there can be no reasonable doubt that Jesus was examined and convicted on charges of disrupting, or at least threatening, the peace of a Roman province. Our problems lie instead in a series of related questions which surround this central fact. *Why* was Jesus convicted of political crimes? Was it simply because the Jews intimidated Pilate into condemning him despite his innocence? Why do we find a large segment of the populace, who had apparently been favorable toward Jesus, suddenly clamoring for him to be crucified? What role in the trial was played by Herod Antipas and by the enigmatic figure Barabbas?

On the first question the Gospels give a uniform answer: Jesus was convicted because the Jewish officials coerced Pilate into acting against him although he believed Jesus innocent. Mark presents this interpretation rather simply, without elaboration. But the later three Gospels intensify it strikingly. In these Gospels the chief dialogue is not between Pilate and Jesus but between Pilate and the Jewish leaders. They plead with Pilate, they cajole and taunt him with threats in order to force his hand against Jesus. Pilate is increasingly insistent that Jesus has done no wrong and is even impressed by Jesus' words and manner. But in the end Pilate weakens. He lacks the will to resist the Jewish leaders and the people who have gathered outside, so he ultimately consigns Jesus to his death. According to the Gospels, Jesus' execution was formally because of his conviction on political charges but actually because of the hatred of the Jewish officials and the Jewish people for Jesus.

Such unanimous testimony is a strong argument for the accuracy of the Gospel records. Whenever all four Gospels agree on a specific point the presumption always favors their reliability. But the evidence against this Gospel claim is so strong, and the motives for its development so transparent, that it must be rejected as a piece of theological and apologetic fiction. The nature of these motives has been explored in Chapter 7 and again in the analysis of the Jewish proceedings. A central aim of the Church's trial narratives was to show that Jesus had not been a political criminal and that he had died only because of the hostility of the Jewish people and their leaders. This dual interest inevitably led the Church to recast the roles of Pilate and the Jewish authorities: Pilate was made a weak, subservient ruler and the Jewish officials became the vicious and overpowering opponents who bent the governor to their will.

Neither of these portraits will bear close examination. It completely reverses the historical circumstances to suppose that the Jewish temple officials were at liberty to enter the praetorium and to demand that the Roman governor do their bidding. Even if they had been able to do so, there would have been no reason for these officials to strive heatedly for Jesus' execution over the objections of Pilate. The Sadducean priests seized Jesus and took him to Pilate in their capacity as political allies of the governor. They considered Jesus dangerous and they fulfilled their responsibility by alerting the governor. But having delivered Jesus to Pilate there was no cause for them to become rabidly intent on his execution even to the point of badgering and threatening Pilate over his reluctance to kill Jesus! The Sadducees were acting as Pilate's agents, not as his enemies. Nothing required them to force Pilate into executing one of their own people when the governor was convinced of his innocence. Given the historical circumstances of the trial, the frenzied bloodthirstiness of the Jewish political leaders toward Jesus cannot be reasonably explained.

Equally inexplicable is the conduct of Pilate as described in the Gospels. If this description is accepted at face value it becomes very hard to explain how he could have maintained any control over the province. The Gospels insist that Pilate permitted Jesus' execution because he was overwhelmed by the Jews. Pilate was confused, afraid, utterly unable to act on his own judgment, subject only to the whims of the authorities and the crowd outside the chambers. He even agreed, under pressure, to set free an insurrectionist who was awaiting execution. This description would seem strange in the case of any procurator but it is especially incredible as a representation of Pilate.[6] As we have seen, Pilate's unrelenting determination was the hallmark of his ten-year rule. He continually showed his contempt for any Jewish attempts to influence him, and he was eventually recalled because of his excessive cruelty and iron-handedness. It would be hard to find anywhere in ancient literature more specific information about a leader who was unswayed by the opinions of his subjects. Yet in the Gospels Pilate is hapless in the face of the Jewish demands.

It is obvious that the Gospel pictures of Pilate and the Jewish leaders are not accurate portraits but caricatures. The Gospel description developed gradually from the needs of the Church rather than from actual recollections of the Roman proceedings. Faced with the problem of explaining how their Master could have died as a convicted seditionist, the Church found it urgent to convince Gentiles of his innocence; otherwise the crucifixion could only remain, in Paul's words, a stumbling block to the conversion of Gentiles. The most effective argument lay in the claim that even the governor who had condemned him had realized that he was innocent. Although the early Christians could not alter the result of the trial, it was possible for them to throw a distinctive light on the causes of Jesus' conviction. This Christian reinterpretation is especially noticeable in the reports of Luke and John. Mark and Matthew state simply that Pilate delivered Jesus to be crucified and the Roman soldiers carried out the execution. But as we have seen, John revises the wording slightly so that Pilate actually turns Jesus over *to the Jewish officials themselves* to be crucified. Luke goes even further: he states that Pilate simply gave Jesus over "to their will." [7] The implication is that Pilate did not order Jesus' execution at all; he released Jesus to the Jews to deal with as they pleased. It is hardly necessary to argue that these two versions are unhistorical. Jesus was condemned by the governor, then was turned over to Roman soldiers who conducted him to Golgotha and carried out the sentence. But two of the Gospels extend the Christian indictment to its ultimate limits by making the Jewish officials responsible for the act of crucifixion itself.

Again we must avoid any supposition that this Christian reinterpretation resulted from a capricious desire to indict the Jewish nation. By the middle of the first century A.D., when the Gospels were in their formative stage, all Christians undoubtedly believed that the Roman governor who sentenced Jesus had thought him innocent. After all, how could he have believed otherwise? Jesus

was no common insurrectionist like Barabbas and the two men crucified alongside him. Surely the governor had realized this. It was
inconceivable to the early Christians that Pilate could so have misunderstood the mission of Jesus. Inevitably, they came to believe
that Pilate had acted because of the pressure brought to bear by
the vengeful Jews.

.   .   .   .   .

But if Pilate was not cowed into pronouncing Jesus guilty, why
did he do so?

It would not have required overwhelming evidence for Pilate
to believe that Jesus was actually guilty of political crimes. Pilate
was faced continually with the problem of Jewish resistance. The
recent insurrection, with the threat of further violence at the Passover feast, probably heightened his concern over potential rebellion.
When still another Jew was arraigned before him and charged with
political crimes, Pilate must have taken it for granted that he was
much like those who were already awaiting death.

If not overwhelming, the evidence against Jesus was at least
adequate. He had entered the city with his followers in dramatic
fashion shortly before the feast. He had stirred the people to pro-
claim him in excited nationalistic terms. He had ejected the Jewish
authorities from the temple grounds and apparently had controlled
the temple court for a time. He had been arrested by force, at which
time his disciples had offered a brief resistance with swords. Now
he was charged by the Jewish leaders with three specific political
crimes: perverting the people, urging them not to pay the Roman
tax, and claiming to be their king.[8] To Pilate the evidence must
have seemed more than sufficient. It is unlikely that he took any
special pains to dig deeply into the charges. He accepted the case
at face value and gave the order that Jesus was to be executed along
with the others. However, it is quite possible that an additional
factor influenced Pilate to condemn Jesus, namely, Jesus' own con-
fession of kingship.

We can never know with certainty what Jesus said before
Pilate. The Gospels have to be read with special caution at this

point, because again there were no Christian eye-witnesses nor official reports. It was natural for the Church to shape Jesus' words at this moment to fit its own convictions about his Lordship. So we cannot speak with assurance about just what Jesus said or about the effect of his words on Pilate, but the most reasonable interpretation of the events is that Jesus confessed to, or did not positively deny, a kingly mission to the Jewish nation. We have touched on this subject in connection with the Jewish inquiry. Now on the basis of the trial before Pilate we can affirm the strong probability that Jesus was condemned at least partly because he gave an affirmative answer to the questions about his claim to be king. The following facts bear out this judgment:

1) The Jewish inquiry centered largely about the term "Messiah" and the Roman trial about the term "king." As we noted previously, these two discussions were very probably related. It seems likely that Jesus claimed a special Messianic mission before the Jewish authorities, and that these authorities, in the Roman trial, put a political connotation on Jesus' words. This would explain why Pilate asked Jesus directly about his claim to be king.

2) At the end of the Roman trial the soldiers made sport of Jesus' kingship by their taunts ("Hail, King of the Jews!") and by arraying him in a mock crown and robe. What could have inspired this treatment, except Jesus' own claim to kingship during the course of the trial? If Jesus had expressed no kingly (or Messianic) pretensions whatever, this mockery would hardly have suggested itself to the soldiers.

3) The charge printed on Jesus' cross, "King of the Jews," must reflect Jesus' own claim to be king. If Jesus' execution had been ordered merely because of alleged revolutionary activities, there would have been no reason to imprint such an indictment on the cross. Other insurrectionists and troublemakers were undoubtedly crucified without this distinctive charge etched into the cross. The words placed on the cross are best explained as a summary of Jesus' own claim, or at least what Pilate understood that claim to be.

What do the Gospels themselves say about Jesus' words before Pilate?

When asked by Pilate, "Are you the King of the Jews?" Jesus replied (according to all four Gospels), "You say so." [9] The meaning of this enigmatic reply has stirred considerable debate. Is it affirmative, negative, or noncommittal? The first point to be remembered is that this is probably the Church's phrase, not Jesus'. It is extremely improbable that the later Church knew the exact words of Jesus' reply. Christian tradition created this answer, which is deliberately evasive. Jesus cannot say, "No" to Pilate and thereby deny his own kingship; but he cannot say, "Yes" and affirm a kingship of the kind which Pilate has in mind. So the question cannot be answered as Pilate asks it; therefore, the Church supplied an answer which must be interpreted as a conditional affirmative. John's account emphasizes this by stressing that Jesus' kingship is ethereal, not earthly (18:36). Jesus' reply is, in effect, "I am a king, but not in the sense you imply." That is what the Church meant by, "You say so."

Whatever Jesus' exact words, we can feel sure that Pilate judged him guilty because of the circumstantial evidence against him;[10] and we can reasonably speculate that Jesus added to the case against himself by refusing to disavow his kingly mission.

.   .   .   .   .

The most serious divergence in any Gospel in describing the Roman trial is Luke's claim that Jesus stood trial also before Herod Antipas, the Jewish ruler of Galilee. Luke's singular claim reads as follows:

When Pilate heard this (that Jesus had worked in Galilee), he asked whether the man was a Galilean. And when he learned that he belonged to Herod's jurisdiction, he sent him over to Herod, who was himself in Jerusalem at that time. When Herod saw Jesus, he was very glad, for he had long desired to see him, because he had heard about him, and he was hoping to see some sign done by him. So he questioned him at some length; but he made no answer. The chief priests and the scribes stood by, vehemently accusing him. And Herod with his soldiers treated

him with contempt and mocked him; then, arraying him
in gorgeous apparel, he sent him back to Pilate. And Herod
and Pilate became friends with each other that very day,
for before this they had been at enmity with each other.
(23:6–12)

Such a course of events is unknown in any other Gospel. This
is highly surprising, if the scene is authentic, because it is very hard
to see how such a dramatic and important episode could have been
lost from the common memory.[11] It has been suggested that the
incident was overlooked in some quarters because the disciples had
fled.[12] But the removal of Jesus from the praetorium to the residence
of Herod and back again would have been the most easily ob-
servable part of the proceedings. Even if the disciples had not seen
the events themselves, other eye-witnesses would certainly have
provided a description in the days that followed. Yet the tradition
certainly was not a part of the common early description of the
trial. Mark, Matthew and John leave no room for such an incident
and in their understanding the trial was conducted in its entirety
before Pilate.

These other Gospels would hardly have omitted this story if
they had known or accepted it. But it is easy to see how this tradition could have found its way into Luke's Gospel even though it
was not historical. The tradition probably arose as a result of an Old
Testament passage which was quoted by the early Church in connection with Jesus' death. In Acts 4:23–30 Luke again cites Herod
Antipas' involvement in the trial, then he quotes Psalm 2:1–2, which
concludes: "The kings of the earth set themselves in array, and the
rulers were gathered together against the Lord and against his
Anointed . . ." The early Church put the greatest stress on Jesus'
fulfillment of the scriptures, particularly in the passion events. They
combed the Old Testament literature for possible allusions to the
ministry and death of Jesus. These verses were undoubtedly repeated
over and over, since they seemed to fit Jesus' death so well. The plural
terms "kings" and "rulers" found in these verses easily suggested
the view that not only Pilate but another ruler had been involved

in Jesus' death. The likely candidate was the Jewish tetrarch Herod, who was probably in Jerusalem for the Passover. Since it was known that Antipas had shown opposition to Jesus during his career,[13] it was natural to suppose that he had also shared in prosecuting Jesus. It is certainly possible that the Church cited this text because of an actual involvement by Herod in the trial, but the reverse is more likely true.[14]

Another motive aided in the development of this tradition. The introduction of Herod Antipas drew a representative of the Jewish people themselves directly into the condemnation of Jesus. It could not be stated by the early Christians that a Jewish ruler had actually condemned and sentenced Jesus, since this would have required a restructuring of the entire trial narrative. But in this Lukan tradition Herod is made one of Jesus' judges and is drawn into the responsibility for Jesus' execution, if only indirectly. Herod mocks Jesus, fails to absolve him of guilt, and permits his soldiers to abuse Jesus. His conduct is even more reprehensible than Pilate's. Including a Jewish ruler in the trial events had the effect of shifting the focus still further away from the Romans toward the Jews. The tradition was used for just this purpose in the early Church, as is evident in the Gospel of Peter (see Chapter 7), in which Jesus is actually *condemned* by Herod rather than by Pilate.[15]

Two literary observations strengthen the belief that this tradition is not historical and was not part of the early passion narrative. In Luke 23:10 the Jewish authorities are said to be present at the trial before Antipas, denouncing Jesus. But in 23:15 Pilate's words to these authorities assume that they remained with him at the praetorium.[16] This incongruity probably arose because Luke inserted the Herod scene into his narrative without reconciling it fully to the rest of his material. More important, Luke's description of the mockery by Herod's soldiers has simply been transplanted from the trial before Pilate. The other Gospels describe Jesus' abuse by Pilate's soldiers, but Luke omits this contemptuous treatment before Pilate and transfers it to Herod's attendants. This is a strong indication that Luke's scene is made up of material borrowed from the trial before Pilate, not material which existed separately from the earliest days of the narrative. There is little justification for supposing that this unique reference in Luke represents an actual stage in Jesus' prosecution.

.   .   .   .   .

The most unusual episode in the prosecution of Jesus revolves around a man who had no direct relationship with Jesus, none with the Sadducean priests, and none with Pilate. He became a key figure in Jesus' trial wholly by chance. This man was Barabbas.

The exact nature of Barabbas' involvement in the trial was not clearly understood in the developing Church. This uncertainty is reflected in the Gospels, which give three very different versions of the story. Mark explains the incident as follows: It was the governor's custom each year at the feast to release a prisoner at the request of the Jews. A rebel named Barabbas, who had committed murder in a recent insurrection, happened to be in prison at the time when Jesus was on trial. In the midst of Jesus' prosecution a crowd appeared and asked Pilate to observe the customary amnesty. Mark clearly implies that the Jews' request was general in nature: they wanted someone, anyone, to be released. So Pilate asked them if he should release Jesus, but the priests incited the crowd to ask for Barabbas instead. Pilate then asked what should be done with Jesus, and the crowd cried, "Crucify him!" When Pilate defended Jesus' innocence the crowd again demanded that he be crucified, and Pilate, to satisfy them, released Barabbas and delivered Jesus for crucifixion. Matthew follows this account closely.

But in Luke the episode has an entirely different flavor. As we saw in Chapter 7, in Luke's account no Jewish crowd appears during the proceedings. A crowd is present from the beginning as part of the prosecuting assembly which presents Jesus to Pilate. Their sole purpose is to seek the execution of Jesus, not the release of Barabbas or anyone else. Here, fittingly, there is no mention of any annual custom; no such explanation of the crowd's presence is required, since they have come for entirely different reasons. Barabbas' name arises incidentally in the later stages of the trial, with only a bare explanation of his identity. Luke apparently mentioned Barabbas only because his name was part of the passion tradition.

John gives still another version. In this Gospel there is no mention of a crowd at any time. Pilate repeatedly engages in conversation with "the Jews" outside the praetorium, but these are apparently only the priests who (John explains) have declined to enter the building for reasons of ritual purity at the feast time. If John is thinking of a large group from among the populace, as in the other Gospels, he makes no mention of the fact. In John it is *Pilate* who brings up the subject of the custom, and he mentions it as a *Jewish* practice. Pilate reminds the Jews of the custom and offers to release Jesus on that basis. But the Jews ask for Barabbas, whom John identifies simply as a *lestes*. The trial then proceeds without further mention of Barabbas by either side. As in Luke, Barabbas plays only an incidental role in the proceedings.

Because of these considerable differences it is very difficult to determine what effect, if any, Barabbas and the "crowd" had on Jesus' execution. It is also hard to understand the custom which supposedly lies at the base of the incident. Such an annual amnesty is unknown in all our other sources. The search for some substantiating evidence has been pursued to the remotest corners of Greek, Roman and Jewish history,[17] but on close examination none of the suggested references stand up as parallels to the Gospel accounts.[18] The Gospels themselves seem very uncertain about the nature of the practice. John ties it to the Passover, Mark and Matthew are vague about the feast,[19] and Luke omits it entirely. If the custom was Jewish, it is strange that no reference to it is found anywhere in Josephus or the rabbinic literature, especially if the practice was traditional. Yet it seems equally unlikely as a creation of the procurators generally or of Pilate in particular.

Doubts over this annual custom and the serious discrepancies in the Gospel accounts have caused some scholars to claim that the whole incident of Barabbas is fictitious.[20] According to these critics, the story is only symbolic; it arose in the early Church as a dramatic illustration of the Jews' rejection of their spiritual Messiah in favor of militant nationalism. Symbolically, the Jews shun God's Anointed One and embrace rebellion and violence as a way out of their troubles. Undoubtedly, the story did bear this significance. The closing words of Luke's trial narrative capture the frustration and bitterness felt by the first Christians as they described the incident: "He (Pilate) released the man who had been thrown into prison for insurrection and murder, whom they asked for; but Jesus he delivered up to their will" (23:25).

But it is excessively skeptical to suppose that the early Christians created this incident out of whole cloth.[21] Its roots are firmly historical, although the details soon became hazy in the early Church. Notice the difference between this incident and that of Herod Antipas in the Roman trial. The latter story occurs in only one Gospel, it was almost certainly inspired by an Old Testament passage and, in part, it is obviously a duplication of other material. Also the Herod story has no effect on the outcome of the trial. But the Barabbas incident is found in all four accounts, it did not develop from any identifiable Old Testament motif, and in two of the Gospels it is central to Jesus' condemnation. We should have no hesitancy in affirming that Barabbas was involved somehow in Jesus' trial—but how and why? Ironically, the answers may lie partly in Barabbas' own name.

In several ancient manuscripts of Matthew Barabbas is called "Jesus Barabbas." [22] It is possible that the name of Jesus has accidentally crept into the text at this point because of a copying error which textual scholars call "dittography." [23] However, there is a good possibility that this was actually Barabbas' name.[24] It seems very unlikely that any Christian scribes could accidentally have included Jesus' name at this point in the text, but it is easy to see why Christian copyists would intentionally have *deleted* the name Jesus as a designation for the murderous Barabbas. The name Jesus (Hebrew pronunciation, Yeshua) was a common one in first-century Judaea, much like James or John today. It is quite possible that Barabbas bore this name. But since the name Jesus was especially sacred to the early Church it would have been most natural for the early Christians to dissociate it from the murderer Barabbas. This would have been accomplished by gradually omitting Barabbas' given name from the oral and written records of the trial. If this suggestion is correct, the few manuscripts which give the name

Jesus Barabbas are the only surviving evidence of the insurrectionist's full name. Following this reasoning, we can cautiously suggest the following reconstruction of the incident of Barabbas:

Barabbas had recently been involved, along with several others then in prison,[25] in an uprising[26] against the Roman government. This uprising had probably occurred just prior to or during the Passover season. We do not know whether Barabbas had yet been tried and sentenced.[27] In the eyes of many Jews gathered for the Passover Barabbas was a national hero, and as the day arrived for the execution of some of those involved in the revolt a crowd of Jews swarmed about the praetorium. Stirred by intense nationalistic feelings, they demanded the release of the patriot, Jesus Barabbas.

At that moment Jesus of Nazareth was on trial before the governor. Hearing the crowd chant Barabbas' name, Pilate stopped to ask whether this Jesus was the man whose release they sought.[28] Barabbas' supporters then expressed their indifference to Jesus of Nazareth, perhaps even saying, "Let him be crucified, but release Barabbas." To the followers of Jesus, who presumably were also outside the praetorium, this cry seemed perverse and inhuman. Jesus was innocent of any political crimes, yet the crowd sought only the release of the murderer who deserved to die. Subsequently, the indifference of Barabbas' supporters to Jesus was gradually reinterpreted as the open and bitter hostility of the people as a whole. Needless to say, such popular hostility is unhistorical.[29] The Jews gathered for the Passover would never have begged a Roman procurator to kill a fellow countryman simply because they did not agree with all his teachings or doubted that he was the Messiah. The Gospels are probably correct in reporting that Jesus was well received in Jerusalem and made a deep and favorable impression on many of the people. Why then should a representative crowd suddenly appear, demanding that he be crucified, a death so abhorrent to the Jews that the victim was thought to be accursed? Some commentators have supposed that the mob sought Jesus' death because they were disappointed that he had not taken a firm stand against Rome; they hated him because he had frustrated their hopes. Such idle speculation is necessary only if we accept the Gospel description of the mob scene. Nothing in the historical situation justifies such a view.

Over the years the Barabbas story was enriched in the Church's memory. In some quarters the story grew until the clamor of the crowd became the decisive factor which led Pilate to rule against Jesus. This tradition is reflected in Mark and Matthew, where it is the crowd's demands which cause Pilate finally to execute Jesus. In other circles the incident remained only a minor sidelight of the proceedings, as Luke and John suggest. The reference to a custom may have arisen secondarily as an explanation of the presence of the crowd and their cries for Barabbas to be released. It is possible that this custom is historical and that it somehow escaped mention in all our other sources. But it is more likely that, as the Church moved away from Palestine, the mention of a custom developed through a simple misunderstanding. Given the appearance of a Jewish crowd pressing for the release of a prisoner, non-Jewish Christians might easily have supposed that their demands were based on an old Jewish custom.

In summary, we can feel confident that Barabbas was a real person and that by an oddity of circumstances, perhaps involving his name, he became involved in the proceedings against Jesus. But it is unlikely that the episode had a serious effect on the outcome of the trial. Jesus did not die because certain Jews stood outside the trial chambers asking that he be killed or that an insurrectionist be freed. Pilate executed Jesus because he thought him guilty. The vast majority of Jews in Jerusalem must have mourned Jesus' death just as they mourned many others who died in this manner under the procurators. Because of its special convictions, the early Church eventually revised the story so that a crowd of Jews was made to share in the blame for Jesus' condemnation. Regrettably, many modern readers of the New Testament find no difficulty in accepting this bitter calumny against the Jewish people of Jesus' day. This is evidence of how effectively the Gospels have laid the blame for Jesus' death at the feet of his own people.

12

THE EXECUTION

"And they brought him to the place called Golgotha . . ."

Mark 15:22

Once Pilate had pronounced sentence against Jesus, the execution lay only minutes away. For a Jew convicted of treason in Roman Palestine there were none of the delays which, in our own day, normally separate the time of condemnation from the time of punishment. In the case of Jesus, the means and the site of death were near at hand. There remained only certain barbaric customs to be observed before he could be raised onto the cross.

Evidently, the hour was still early when the governor completed the proceedings and turned Jesus over to his soldiers. Mark tells us that the crucifixion began at the third hour, that is, the third hour after dawn, or about 9 A.M.[1] This means that the Jewish officials would have delivered Jesus to the governor shortly after dawn. John sets the time of crucifixion somewhat later.[2] He states that it was already noon—the sixth hour—when Pilate completed the trial and sent Jesus to the cross. This disagreement is not very significant; what matters is that, from the moment when Jesus was first brought before the governor, the events moved very swiftly toward the execution.

We are tantalizingly close to being able to pinpoint the site in ancient Jerusalem at which the governor condemned Jesus and let the soldiers take command of him. It would be of the greatest interest if we could make this identification. In bringing historical events to life, nothing is more useful than being able to stand, at least with the mind's eye, on the very ground where those events took place. This is particularly true as we trace the final movements from the praetorium to the place of execution and thence to the tomb where Jesus' body was laid. We can feel sure that Pilate passed sentence against Jesus at one of two places, both of which can be located today. One was the palace of Herod I, near the north-west corner of the upper portion of the city, which Herod had built to his own glory about 23 B.C. After Judaea was converted into a province, the palace became the customary residence of the procurators when they were in Jerusalem. It is probable that Pilate was housed at the palace during his trip to the city at the time of the Passover feast, and it may have been here that he conducted the prosecution of Jesus.[3]

The alternative site is the Tower of Antonia. This fortress, rebuilt by Herod and named by him in honor of Mark Antony, stood in a conspicuous spot within the city, at the northwest corner of the temple grounds. The tower housed Roman troops during the procuratorial period[4] and also served as an occasional residence for the procurators. Even if Pilate was then residing at the palace, he may have used the tower as his "praetorium," where the trial took place. This word praetorium, used in three Gospels as the site of the trial, designates not a specific building but anyplace where a provincial governor resided or conducted official business.[5] A modern archeological discovery has added to the speculation that Antonia may have been the site of the trial.[6] The traditional *Via Dolorosa*, tracing the steps of Jesus from the trial to the cross, also begins at the *Ecce Homo* arch at the Tower of Antonia. However, this tradition arose centuries after the death of Jesus, and the supposed archeological evidence is very doubtful. In truth, we have no firm grounds for choosing between these two locales.[7]

When Pilate had completed the proceedings, he delivered Jesus into the hands of the soldiers who stood nearby. The trial appears to have been conducted just outside the praetorium proper, since Mark and Matthew indicate that, after the sentencing, the soldiers took Jesus inside the building. There they began to make sport of him, in a scene which is one of the most graphic in the New Testament. The soldiers' mockery centered around Jesus' claim of kingship, since this had been the basis of his condemnation. The soldiers[8] found amusement in the fact that this man, who had none of the trappings or the military support of royalty, imagined himself a king. They naturally supposed, as Pilate had, that Jesus had intended to mount a rebellion against the state. To them he seemed a ludicrous rival to Caesar, and they indulged themselves in coarse mimicry of his kingship. Stripping him down, they draped one of the soldiers' purple cloaks about him in imitation of the royal scarlet. Then they plaited a mock crown from the vines of a thorny bush and placed it on his head and, according to Matthew, put a reed in his hand as a mock sceptre. Then they did obeisance before him, revelling in the spectacle of their Jewish "king." The Gospels add that they also beat and abused Jesus physically before putting his own clothes back on him and leading him away to be crucified.

This mockery arose spontaneously because of the particular nature of the charges against Jesus, but the scourging itself was a customary preliminary to the act of crucifixion.[9] Such punishment was ordinarily meted out to those condemned to die on the cross, and the soldiers merely added their personal insults to the blows and lashes. Although this mockery is found in some form in all the Gospels, the tradition was not precise. Mark and Matthew indicate that this abuse followed the completion of the trial.[10] John places the scene, inexplicably, in the midst of the proceedings, before Pilate has even decided the case. Luke omits this maltreatment altogether in the Roman trial, having described a very similar scene before Herod Antipas. Luke apparently wanted to avoid any further emphasis on the Roman hostility toward Jesus. He also had no logical place for the soldiers' scourging; in his account, Pilate released Jesus directly to the Jewish officials, to do with as they pleased, rather than to the soldiers.

It was a long-established practice that the condemned criminal should be required to carry his own cross to the place of hanging.[11] The intent was to add to both the pain and the humiliation of this means of death. The route to the death-site was often not the most direct, but was selected to lead the condemned man past a large segment of the populace, so that his fate might serve as an object lesson. The victim did not actually bear the whole cross, but only the crossbeam which was to be nailed to the upright at the place of execution. It was also customary for the victim to carry about his neck the *titulus*,[12] a sign which designated the charge on which he had been condemned. This was done in the case of Jesus. No two Gospels are alike in recording the exact words of the *titulus*, but all agree that the phrase "King of the Jews" appeared in one form or another.[13] It is possible that later Christian belief in Jesus' kingship has affected the record at this point, but it is much more likely that the Gospels' report is correct. The charge written on the cross would hardly have been forgotten in substance, and this charge fits the historical situation well. Jesus was being executed because he had claimed to be—or in Roman eyes, had acted as if he were—King of the Jews, an act which made him guilty of treason.

John states that Jesus bore his own cross, in accordance with custom. It was important to John to show that Jesus was in command of the events and that he needed help from no one.[14] But the Synoptics declare that a man by the name of Simon, from the city of Cyrene in North Africa, was pressed into service and made to carry Jesus' cross at least part of the distance. The selection of Simon was wholly by chance; he was entering the city from the country-side and happened to pass near the procession.[15] Although the Gospels do not say so, the natural explanation is that Jesus was unable to bear the weight himself, perhaps because of the physical beating he had absorbed at the hands of the soldiers. Therefore, when he collapsed under the weight, the Romans forced Simon to give assistance.[16] There is no reason to doubt that this Synoptic record is accurate. Simon's assistance is just the kind of detail which would have been remembered later.

Luke alone gives further information about the journey to Golgotha. He states that a large crowd followed Jesus, including women who cried out in mourning. Luke supplies extended remarks spoken by Jesus to these women. Their grief, he says, should be for themselves and their children, because of the disasters which are to fall upon the country. So great is the impending tragedy that the women will wish they had never borne children to witness it.[17] Indeed, they themselves will pray for death, for if Jesus, who is innocent, is subjected to crucifixion, what will become of those who are guilty? [18] These words, which arose later in the death narratives, represent the Church's comment on the fate of the Jewish nation, perhaps in the aftermath of the disastrous war of A.D. 66–72.

Luke also adds that two other men were led away to be crucified with Jesus.

·   ·   ·   ·   ·

The narratives of the crucifixion are among the most vivid and compelling in the Gospels. Moving from the trial of Jesus to the execution, one emerges from sometimes difficult and shadowy accounts into a well-illumined and graphic story. It is fortunate that no significant problems detract from the quiet force of the Gospel records and from this drama which is central to the faith of the Christian Church. The agreement of the Gospels on the core events reflects the primitiveness and reliability of the main elements in the death and burial stories.

Yet the specific details surrounding the central events are remarkably varied. There is hardly a single incident in Jesus' crucifixion and burial which is reported identically in all four Gospels. Often we have three or four different versions of the same vignette. There are two reasons for this abundance of minor variations. First, by their very nature the death stories contain a great many details of narrative and dialogue. It was inevitable that these details should have come to be recited in several different ways in the early days of the Church. Our Gospels reflect the variety with which individual incidents were described throughout the Church. Secondly, these stories of Jesus' death had such profound spiritual meaning that the Church added fresh insights and elaborations to them as the years passed. Here, as in all the Gospel material, faith has left its impact on history and the narratives have been seriously conditioned by the emerging convictions of the Church. Fortunately, in the crucifixion stories this conditioning has had only a peripheral effect. Nowhere do these elaborations obscure the essential historical events. In describing Jesus' death the Church has not painted over the whole historical canvas. It has merely touched up the picture here and there, in order to highlight the spiritual meaning of Jesus' sacrifice on the cross.

The chief source on which the early Christians drew in interpreting and expanding the stories of Jesus' death was the Jewish Scriptures. These first Christians were Jews who considered themselves full heirs of the Jewish faith. They saw in Jesus the fulfillment of that faith and of its sacred writings. This belief formed the heart of the first Christian sermons. Jesus was proclaimed as the One promised of old, and the pages of the Scriptures were combed for evidences which demonstrated that Jesus had in fact fulfilled the ancient prophecies. It was especially important to show that his death, which seemed to contradict the hope of a triumphant Messianic reign, was actually a fulfillment of the Scriptural promises. It was inevitable, therefore, that the Church's records of Jesus' death should have been seriously influenced by relevant references which these Jewish Christians uncovered in their Scriptures. The crucifixion stories are replete with open or covert references to Scriptural passages which the Christians believed had been fulfilled by some final incident or word of Jesus.

This fact creates the only serious difficulty in analyzing the crucifixion events. Did the early Christians simply find in their Scriptures certain passages which *coincided* with the crucifixion events? Or did they gradually alter the details of this story so as to bring it into line with these Scriptural references? The choice between these alternative interpretations is often extremely difficult. In some instances, there can be little doubt that an Old Testament reference has led to the development of the record itself, as Christians sought to increase the number of Scriptural witnesses to Jesus and his sacrifice. The crucial Old Testament passage is Psalm 22: this psalm obviously had a major influence on the Gospel stories of the cross. Indeed, it is almost a prolonged proof-text for the key elements in this narrative. Christians also found parallels in other Old Testament passages. These various Scriptural allusions will be noted as they occur in the crucifixion narratives.

Broadly speaking, the Gospels show the same pattern of agreement they demonstrated in the trial narratives. Mark and Matthew are closely similar; Matthew seems wholly dependent on Mark, making only three significant additions.[19] Luke again omits much of Mark's record and introduces extensive new material, almost certainly derived from his non-Markan source. As before, John follows the main outline of the Synoptics, but shapes all the details so as to bring them into harmony with his special theological aims.

.   .   .   .   .

The place of execution was located not far outside the city walls.[20] The Gospels call the execution site Golgotha,[21] meaning "skull." Our modern word, "Calvary," is derived from the Latin word for skull, *calvaria*. It is not clear why the Jews called the place "The Skull" or "Place of the Skull." The best guess is that the terrain had the appearance of a human head.[22] However the name arose, it formed a fittingly macabre designation for this place where executions were probably frequent. The exact location of Golgotha—and of the tomb of Jesus, which John says was nearby—are unknown. Under instructions from the emperor Constantine, some 300 years after the crucifixion, Christians erected a church on a site believed to have been the locale of both the cross and the tomb.[23] The present Church of the Holy Sepulchre stands on the same spot, where various Christian edifices have stood for more than sixteen centuries. However, this traditional site is doubtful. There are no records of this site for three centuries after the event, and in some periods during those centuries there was no Christian community in Jerusalem which could easily have maintained an accurate tradition. A good case can be made out for this traditional locale,[24] but today there is little certainty about the location of either Golgotha or the burial place. Although Golgotha is commonly depicted as a hill, this tradition also arose in later years and is not found in the Gospels. However, it is likely that an easily visible site was used for these executions, so that they might be seen by the populace.

Crucifixion was regarded in Jesus' day as the most agonizing of deaths. This form of execution had arisen several hundred years before Jesus and continued in use until outlawed by Constantine. In Jesus' time the Romans normally reserved it for certain types of crimes and criminals. Slaves might be crucified for any serious offense, and others were crucified particularly in cases of insurrection or murder, particularly in the provinces. Roman citizens were rarely if ever crucified, whatever their crimes.[25] Not only was the cross the most painful of deaths, it was also considered the most debasing. The condemned man was stripped naked and left exposed in his agony, and often the Romans even denied burial to the victim, allowing his body to hang on the cross until it disintegrated. It is understandable that, according to Jewish law, anyone who was crucified was considered cursed.[26]

Crosses were of various shapes.[27] The most common consisted of a vertical stake and a horizontal crossbeam placed either across the top of the stake or somewhat below; X-shaped crosses were also known. There is no definite evidence about the shape of Jesus' cross, but it was probably a vertical stake and a crossbeam. This is indicated by the placing of the *titulus* over the head of Jesus,[28] evidently along the crosspiece.

The victim's arms were secured to the crossbeam by either nails or straps. When nails were used they were normally driven through the wrists rather than the hands, so as to support the body's weight. The feet were usually strapped to the upright, and sometimes the body straddled a small peg. This peg provided support and helped prevent a more rapid death, the very purpose of crucifixion being to prolong the victim's pain for as long a time as possible. Death usually resulted from sheer exhaustion; the body eventually wore out from both the pain and the unnatural suspension of the organs and muscles. As Harvie Branscomb summarizes:

> Few more terrible means of execution could be devised. Pain, thirst, the torture of insects, exposure to brutal spectators, the horror of rigid fixation, all continuing interminably, combined to make it a supreme humiliation and torture.[29]

The most remarkable feature of the Gospels' description of Jesus' death is the brevity and simplicity with which they depict the act of crucifixion itself. The Gospels provide almost no details. Only John, for example, indicates the use of nails in the hands of Jesus.[30] To the first readers of these Gospels, crucifixion needed no elaboration, and it was unnecessary for the Gospels to elaborate on Jesus' suffering. Indeed, the Gospel writers seem anxious to hurry past the mention of the fact, not from shame over the fate of Jesus, but because the Church found no pleasure in dwelling on his final agony. Mark, after stating that Jesus had been brought to Golgotha and had been offered a drink of wine and myrrh, states with stark simplicity,

> And they crucified him, and divided his garments among them, casting lots for them, to decide what each should take. (15:24)

Only these four words—"And they crucified him . . ."—are used to describe the act itself. The other Gospels follow suit, subordinating the actual crucifixion in brief clauses and quickly moving on.

Mark observes that, just prior to being placed on the cross, Jesus was offered a mixture of wine and myrrh, an opiate intended to dull his pain.[31] Mark's language suggests that the soldiers made this gesture, though this seems surprising. It was customary for Jewish women, as a gesture of charity, to offer sympathy and help to victims of crucifixion. It may have been these women who offered the potion to Jesus. We are told that Jesus declined to drink, either so as not to lose control of his senses or because of the bitter taste. Matthew repeats the scene but changes the wine to gall in order to tie the event to an Old Testament passage.[32] It appears that there was some uncertainty in the traditions about the drinks offered to Jesus on the cross, since wine and vinegar are tendered by various people in varied circumstances in each Gospel.[33]

The division of Jesus' clothing among the soldiers who conducted the execution was also in line with common practice. There is no reason to doubt this record, although the detail that they made this division by casting lots may have arisen from Psalm 22:18: ". . . they divide my garments among them, and for my raiment they cast lots." [34] John mentions that four soldiers were involved; it was customary to assign four men to carry out a crucifixion.[35] Since three executions were to take place, there were probably twelve soldiers present at Golgotha, plus the centurion in command, who is mentioned later in the accounts. The other two men were crucified on opposite sides of Jesus.[36]

Instead of focusing on Jesus' anguish, the Synoptic Gospels avert our gaze to the people and incidents around the cross. Through brief vignettes they describe the reaction of various groups to the gruesome spectacle taking place before them.

According to Mark and Matthew, most of those who viewed Jesus' suffering responded by showering him with insults. Mark first reports that certain passers-by[37] wagged their heads at Jesus and cried out: "Aha! You who would destroy the temple and build it in three days, save yourself, and come down from the cross!" (15:29b–30). These passers-by are undoubtedly intended to represent the Jewish populace in a broad sense. Mark's implication is that Jesus' countrymen were indifferent and insensible, hurling his own words back at him in his last hours.[38] But this popular antipathy is wholly lacking in Luke, who twice refers to the crowd of Jews at the foot of the cross. He first reports that, during the execution, they stood by watching. The meaning is that they watched quietly, soberly, for Luke immediately adds that the Jewish leaders, by contrast, openly reviled Jesus. Then, at Jesus' death, Luke adds: "And all the multitudes who assembled to see the sight, when they saw what had taken place, returned home beating their breasts (23:48)." That is, they returned grieving deeply over the events they had just witnessed. It is not clear why Luke presents the Jewish people in a more favorable light, except that his special source emphasized the sympathy and despair felt by many of Jesus' own people at his death.[39] This is just what we would expect to be the case. Why should the Jews have taken pleasure in the misery of one of their own people, dying wretchedly at the hands of the hated Roman soldiers? Mark's and Matthew's record has undoubtedly been influenced by Psalm 22:6,7: "All who see me mock at me, they make mouths at me, they wag their heads . . ."[40] It is noteworthy that only Luke provides the words of Jesus, "Father, forgive them; for they know not what they do (23:34a)." This saying is not found in some ancient manuscripts of Luke.[41] It is interesting to speculate whether this saying arose in later years as an example of Jesus' forgiving spirit, or whether it was part of the early traditions and was later deleted because Christians found it so difficult to forgive the Jews for their deed.[42]

Mark and Matthew also state, this time with Luke's agreement, that certain Jewish leaders were also present, and that they taunted Jesus, urging him to prove his kingship by saving himself.[43] Despite this unanimity, it is very hard to believe that a representative contingent of the leading Jewish officials pursued Jesus to the cross in order to vent their malice toward him. This was hardly the place for these national figures, especially since the Sabbath of Passover week was so near. It is possible that some officials did go with the procession to Golgotha, but the Gospel record probably reflects the later hostility between the Church and the Jewish leaders.

Luke's record of the Roman soldiers and the two men condemned alongside Jesus is also different from the first two Gospels. Luke states that the soldiers offered Jesus vinegar in order to mock him, and that they also yelled at Jesus to save himself. Their words are almost identical to those placed on the lips of the Jewish leaders in Mark and Matthew. As with the drinks offered Jesus, there seems to have been some uncertainty in the early traditions about the insults yelled at Jesus on the cross.[44] Luke also has a very different remembrance of the two insurrectionists. Only one of the criminals reviles Jesus, and he is rebuked by the other for not recognizing that

Jesus is suffering unjustly. Then follows one of the most famous exchanges in the Gospels:

> And he said, "Jesus, remember me when you come in your
> kingly power." And he said to him, "Truly, I say to you,
> today you will be with me in Paradise." (Luke 23:42,43)[45]

Mark and Matthew know nothing of this tradition; they state that both criminals joined in yelling derisively at Jesus.

During the hours of Jesus' suffering, no other groups are mentioned at the cross. But at the moment of death, the Synoptics describe the response of the Roman centurion who had supervised the executions. In Mark's words:

> And when the centurion, who stood facing him, saw that
> he thus breathed his last, he said "Truly this man was the
> (or a) Son of God!" (Mark 15:39)[46]

Luke softens the expression to: "Certainly this man was innocent!" (23:47b). Whatever the exact words, in the eyes of the Church the scene demonstrated that even a hardened soldier who had no interest in Jesus could see in him, at this final moment, the quality of deity, or at least innocence.[47] Symbolically, this centurion was a prototype of the many Gentiles who would come to recognize the divinity of Jesus in the years to come.

Thus, the Synoptic Gospels build their accounts around the people clustered about the cross. But once again, John shows both his independence and his genius for developing his major themes from the material at hand. For John, the outward crucifixion events are only the raw ore from which the deeper spiritual truths must be refined. It is highly illuminating to see how John works out, in the crucifixion scene, his emphasis on Jesus' deity and his mastery over the events. In John there is no reference to any insults or abuse showered on Jesus at the cross. There are no hostile Jews or their leaders, no Roman soldiers or condemned criminals. There are no taunting shouts, no drinks offered in mockery. Such references would have detracted from the majesty of Jesus in his last moments. No one must be allowed to speak ill of Jesus or draw attention away from him. In this Gospel, Jesus remains at the center of the cruci-fixion narrative.

The only incidents supplied by John were carefully selected to show how Jesus' death fulfilled the Scriptures, or how Jesus other-wise manifested his divine nature on the cross.[48] All else was elimi-nated, and John's account is remarkably brief. John is moving rapidly toward the resurrection, on which he will place much greater emphasis. John mentions the soldiers' casting of lots only because their act fulfilled Psalm 22:18, which John quotes. He adds that Jesus' tunic, for which the soldiers cast lots, was seamless. His Jewish readers would have seen the parallel to the seamless garment of the high priest, whose spiritual function was now taken over by Jesus.[49] John alone supplies Jesus' words, "I thirst," again as a fulfillment of Scripture,[50] and he adds the offer of vinegar to Jesus in response. Although John does not specify the Scripture, it is obvi-ously Psalm 69:21: "They gave me poison for food, and for my thirst they gave me vinegar to drink." John adds that the bowl of vinegar was raised to Jesus' lips on hyssop. This plant was a short, spindly shrub with no firm limbs which might well have conveyed the drink upwards.[51] Yet John introduces the hyssop because this plant was used for sprinkling blood on the doorposts in the ancient Passover ritual. John has already shown that Jesus was slain as a symbolic Passover lamb, and here he adds to that imagery. Again the details are molded so as to increase the spiritual impact, in ways more obvious to the early readers of the Gospels than to moderns.[52]

John also includes the following scene:

When Jesus saw his mother, and the disciple whom he loved standing near, he said to his mother, "Woman, behold your son!" Then he said to the disciple, "Behold your mother!" And from that hour the disciple took her to his own home. (John 19:26–27)

Catholic theology finds in these verses a veiled reference to Mary's spiritual motherhood over the Church and her participation in Jesus' work of redemption. For John the significance is that, even at a time of physical anguish, Jesus' thought was not of himself but of his

family and friends.[53] The "disciple whom Jesus loved" has been regarded throughout the Church's history as John, the traditional author of the fourth Gospel.

.   .   .   .

The death of Jesus came with surprising quickness. Victims of
crucifixion often hung on the cross for as long as two days or even
more. Ordinarily, nothing was done to hasten death, and the victim
might survive long after he wished for life to end. The Gospels
supply no explanation of Jesus' death within six hours after he had
been placed on the cross. It can only be supposed that the severity
of the scourging, which evidently made him unable to carry the
cross, also speeded his death.

Jesus' last words from the cross are variously recorded in the
Gospels. Mark, followed by Matthew, gives this account:

> And at the ninth hour Jesus cried with a loud voice, "Eloi,
> Eloi, lama sabachthani?" which means, "My God, my God,
> why hast thou forsaken me?" And some of the bystanders
> hearing it said, "Behold, he is calling Elijah." And one ran
> and filling a sponge full of vinegar, put it on a reed and gave
> it to him to drink, saying, "Wait, let us see whether Elijah
> will come to take him down." And Jesus uttered a loud cry,
> and breathed his last. (Mark 15:34–37)

Jesus' words, "My God, my God, why hast thou forsaken me?"
have given rise to the most intense analysis and speculation. The
words are the opening sentence of Psalm 22. But why should Jesus
have voiced this sentiment? In what sense should he have thought
of himself as separated from God, at the very moment when he
was fulfilling God's plan? The question is more difficult for the
theologian than the historian. In the historical circumstances, nothing is more natural than that Jesus, crying out in a moment of
great physical torment, should have uttered these words which
were undoubtedly recited often by Jews in moments of despair.
The record has strong credibility; there is little room to suppose
that the Church borrowed this cry from Psalm 22 and added it to

the crucifixion story. Rather, it was probably because Jesus spoke these words that the Church's attention was directed to this psalm, which then became a source for elaborating the crucifixion events. Luke and John omit this cry of Jesus, probably because it raised the same difficulties for them that it raises for commentators today. To explain Jesus' words, Christian interpreters have often emphasized that Psalm 22 ends on a note of confidence and trust in God, and that Jesus' cry must be interpreted in this light. But this misses the point. Jesus did not quote the final words of hope, but precisely the initial words of despair. Jesus would of course have known the theme of the full psalm, but the vividness of Jesus' cry, and the insight it gives into the humanity of Jesus, are lost in any attempt to explain away the natural meaning of these words.

Mark and Matthew add an interesting aftermath to Jesus' cry. Hearing the words "Eli, Eli," [54] some of the people thought that Jesus was calling Elijah. Their mistake was natural enough, not only because of the similarity of sound, but because in Jewish thought Elijah was an aid and comforter of those in distress. Responding to his words, one of the bystanders rushed toward Jesus to offer him vinegar to dull his pain; but others[55] restrained him, saying, "Wait, let us see whether Elijah will come to take him down." [56] But Jesus then uttered a loud cry and breathed his last. The Synoptics emphasize that Jesus' life ended not quietly but with a shout. It seems surprising that there was strength remaining for such a forceful cry. It has been speculated that the quickness of Jesus' death, and the shout at the final moment, indicate that Jesus died not from exhaustion but from the rupture of some vital organ. In the minds of the Gospel writers, his cry suggested not only strength but a sense of completion. Luke, who says nothing of "Eli, Eli . . . ," states that the final cry was a prayer: "Father, into thy hands I commit my spirit!," which is derived from Psalm 31:5. John supplies a different version; at the moment of death Jesus says simply, "It is finished." [57] John has shown in his first chapter how Jesus entered the world on a divine mission. Now at the end Jesus pronounces his work complete. Life is not taken from him: rather, ". . . he bowed his head and gave up his spirit."

The Synoptics declare that Jesus' death was attended by miraculous signs which reflected both the tragedy and the victory of the crucifixion. They state that darkness covered the land—or perhaps the whole earth[58]—from the sixth to the ninth hour, the hour of Jesus' death.[59] Sudden darkness or similar portents were commonly associated in ancient times with the deaths of important or God-like men. But John omits this representation of divine displeasure; for him, Jesus' death is in no sense a tragedy, and no signs in nature must suggest defeat or despair. The Synoptics add that, at the moment of Jesus' death, the curtain of the temple was torn in two. This evidently refers to the curtain which separated the Holy Place from the Most Holy Place in the temple.[60] The symbolism is clear: through Jesus' death the barrier which has shielded men from the immediate presence of God has been removed, and the old Jewish religious system, in which the high priest was the chief intermediary between God and the people, has been replaced by Jesus' own mediation.

Matthew carries the miraculous signs much further, in language not paralleled in any other account. He describes a severe earthquake which shook the ground, splitting rocks and opening tombs. From these opened tombs emerged the bodies of many saints who, after the resurrection of Jesus, went into Jerusalem and appeared to many people. This somewhat startling passage is reminiscent of the sort of expansion which appears in the later apocryphal Gospels and other Christian writings.

After relating Jesus' death, the Synoptics again direct our attention to a group gathered at the cross. This time it is the women followers of Jesus who had been gathered some distance away. John has introduced the women earlier and has placed them very near the cross. The names of the women vary in the Gospels; again, this is the sort of incidental detail which would naturally have become obscured over the years. Mary Magdalene's name is fixed firmly in the tradition, however, along with another Mary, or perhaps two, who are variously identified.[61] More important than the women's names is the role they play in the narratives. These women become the connecting link in the accounts of Jesus' death, burial and resurrection. They are the eye-witnesses who provide an unbroken chain of testimony, giving continuity and substantiation to the death events and the Easter events. This role is readily evident in the Synoptics, where the reference to the women serves as the end of the crucifixion story and the beginning of the burial accounts.

But why should the disciples not have filled this role? It was they who had been Jesus' main followers, and they who would lead in proclaiming him risen. Why are they missing from these scenes? The answer is that, having fled at Jesus' capture, they have remained hidden, free from danger. Only John's reference to the beloved disciple contradicts the impression that these main followers stayed far in the background. Whatever minor changes the first Christians introduced gradually into the death narratives, they remained faithful to the firm memory that Jesus' principal followers had defected. Indeed, the disciples themselves undoubtedly perpetuated this memory, freely confessing their failure. Although it was they—or at least some of them—who built the Church, it was only these women who had been near during the last hours of Jesus' life.[62]

.   .   .   .   .

In another province, the body of Jesus would have remained on the cross indefinitely. But Jewish law forbade leaving a body hanging overnight,[63] and evidently the Romans allowed the Jews to observe their customs. In this case, there was a special urgency for lowering the three bodies and burying them. It was approaching sundown, the hour when the Jewish Sabbath began. Further, this Sabbath was the Sabbath of Passover week, when the observance of the law was particularly important.

This urgency is clear in the Gospel accounts.[64] John reports that a delegation of Jews asked Pilate to have the legs of the condemned men broken, in order to hasten death and thus permit a quick burial. Pilate complied,[65] and John says that soldiers broke the legs of the other two men. But they found this unnecessary in the case of Jesus, since he had already died. John is anxious to show that a Scriptural passage—"Not a bone of him shall be broken"—was fulfilled by this incident.[66] He also adds that one of the soldiers pierced the side of Jesus with a spear, and that blood and water flowed from the wound. John's purpose again was to show a fulfillment of Scripture, "They shall look on him whom they have pierced." [67] Modern medical spokesmen have emphasized that the reference to blood and water is plausible physiologically.[68] But for John, who emphasizes that the report came to him from an eye-witness, these two elements had spiritual, not physical, significance. The blood represented the life of Jesus, poured out for man. The water undoubtedly symbolized God's spirit, which now became, with Jesus' departure, the vehicle of God's contact with man.

The family of Jesus owned no burial place near Jerusalem, since their home was in Galilee. Unless someone had intervened it is likely that Jesus' body would have been placed in a potter's field. This is probably what happened to the two men who died alongside him. But a well-to-do and prominent countryman of Jesus stepped forward to provide decent burial. This man was Joseph, from the village of Arimathea, a town which can no longer be located with certainty.[69] The Gospels provide varied information about Joseph; once again the details of the tradition were somewhat unstable. Mark and Luke indicate that he was a member of the Sanhedrin, Luke adding that he had not consented to the Council's action against Jesus. These two Gospels explain Joseph's charitable act by stating that he was a pious man "who was looking for the kingdom of God." But in Matthew and John (which make no mention of his membership in the Sanhedrin) Joseph is made a disciple of Jesus—a secret disciple, John adds, from fear of his fellow Jews. John also associates Joseph with Nicodemus, the Sanhedrin member who had earlier sought out Jesus at night. John states that the two men shared in preparing the body for burial. Only Matthew comments that Joseph was rich, but it seems implicit in all the stories that he was a person of substance.

Mark calls attention to the fact that Joseph's act required courage. This would seem to be so. To obtain the body, Joseph had to make request of Pilate personally. Since Jesus had died as an enemy of the state, Joseph could easily have come under suspicion as a revolutionary. However, he probably gave a simple explanation:

as a prominent citizen, he wanted to be certain that the religious regulations for the Sabbath and the Passover were observed, and he was willing to provide a sepulchre for this purpose. It was not unusual for devout Jews to provide proper burial for the poor and dispossessed. It has often been suggested that Joseph intended to supply only a temporary tomb, so that the body could be hastily buried, to be removed and reburied at a later time. A verse in John[70] implies that Jesus was laid in Joseph's tomb only because the tomb was close at hand and the hour was late. This may indicate the temporary nature of the arrangement; it is impossible to settle the question with certainty.[71]

As noted, we do not know the location of Joseph's tomb. John gives the only geographical information, stating that it was in a garden not far from Golgotha. As sundown neared, the body of Jesus was removed from the cross and taken to the sepulchre. Through the aid of modern archeological investigations in Palestine, it is possible to gain a good indication of what the tomb must have been like. Three Gospels mention that the tomb was hewn from rock, and all refer to a stone rolled in front of the doorway. In the Easter story all the Gospels indicate that those who discovered the resurrection went *into* the tomb itself, and John mentions that the disciple who was with Peter had to stoop down in order to see in, before entering. All these references fit very well with a type of tomb commonly used in Palestine in ancient times, of which several good examples have been discovered.[72]

The tombs were created by chiseling into hillside rock. The outermost part of the tomb was an ante-chamber, which led into an inner, lower portion which one could enter only by crouching. Here, in this inner chamber, the bodies were placed, often in ledges hewn into the rock.[73] The stone used to seal the tomb stood between the ante-chamber and the inner recess where the body was actually buried. Tombs were of various sizes; often whole families were buried in a single sepulchre. The size and location of the tomb reflected the wealth of the family interred there. In Jesus' case, all the Gospels but Mark mention that Joseph's tomb was new; that is, no body had previously been placed there. Joseph had undoubtedly obtained the tomb for himself (as Matthew notes) and perhaps his family. However, had Jesus' body remained in the tomb, Joseph's family could not have been buried there, for it violated Jewish custom to bury in the tomb of one's fathers a man who had been executed.[74]

The proper preparation of the body for burial was specified by Jewish custom. This involved wrapping the body in a shroud of cloth and anointing it with spices and ointments. Each Gospel relates that the body of Jesus was wrapped in linen obtained by Joseph,[75] but John disagrees with the Synoptics as to whether Jesus' body was anointed before being placed in the tomb. John emphasizes that Nicodemus, assisting Joseph, brought a huge measure[76] of spices and anointed Jesus. But in the Synoptics no mention is made of anointing by Joseph or anyone else prior to the burial. Instead, Luke says that the women, after seeing where Jesus had been entombed, went directly to prepare spices and ointments so as to anoint the body. Then, on the day after the Sabbath, Mark and Luke both explain that the women came to the tomb early, bringing spices for this same purpose.[77] It is clear in these two Gospels that the anointing had not been done previously. If this record is correct,[78] the explanation is clearly the pressing time-problem after the crucifixion. In order to complete the burial before sundown the body was hastily wrapped, but there was not time for the ointments to be prepared and applied. The anointing could not be done on the following day, the Sabbath, as Luke notes. Therefore, the women—the same who had witnessed the execution—returned to the tomb at dawn on the morning after the Sabbath in order to perform this act. But according to the Gospels, instead of completing their mission they became the first witnesses to the Easter event.

A final postscript is supplied by Matthew. He adds that, on the day following the Sabbath, the chief priests and the Pharisees[79] gained audience with Pilate. They reminded him that Jesus—the "impostor"—had said that he would rise again in three days. Therefore, they requested that the tomb be secured, so that the disciples could not steal the body and claim that Jesus had risen. Pilate gave permission, and the tomb was sealed and a guard posted outside.[80]

Matthew later notes that, after the resurrection had occurred, some members of the guard returned to the city and informed the chief priests of what had taken place. After conferring, these officials bribed the soldiers to say that Jesus' body had been taken by his disciples at night while the soldiers slept. Matthew adds that this claim, that Jesus' body had been stolen by his followers, was still common among the Jews at the time when his Gospel was composed. This tradition provides a very interesting insight into the arguments which continued through the years between Christians and Jews over the resurrection of Jesus.

. . . . .

Death and burial commonly represent an ending. But in the New Testament, the trial, execution and burial of Jesus are only prologue. The central story begins after Jesus is laid in the tomb.

It is regrettable that, in the period just after the death and burial of Jesus, the Gospels do not focus attention directly on the disciples. No doubt, during these long hours they were victims of a dual despair: their grief over the loss of Jesus, and their shame for their personal cowardice in the last critical moments.

They must have been seized by a sense of hopelessness and bewilderment. Then and now the death of a righteous man, particularly at an early age, is tragic enough. But for the disciples this sense of tragedy was immeasurably deepened by their conviction that *this* man had borne the message of God in a special way, and that his death signified a defeat of that message.

The Easter faith was to transform this despair. The disciples' grief was converted into enthusiasm and hope. It is fitting that the resurrection narrative begins at dawn. In the eyes of the disciples, the resurrection of Jesus symbolized the emergence of themselves, and the world, from darkness into light.

CONCLUSION

LEGALITY AND RESPONSIBILITY

> ". . . he delivered him to be crucified."
> *Mark* 15:15

The execution of Jesus of Nazareth as a political criminal is one of the strange ironies of history. It is a tragic paradox that one who had opposed forceful opposition to Rome, and who today is worshipped by millions as the Prince of Peace, should have died as a common revolutionary. Although he doubtless shared the concern of his countrymen over the Roman occupation, Jesus' message centered around man's spiritual struggle with himself, not his nation's struggle against foreign rule. For Jesus, the enemy to be overcome was Satan, not Caesar. Like the Pharisees with whom he had much in common, Jesus counselled patience and forbearance under the Roman yoke. He came to Jerusalem in order to announce the imminent arrival of God's spiritual kingdom, not to bring in that kingdom by violence. Yet he was convicted of crimes against Rome and died alongside two others who were also condemned as insurrectionists.

Our first impulse is to insist that Jesus' prosecution was grossly illegal, as an endless list of writers has done.[1] But although Jesus' conviction was clearly unjust, it may well have been legal in a formal sense.[2]

The trial of Jesus occupied two stages: the preliminary Jewish investigation and the Roman trial. It is quite possible that the customary judicial practices of first-century Judaea were observed in both. Obviously, the formal Jewish trial described by Mark and Matthew would have been illegal; even if many of the judicial regulations set down in the *Mishnah* did not apply in the time of Jesus, no law code of any kind could have countenanced the judicial methods described by Mark. But this Mark/Matthew description is a secondary and fictitious tradition. It cannot be used as a basis for berating the Sanhedrin over its conduct of a kangaroo court. The Jewish proceedings were only an inquiry of a grand-jury nature, designed to prepare charges against Jesus to be presented to the Roman governor. The rules of procedure for such a hearing were probably informal. It is not even certain that a true judicial session was held at all. Some of those in the influential group around the high priest may simply have taken it upon themselves to seize Jesus, to question him privately, and to take him to the governor. This interpretation is suggested directly by John's Gospel, in which Jesus is interrogated by only two members of the temple priesthood. Probably, however, the Sadducean priests and their allies convened a regular judicial hearing for the purpose of arraigning Jesus. We have no idea what rules should have governed this hearing, and for that reason there is no way of determining whether the indictment was prepared legally.

In the Roman trial we are again handicapped by the fact that the Gospels have no interest in judicial questions. The Gospels supply us only sketchy summaries of the proceedings, summaries seriously conditioned by the concerns of the early Church. Further, no surviving information from Roman sources provides a sure basis for judging Pilate's handling of the case. We know only that the conduct of provincial trials was informal and expeditious, and that Roman governors were permitted to exercise their own judgment

within the broad pattern of justice observed in Rome.[3] The format
of the trial was probably simple and practical. It appears that the
Sadducean priests not only presented the charges to Pilate but also
acted as prosecutors, arguing the case against Jesus. There is no
record of any advocate or witnesses in behalf of Jesus, but we do
not know what practices were customary and we cannot assume
that our records of the trial testimony are complete. Evidently, Jesus
was required to answer the charges personally; such self-defense
may have been considered adequate in the circumstances.

The question of legality in the Roman trial thus comes down to
Pilate's personal respect for the principles of justice. Our only evidence on this issue is contradictory. Agrippa declares that Pilate
crucified many Jews without due legal process, and his testimony is
apparently based on very real grievances against the procurator.
Yet Pilate survived ten years as procurator of Judaea and it is unlikely that any governor who served a full decade in an imperial
province could have made it a practice to dispose of his subjects
without any judicial restraints. We are left with conjectures, and on
the basis of our limited evidence it is impossible to assert with assurance that Pilate's prosecution of Jesus was outside the accepted
legal bounds. It cannot be assumed lightly that either the Jewish or
the Roman proceedings against Jesus were illegal.

But if we cannot affirm definite illegalities, we can obviously
uncover injustice. A searching examination by Pilate would have
revealed that Jesus was no political pretender and that the charges
against him were superficial. It is impossible to believe that Pilate
made a careful and compassionate investigation into the charges
against Jesus. He almost certainly judged Jesus summarily after the
briefest investigation. His pronouncement of guilt resulted from the
priests' description of Jesus' actions and from the recurrent pattern
of political turmoil within the province. In another period, Jesus'
innocence of political plotting might have been obvious. But in the
prolonged crisis which gripped Judaea, particularly amidst the tension of the Passover season, it was too easy for Pilate to identify
Jesus with all those others who had plagued him by spreading rebellion in the country. The best guess is that Jesus also strengthened

the case against himself by affirming his Messianic role, which Pilate could hardly have distinguished from political ambitions.

What Roman law lay at the basis of the condemnation of Jesus? If Pilate made reference to a formal offense in sentencing Jesus, it was probably *laesa majestas,* "offense against the majesty" (of the people of Rome), the customary designation for treason.[4] But Pilate may have condemned Jesus without reference to a formal statute, citing only his supposedly revolutionary activity or his challenge to the peace of the country.[5]

In summary, the supposition—and it is only that—must be that Jesus was subjected to a formal trial within the customary practice of the period. He was arraigned by the Sadducean priests, presented to Pilate and charged with seditious activities in Jerusalem, examined perfunctorily by Pilate, and condemned by him for insurrection or a related offense. The legality of his prosecution will always remain uncertain because of the inadequacy of the evidence. But even if the trial of Jesus was conducted within accepted judicial practice, his very condemnation shows that the proceedings had only the form of justice and not the substance. No wonder the first Christians were so anxious to show that Jesus had been wrongly condemned and was innocent of the charges which led to his death.

A final point remains in this connection. In Chapter 1 an extensive investigation was made into the question whether the Jewish courts of Judaea in the time of Jesus had the legal right to try capital cases and to execute death sentences. It was argued that this privilege was denied the Jews, as it was evidently denied the citizens of all other provinces. The debate will certainly continue, but it is of the greatest importance to recognize that, once the events of Jesus' death have been properly reconstructed, the question whether the Jews held such authority actually becomes *irrelevant.* The issue of the Jewish judicial competence is important only if the Jews seized Jesus for violating their own laws and sought his death for such violations. The dilemma of interpretation would then be whether the Jews lacked full authority, and so were forced to take Jesus to Pilate, or whether they took him to the governor *in spite of* having the power to execute him. But neither of these two alternatives is correct. Jesus was not seized because of any violations of the Jewish religious laws, and there was never any cause for him to be subjected to a capital trial in a Jewish court even if such a trial had been possible. Jesus was apprehended because of alleged political crimes and the only function which could have been served by the Jewish officials was that of establishing the evidence against Jesus and preparing an indictment for the governor. There is no doubt that the Jewish courts had full authority for conducting such a preliminary hearing, and it is equally sure that the Sadducean priests often performed this function as part of their close league with the governor. The competence of the supreme Sanhedrin is an issue of importance which will inevitably arise in any discussion of the death of Jesus. But despite the rivers of ink which have been expended in examining it, the issue actually has little consequence for understanding the prosecution of Jesus. The Sanhedrin may or may not have had unlimited powers, but those powers were not required in the case of Jesus. Jesus was tried in a Roman court on charges prepared by Jewish authorities, and the basis of the trial was wholly political. The case did not belong in a Jewish court and would never have been tried there.

.   .   .   .   .

On whom does the moral responsibility for the crucifixion of Jesus lie? Regrettably, it has become necessary to observe that no legal or moral guilt extends to the Jewish people of Jesus' time or of any other. Tragic as the death of Jesus was, its tragedy has been surpassed by the unspeakable abuse suffered in its wake by Jews of all eras because of the blame assigned them for the crucifixion. This inclination to indict an entire people for the act of a handful has constituted the most malignant tendency in the Church's history. Although anti-Semitism is still with us in all its forms, it is now somewhat rare to hear this responsibility imputed to the Jewish people as a whole. After 1,900 years the Church hopefully is ridding itself of this strange compulsion.

Nor can the responsibility be laid on the majority of Jews who were gathered for the Passover in Jerusalem. Even if a crowd actually stood outside the praetorium calling for Jesus' death, this group constituted only a minute portion of those present in the city. But there is no reason to blame even such a limited number from among the people. It is extremely unlikely that any sizable group of Jews railed at the governor to do away with Jesus. The Gospel records are clearly prejudicial at this point; they reflect the rapidly developing practice in the early Church of blaming the entire Jewish nation because of its rejection of Jesus' Messiahship.

It is particularly unfortunate that the Pharisees have so commonly been blamed for Jesus' execution. Because the earlier opposition of some members of this group has been confused with the climactic hostility of the Sadducean priests, it has been wrongly supposed that religious bitterness lay at the roots of the crucifixion. The Pharisees have been denounced with special fervor because it has been assumed that they not only objected to elements in Jesus' message but pursued their objections to the cross. This reconstruction is imaginary and is not supported by the Gospels. Condemnation of the Pharisees for their part in Jesus' death has long obscured the essential nobility of Pharisaism, which despite its excesses was the vital and cohesive force which saved Judaism from extinction.

The central responsibility rests on the governor who dispatched Jesus to his death, and on the small group of priests who lent themselves to his support. It was they who arranged the arrest of Jesus and who pressed the case against him, and it was not their personal religious quarrel with Jesus which inspired their actions.

However dishonorable it appears in our eyes, the alliance of these priests with the procurator served a useful national purpose. They helped maintain a practicable government without which political conditions in Judaea might have been gravely worsened. It was, after all, not these Sadducees but the Zealots who led the nation to near-extinction in the war of A.D. 66–72. The priests' cooperation with the governor, and their willingness to act as his agents when necessary, aided in preserving the relative peace of the province.

It was this role which set them in opposition to Jesus. Despite his intentions, Jesus' activity in Jerusalem had enough of the appearance of violence, and enough promise of arousing and exciting the people, that the authorities regarded him as a threat to the restless calm of the Passover season. It is easy to imagine the worst of these priests; the execution of Jesus naturally suggests the most unprincipled villainy. But it is not in the least impossible that the Jewish national officials who sought the death of Jesus did so because they actually believed, as the Gospel of John suggests, that the death of one man might avert political disaster for the whole nation. He who came to Jerusalem to bring the nation nearer to God evidently lost his life because of the mistaken fear that he might lead it instead to destruction.

NOTES

Chapter 1

1 W. E. Filmer has recently argued that this traditional dating is in error and that Herod lived until 1 B.C. ("The Chronology of the Reign of Herod the Great," *J.T.S.* 17 (2, 1966), 283–298). This view is effectively refuted by T. D. Barnes, "The Date of Herod's Death," *J.T.S.* 19 (4, 1968), 204–209. See also T. Corbishley, "The Chronology of the Reign of Herod the Great," *J.T.S.* 36 (1935), 222–32; J. Finegan, *Handbook of Biblical Chronology,* Princeton, 1964, 230–234.

2 Josephus is the chief source for the information which follows, chiefly *Ant.* XVII–XVIII; *Bell. Jud.* I–III.

3 See T. Mommsen, *The Provinces of the Roman Empire from Caesar to Diocletian,* New York, 1887, vol. II, 199–200.

4 Augustus personally created this distinction: Suetonius *Aug.* 47; Strabo xvii.3, no. 25; Dio, liii, 12. Theoretically, the imperial provinces were those in special need of a military garrison because of internal or external threats. The clear-cut distinction between senatorial and imperial provinces often broke down in practice. See W. T. Arnold, *The Roman System of Provincial Administration,* Oxford, 1914, 104; G. H. Stevenson, "The Imperial Administration," Chapter VII of *Cambridge Ancient History,* Cambridge, 1923 seq., vol. X, 211–212.

5 Technically, these officials were called *prefects* at the time of Judaea's conversion into a province; the term *procurator* came into use only later in the first century. However, procurator is the most common designation for this office and is used here according to usual practice. Prefects/procurators were members of the equestrian class and were most commonly minor finance-officials—*procuratores fisci.* When serving in the place of legates they assumed full governmental authority and became *procuratores Caesaris pro legato.* See A. H. Greenidge, "Procurator," *Dictionary of Greek and Roman Antiquities,* London, 1901, vol. II, 496. For the title "procurator" Josephus uses interchangeably ἐπίτροπος, ἡγεμών, ἔπαρχος.

6 Egypt was the most significant such province; others included Raetia and Noricum.

7 Except for the brief interruption in A.D. 41–44 when Herod Agrippa I ruled briefly

as a client-king. After Agrippa's rule the procurators were given the responsibility for all of Palestine.

[8] There has been extended discussion over the relation of the Judaean procurators to the legates of Syria. Josephus states that Judaea was made a part of Syria (*Ant.* XVIII,i,1; XVII,xiii,5; but cf. *Bell. Jud.* II,viii,1, where he says that Judaea itself was made into a province) and he records the intervention of the Syrian legate in the internal affairs of Judaea (*Ant.* XVIII,i,1; iv,1f. Cf. also *Ant.* XVIII,viii,2-9; XX,i,1; *Bell. Jud.* II,xiv,3; xvi,1; xviii,9). But Josephus' statement is almost surely incorrect. Judaea was technically independent of Syria and the control exercised by Syrian governors over Judaea (as when Vitellius deposed Pilate in A.D. 36; *Ant.* XVIII,iv,2) is found only in extraordinary cases and seems to have been *de facto* rather than *de jure* control. It was inevitable that the emperors would call on the legate of nearby Syria to intervene in Judaean affairs when there was some special need for it. The clearest statement of this problem and its correct solution are found in Mommsen, *op. cit.* 201, note 1. See also R. W. Husband, *The Prosecution of Jesus,* Princeton, 1916, 174f; A. N. Sherwin-White, *Roman Society and Roman Law in the New Testament,* Oxford, 1963, 11.

[9] μεχρι του κτεινειν εξουσιαν: *Bell. Jud.* II,vii,1. The term clearly implies the *ius gladii* or *potestas gladii* commonly exercised by Roman governors.

[10] See particularly Sherwin-White, *op. cit.,* 1-11.

[11] R. H. Stevenson, *op. cit.,* 209: ". . . all that Rome could hope to do was to maintain internal peace and win the gratitude of her subjects by protecting them against invasion . . . no attempt was made to impose municipal institutions on unwilling subjects."

[12] Analyses of the history and character of the Sanhedrin are available from many modern writers; for a recent and detailed review, see H. Mantel, *Studies in the History of the Sanhedrin,* Cambridge, Mass., 1961. Some Jewish scholars have argued that there were *two* supreme Sanhedrins in Jerusalem in Jesus' day: a "religious" Sanhedrin and a "political" Sanhedrin. This duality is suggested by the wide differences between the Sanhedrin described in the rabbinic sources and that described in Josephus and the New Testament. Despite the prominent names associated with this theory, it has an almost fantastic character and has never become a serious factor in the interpretation of Jesus' prosecution. It is incredible to suppose that this duality could have existed without the slightest mention in our sources. The differences between *Mishnah Sanhedrin* and the Josephus/New Testament evidence can be explained without the necessity of multiplying the Sanhedrins. First, the Mishnaic description is largely academic, not a description of an actual functioning body (see note 35 below). Second, the Gospel descriptions of the Sanhedrin's conduct in prosecuting Jesus also have unhistorical elements (see Chapters 7 and 10). For the theory of multiple Sanhedrins, see A. Büchler, *Das Synhedrion in Jerusalem,* Vienna, 1902; J. S. Lauterbach, article "Sanhedrin," *The Jewish Encyclopedia,* ed. by G. Adler *et al,* New York, 1905, vol. XI, 184-185; S. B. Hoenig, article "Sanhedrin," *The Universal Jewish Encyclopedia,* ed. by I. Landman, New York, 1943, vol. IX, 361-363; Hoenig, *The Great Sanhedrin,* New York, 1953; S. Zeitlin, *Who Crucified Jesus?,* New York, 1942, 69-78; H. Mantel, *op. cit.,* 54f. On the function of the Sanhedrin generally, see J. S. Kennard, "The Jewish Provincial Assembly," *Z.N.T.W.* 53 (1962), 25-51.

[13] *Mishnah Sanhedrin* 1:6. Membership was evidently for life, and although we do not know the exact method of replacement, vacancies were probably filled either by the Sanhedrin itself or by nomination of the Roman governor; see E. Schürer, *The Jewish People in the Time of Jesus Christ,* Edinburgh, 1901, Div. II, Part I, 175. The former method was theoretical and ideal, but the Roman governor may have preempted this right in the provincial period.

[14] Josephus implies as much when he says that the Sadducees were forced to reach their decisions according to Pharisaic principles, at the insistence of the populace (*Ant.* XVIII,i,4). Actually, our evidence does not permit us to determine which group, if either, dominated the Sanhedrin at the time of Jesus. This point is sometimes debated on the assumption that if the Sadducees controlled the Council its rules of judicial practice were probably more harsh than would have been the case

under Pharisaic control; e.g., J. Blinzler, "Das Synedrium von Jerusalem und die Strafprozessordnung der Mischna," *Z.N.T.W.* 52 (1961), 54–65. Also D. Chwolson, *Das letzte Passamahl Jesu*, 118f., reference from A. E. J. Rawlinson, *The Gospel According to St. Mark*, London, 1925, 218.

[15] Mk. 11:27par.; Mk. 14:43par.; Mk. 14:53par.; Mk. 15:1par.; Mt. 2:4; Mt. 20:18; etc. See E. Schürer, *op. cit.*, 177, note 481.

[16] In later Jewish tradition the president of the Sanhedrin is said to have been the head of one of the Pharisaic schools, rather than the high priest. For the many rabbinic citations to this effect see H. Danby, "The Rabbinical Criminal Code and the Jewish Trial Narratives in the Gospels," *J.T.S.* 21 (1920), 67–68. But as we learn from Josephus (*Ant.* IV,viii,14; XX,x,5; XIV,ix,3–5; XX,ix,1; *Apion.* ii,23) and the New Testament (citations listed by Schürer, *op. cit.*, 182f.; cf. Danby, *op. cit.*, 68) in earlier times the high priest filled this post. There is no dispute that this was true in the procuratorial period.

[17] The office conferred a certain permanency by which a high priest retained not only the title but many of the special privileges and obligations of the office even after the end of his tenure; see H. L. Strack and P. Billerbeck, *Kommentar zum Neuen Testament aus Talmud und Midrasch*, München, 1928, II, 153; J. Jeremias, *Jerusalem zur Zeit Jesu*, Göttingen, 1958, II B, 14f; cf. Luke 3:2, where Annas and Caiaphas are both given this title.

[18] In Josephus (*Bell. Jud.* II,xx,4; IV,ix,11; V,xiii,1; VI,ii,2) and the New Testament (e.g., Acts 19:14; cf. 4:6) several men are designated αρχιερεις whose names are not on the high priestly lists. Also a reference in Josephus (*Bell. Jud.* IV,iii,6) to certain families from whom the high priests were selected indicates a group of privileged families whose members may have shared in the title although not actually serving as high priests themselves.

[19] See E. Mary Smallwood, "High Priests and Politics in Roman Palestine," *J.T.S.* 13 (1, 1962), 14–34.

[20] To be precise, the name of Caiaphas appears only in Matthew and John; Mark and Luke refer to the high priest by title rather than by name.

[21] In fact, Josephus indicates that the Sanhedrin's powers actually *increased* under the procurators, in contrast to the restrictions which had been imposed by Herod I and Archelaus.

[22] Several key works have led to the formation of this view, which is adopted in a great many studies of Jesus' trial. Schürer, *op. cit.*, 184–195 and J. Juster, *Les Juifs dans l'Empire Romain*, Paris, 1914, vol. II, 127f. give two of the most influential statements. See also H. Lietzmann, "Der Prozess Jesu," *Sitzungsberichte der Preussischen Akademie der Wissenschaften*, Berlin, 1931, who is dependent on Juster. It was the appearance of Lietzmann's view (which was actually a minor part of his study of the trial) which ignited much of the debate on this problem. From the side of Roman studies the work of Mommsen, *op. cit.*, 200–204 gives the same picture, although with less detail. For a good bibliography of works which accept this theory in interpreting the trial of Jesus, see J. Blinzler, *op. cit.*, 159f. Paul Winter has been the most important recent spokesman for this view, although he rejects the claim that the Sanhedrin actually exercised its capital powers in Jesus' case: *On The Trial of Jesus, Studia Judaica, Forschungen zur Wissenschaft des Judentums* I, Berlin, 1961; also in several articles, e.g., "The Trial of Jesus and the Competence of the Sanhedrin," *N.T.S.* 10 (4, 1964), 494–499; "The Trial of Jesus," *Commentary* 38 (3, 1964), 35–41; "Sadokite Fragments IX,1," *Revue de Qumran* 6 (1, 1967). See also T. A. Burkill, "The Competence of the Sanhedrin," *Vigiliae Christianae* 10 (1956), 80–96; "The Trial of Jesus," *Vigiliae Christianae* 12 (1958), 1–18.

[23] *Ant.* V,xi,5; *Bell. Jud.* VI,ii,4. This temple notice has of course been recovered. See G. A. Deissman, *Light from the Ancient East*, tr. by L. R. M. Strachan, New York, 1927, 79f. In Acts 21:28 the Apostle Paul is accused of violating this rule.

[24] *Ant.* XX,ix,1. See also Eusebius, *Eccl. Hist.*, II xxiii. For the parallels to this story in later Christian literature see K. Beyschlag "Das Jakobusmartyrium und seine Verwandten in der frühchristlichen Literatur," *Z.N.T.W.* 56 (3–4, 1965), 149–178.

[25] *Ant.* XIV,x,17; XIV,x,21–24; XVII,x,1–2; *Bell. Jud.* II,ii.6.

[26] *Ant.* XVI,vi,2.

[27] *Bell. Jud.* II,viii,9.

[28] See *Mishnah Sanhedrin*. The most important are: capital cases are to be tried by a court of 23 judges; capital cases must begin with testimony for acquittal, not testimony for conviction; capital trials are to be held during the daytime and the verdict reached in the daytime; a verdict of guilt cannot be reached on the same day as the trial; witnesses in capital cases are to be examined with special care and no hearsay evidence is acceptable; after the initial decision is reached in a capital case, the members discuss the case all night and vote again in the morning; if a man is found guilty on a capital charge there are four prescribed methods of execution: stoning, burning, beheading and strangling; another *Mishnah* section, *Makkoth*, describes the punishment to be assigned to false witnesses.

[29] *Mishnah Sanhedrin* 7:2.

[30] *C. Flacc.* 7:8; *Leg. ad Gaium*, 16,24,31.

[31] In *De Specialibus Legibus*, I–IV, Philo treats extensively the problem of harmonizing the Mosaic law code with another legal system which he describes. E. R. Goodenough, in his thorough analysis of the work (*The Jurisprudence of the Jewish Courts in Egypt*, New Haven, 1929) believes this second system is that of the Jews in Alexandria under Roman rule. J. Juster and some others (see Goodenough, 11f.) considered this code only hypothetical, but Goodenough demonstrates persuasively that it is an actual code to which Jews who accepted the Mosaic law had to reconcile themselves in first-century Alexandria (see Introduction and Chapter 5, 22–23, 214f.). If so, this code indicates that the Romans granted extensive judicial powers to the Jews in their own community. Strabo specifically mentions that the Jews in Egypt had special sections in Alexandria where they lived under their own laws and courts (Goodenough, 16). Philo, *In Flacc.* 53 mentions the special privileges of the Alexandrian Jews. Goodenough agrees with Fuchs (*Die Juden Aegyptens*, 91; cited by Goodenough, 17–18) that these privileges included criminal jurisdiction. So also Juster, *op. cit.,* II,114. Although Goodenough admits that the Jews were undoubtedly restricted somewhat in the more serious cases, they may have had the right to pass death sentences subject to the governor's approval (pp. 18–24). Carl Kraeling has described the Jewish legal privileges in another city outside Judaea during this period ("The Jewish Community at Antioch," *J.B.L.* 51 (1932), 130–160.) Kraeling is able to reach no decision about the exact legal status of the Jews, which is the case in all other instances where we know of Jewish communities. See also G. Haddad, *Aspects of Social Life in Antioch in the Hellenistic Period,* New York, 1949, 61.

[32] The right of the Sanhedrin to arrest and imprison is reflected in Acts 5:18,40; 22:4; 26:10; II Cor. 11:24f. See A. T. Robertson, "Luke's Knowledge of Roman Law," Ch. XV, *Luke the Historian in the Light of Recent Research,* New York, 1920.

[33] Acts 22:4.

[34] See also Mt. 10:17,21 and Jn. 16:2, in which Jesus issues warnings to his followers that they may suffer death. These references probably reflect the persecution of the early Christians at the hands of some Jewish officials.

[35] The decisive demonstration of this point is from H. Danby, *op. cit.* Danby showed that the Mishnaic regulations are largely academic and date from a period subsequent to the time of Jesus. Even in cases where no direct comparison can be made between the *Mishnah* and all non-rabbinic sources, ". . . the internal evidence which the Mishnah provides is of a nature which can give us but little confidence in the laws as a practical working code governing the life of the nation before or after the fall of Jerusalem" (p. 71). Danby concluded, "The Mishnah fails to agree with the earlier accounts of the Sanhedrin because the historical Sanhedrin had ceased to exist, and the Sanhedrin which it (the Mishnah) did know, on which it based its description, was a purely academic institution, having purely academic powers and purely academic interests" (p. 75). Danby probably overstates the case; it is likely that some of these regulations are historical and a few probably antedate the time of Jesus; but we have no way of knowing which, and we cannot tell from these rules whether the capital powers they imply were applicable in Jesus' day. For an attempted rebuttal to Danby's view, see I. Abrahams, *Studies in Pharisaism*

and the Gospels, "The Tannaite Tradition and the Trial Narratives," Cambridge, 1924, 129–137; also W. Bacher, article "Sanhedrin," *Dictionary of the Bible,* New York, 1902, IV, 398. In support of Danby's view see J. Klausner, *Jesus of Nazareth,* tr. by H. Danby, New York, 1925, 334; G. Barton, "On the Trial of Jesus Before the Sanhedrin," *J.B.L.* 41 (1922), 205–211; G. D. Kilpatrick, *The Trial of Jesus,* London, 1953, 11–12; A. H. McNeile, *The Gospel According to St. Matthew,* London, 1915, 398; A. E. J. Rawlinson, *St. Mark,* in *Westminster Commentaries,* ed. by W. Lock, London, 1925, 218; J. Blinzler, *op. cit.,* 149–157. Blinzler provides an extensive bibliography. As Blinzler correctly notes, the Mishnaic rules, taken as a whole, are of such "exaggerated mildness" that they could never have been in practical operation (p. 153).

[36] E.g., Philo, *C. Flacc.* 7. A large measure of self-rule was extended, of course, to non-Jews as well (see discussion in text). Cf. H. T. F. Duckworth, "The Roman Provincial System," in *The Beginnings of Christianity,* ed. by F. Jackson and Lake, London, 1920, Part I, Vol. I, 171–217: The Romans ". . . seldom interfered with the religions of their subjects or allies if these religions neither disturbed the peace nor encouraged barbarities. Even so, they interfered only to protect the *majestas* of the Roman people . . ." (p. 199).

[37] See *Ant.* XIV, x, 5–6; iv,4; cf. Mommsen, *op. cit.,* 189–191.

[38] Even Schürer, *op. cit.,* Div. II, Part K, 189 is sure such executions were permissible only by approval of the procurator. See also G. Deissmann, *op. cit.,* 79f. G. Dalman, *Sacred Sites and Ways,* New York, 1935, 290 argues that the inscription indicates only that offending Gentiles would be killed on the spot; no reference to court proceedings was intended.

[39] *Ant.* XX,ix,1. The authenticity of this Josephus passage is disputed. Even if part of the original work, it seems to be a report of an illegal action. See S. G. F. Brandon, *The Fall of Jerusalem and the Christian Church,* London, 1951, 100: ". . . it would accordingly appear that the death of James was the outcome of a piece of high-handed action on the part of the Sadducean aristocracy, led by Ananus, and the crime was effectively condemned by the Pharisees." We have similar evidence of lynch-justice from the same period in the Jewish community in Alexandria. Philo records several instances in which Alexandrian Jews killed their fellow countrymen for crimes against the Jewish religious laws, instead of delivering them to the Roman authorities, as they were required to do. In these cases also the Romans seemed to have turned their backs, since neither Roman laws nor Roman citizens were involved. See E. R. Goodenough, *op. cit.,* 23–34, 214f., 253. Instances in which Christians suffered apparently extra-legal persecution are cited in Acts 5:33; 22:4; 26:10. On the high incidence of lynch-law across the empire generally see Sherwin-White, *op. cit.,* 39–40.

[40] Because of the privileges which attended his Roman citizenship, the Apostle Paul could not legally have been put to death by a Jewish court on its own authority. Yet in Acts we read that certain of the Jews repeatedly sought to lay hands on Paul and to kill him, and would certainly have done so had any opportunity arisen. This is a good example of how the Jews, because of their intense religious affections, would willingly have violated the Roman judicial code in order to punish anyone who flagrantly violated the Jewish religious laws. This example underlines the importance of distinguishing between regular criminal jurisprudence and individual incidents of lynch-law.

[41] Justin Martyr, *Dialogue with Trypho,* 16:4.

[42] Most of the Acts references to the Sanhedrin's attempts to intimidate the early Christian movement show only that the Sanhedrin had *limited* judicial powers. For example, it is not contested that the Sanhedrin had its own police force for arresting offenders (Acts 4:1–3; Acts 5:17–18). But the arrests and attempted arrests described in Acts do not show that the Sanhedrin could lawfully have put on trial and executed those whom they seized. For example, the first arrest of Simon Peter is followed only by a hearing which attempted to discover if there was adequate justification for a trial. The second arrest is followed by the release of the two disciples without a trial. On the lynching of Stephen see D. R. A. Hare, *The Theme of Jewish Persecution in the Gospel of Matthew,* Cambridge, 1967, 20f.

43 A careful documentation of this fact is provided by Sherwin-White, *op. cit.*, 14f., 35f. He summarizes: ". . . the capital power was the most jealously guarded of all the attributes of government, not even entrusted to the principal assistants of the governors . . ."

44 This edict, numbered IV in a collection of edicts from Augustus to local στρατηγοι in Cyrene and Crete, has been published by several scholars; Goodenough, *op. cit.*, 19–20 supplies an English translation.

45 It is often argued that Egypt was not a province at all but, in a unique sense, a personal property of the emperor; further, that this fact explains the very limited judicial powers delegated to the Egyptians. See the argument by M. Nilsson in note 46. The evidence seems to have swung against this view; Egypt was evidently a province in the normal sense and it is clear that it was under the rule of procurators of equestrian rank, as was Judaea.

46 In an important but widely overlooked book (cf. note 8, above,) R. W. Husband based his interpretation of the trial of Jesus largely on the judicial system operative in Egypt in the first century A.D. Since we have very little direct information on the Judaean legal system, said Husband, we should seek information about Roman provincial practices from the (then) recently discovered papyrological evidence concerning the Egyptian system, especially since Egypt was also an imperial province governed by procurators. The Egyptian procurator (prefect) made an annual judicial circuit into the three districts of the country in which he judged a great many cases which had been prepared in advance by lesser officials. He delegated the less significant cases to his Roman subordinates (επιστρατηγοι), and sat personally in all serious cases. The local Egyptian officials (στρατηγοι) merely prepared the evidence, serving a grand-jury function. According to Husband, the various Sanhedrins in Judaea—including the supreme Sanhedrin—performed the same function. The Sanhedrin did not have the power to try serious cases on its own; it merely presented the evidence to Pilate and the other procurators. This is precisely what the Council did in the case of Jesus. H. Danby based his interpretation of the trial largely on the same evidence, following the argument as given by Husband (Danby, *op. cit.*, 51–76). As we will see in Chapter 10, a great many scholars agree that the Sanhedrin actually performed only a grand-jury function in Jesus' case, although few base their argument on the Egyptian papyri. One problem with Husband's and Danby's argument is that Egypt seems to have had less freedom of self-government than any other province in the empire (see M. Nilsson, *Imperial Rome*, tr. by G. C. Richards, London, 1926, 189–90); therefore, it provides a very questionable parallel to Judaea. As Nilsson says, "In contrast with all other provinces it (Egypt) had no provincial diet"; indeed, ". . . the Egyptians were excluded from the management of their own country . . . ," much unlike the practice in other provinces.

47 But see the reservations noted above.

48 *Op. cit.*, 36. He also makes the very interesting observation that the Roman reluctance to grant capital powers to provincial courts arose partly from the fear that these courts might use their powers to intimidate Roman sympathizers. In the hands of the Jews of Judaea such powers would surely have been used to this end.

49 *J. Talmud, Sanhedrin* 18a (1:1, 11, 23–24); 24b (7:2, 1, 44). See also *B. Talmud, Sanhedrin* 41a. Still another primitive Jewish source implies that, under the procurators, the Jews were restricted in the exercise of capital powers. The "Scroll of Fasting" (*Megillat Ta'anit*) is a document dating from the first century A.D. which describes the 35 feast-days of the Jews. *Meg. Ta'anit* 6 declares that five days after the Romans evacuated Jerusalem the killing of "wrongdoers" was reinstituted by the Jews. This reference is probably to A.D. 66 when the Romans were expelled at the start of the Jewish rebellion, and the text may indicate that, when the Romans had departed, the Jews again began to exercise full judicial powers freely. However, this reference is of questionable value: it may mean simply that, when the Romans had gone, the patriotic Jews began to avenge themselves on the hated Roman sympathizers, which they of course had been unable to do previously.

50 Scholars who believe that the Sanhedrin retained its capital powers under the

procurators usually challenge the meaning of this reference; e.g., T. A. Burkill, "The Competence of the Sanhedrin," *op. cit.* 80–96. Burkill's attempt to dispute the meaning of this notice by comparison with a similar report in *Bab. Talmud, Sanh.* 41a (see above) and a related reference in *Bab. Talmud, Ab. Zar.* 8b is unconvincing (p. 83f.). The obvious meaning of the passage stands, and is actually supported by *Bab. Talmud, Sanh.* 41a.

[51] For a bibliography of works which deny that the Sanhedrin had the power, in Jesus' day, to pass and to execute capital sentences, see J. Blintzler, *op. cit.*, 157–163. From the side of Roman studies the most important work is A. N. Sherwin-White, *op. cit.* Sherwin-White gives a brief summary of his views in "The Trial of Christ," in *Historicity and Chronology in the New Testament*, London, 1965, 97–116. See also J. Jeremias, "Zur Geschichtlichkeit des Verhörs Jesu vor dem hohen Rat," *Z.N.T.W.* 43 (1950–1951), 147f.; G. D. Kilpatrick, *op. cit.*, 18–20 (Kilpatrick believes, however, that the Sanhedrin did proceed to try and to condemn Jesus, though it lacked the legal right); C. G. Montefiore, *The Synoptic Gospels*, London, 1927, Vol. II, 352f.; J. Klausner, *op. cit.* 333–4, 340; G. Barton, *op. cit.* 205 (like Kilpatrick, Barton believes the Jewish authorities did try Jesus, though they lacked the right); B. S. Easton, in review of Husband's book, *op. cit.*, in *American Journal of Theology*, 1917, 462f.; F. C. Grant, "On the Trial of Jesus: A Review Article," *Journal of Religion* 44 (3, 1964), 230–237; A. E. J. Rawlinson, *op. cit.*, 218f.

[52] See Chapter 10 for a full discussion of the conflicting theories concerning the Sanhedrin's action in the case of Jesus.

Chapter 2

[1] As H. B. Sharman says, although a procurator or tetrarch might be brought into the story by his direct connection with Jesus, ". . . it did not become a concern of the evangelist to set forth in an adequate way the trend of Roman rule in Palestine, and its far reaching effect upon Jewish and political life . . . ," *The Teaching of Jesus About the Future*, Chicago, 1909, 103.

[2] Lk. 23:4,14–15; Mt. 27:24b; Jn. 19:12a; Mk. 15:14par.

[3] Mk. 15:13par.; Lk. 23:5; Mt. 27:24a; Jn. 19:6,12–14a.

[4] Mk. 15:15par.; Mt. 27:24–26.

[5] *Ant.* XVIII,iii,1–2; iv,1–2.

[6] The account appears in both major histories: *Ant.* XVIII,iii,1; *Bell. Jud.* II, ix,2–3

[7] *Leg. ad Gaium*, 38.

[8] It is quite possible to interpret Pilate's policies as judicious governmental practice rather than as arbitrary high-handedness toward the Jews. See C. Kraeling, "The Episode of the Roman Standards in Jerusalem," *H.T.R.* 35 (1942), 263–289. But even if we take this view, the point is the same: Pilate made little or no effort to accommodate his Judaean subjects and, whether from malice or from justifiable political practice, he ruled with firm decisiveness. See S. Mathews, *A History of New Testament Times in Palestine*, New York, 1913, 172; P. Winter, *On the Trial of Jesus*, 51–61; S. Liberty, "The Importance of Pontius Pilate in Creed and Gospel," *J.T.S.* 45 (1944), 38–56.

Chapter 3

[1] The literature on form criticism is now vast, although the fundamental works can still be numbered on one's fingers. The landmark works are: R. Bultmann, *Die Geschichte der synoptischen Tradition*, Göttingen, 1921 Engl. tr., *History of the*

Synoptic Tradition, tr. by J. Marsh, New York, 1963; M. Dibelius, *Die Formge-schichte des Evangeliums,* Tübingen, 1919, Engl. tr. *From Tradition to Gospel,* tr. by B. L. Woolf, London, 1934 (see also *Botschaft und Geschichte* I, Tübingen, 1953); K. L. Schmidt, *Der Rahmen der Geschichte Jesu,* Berlin, 1919; G. Bertram, *Die Leidengeschichte und der Christuskult,* Göttingen, 1922. In addition, the following works in English are useful: B. S. Easton, *The Gospel Before the Gospels,* New York, 1928; R. H. Lightfoot, *History and Interpretation in the Gospels,* London, 1935; F. V. Filson, *Origins of the Gospels,* New York, 1938; D. W. Riddle, *The Gospels: Their Origin and Growth,* Chicago, 1939; F. W. Beare, *The Earliest Records of Jesus,* Nashville, 1962; F. C. Grant, *The Earliest Gospel,* New York, 1943; M. Dibelius, "The Structure and Literary Character of the Gospels," *H.T.R.* 20 (3, 1927), 151-170.

[2] The battle-lines have too often been determined by theological rather than analytical considerations, since radical form criticism is antithetical to a conservative interpretation of the Gospels. Recently, "redaction criticism" has offered a partial alternative to form-critical premises by focusing attention on the creative roles of the individual Gospel writers or redactors and less on the influence of the community as a whole in the shaping of the Gospels; e.g. H. Riesenfeld, *The Gospel Tradition and Its Beginnings: A Study in the Limits of Formge-schichte,* London, 1957; H. Conzelmann, *The Theology of St. Luke,* London, 1960; G. Bornkamm, G. Barth and H. J. Held, *Tradition and Interpretation in Matthew,* 1963; W. Marxsen, *Der Evangelist Markus,* Göttingen, 1956; G. D. Kilpatrick, *The Origins of the Gospel According to St. Matthew,* Oxford, 1946. A very helpful recent summary of redaction criticism is given by N. Perrin, *What Is Redaction Criticism?,* Philadelphia, 1969.

[3] G. Bertram holds that the passion events were themselves circulated as individual units, *op. cit.,* 8, and Bultmann makes the number of connected events very small, *op. cit.,* 64.

[4] *From Tradition to Gospel,* 179.

[5] See M. Goguel, *The Life of Jesus,* tr. by Olive Wyon, New York, 1933, 58-59.

[6] Dibelius has emphasized the influence of early Christian preaching in the shaping of the individual pericopes in the Gospels; there is no doubt that preaching had a profound effect particularly on the development of the passion narrative. On the use of the connected passion story in worship, see Schmidt, *op. cit.,* 305. The effect of cultic interests on the formation of the narrative has been demonstrated especially by Bertram, *op. cit.* See also D. W. Riddle, *op. cit.,* 95; B. W. Bacon, *The Gospel of the Hellenists,* New York, 1933, 228; P. Carrington, *The Primitive Christian Calendar,* Cambridge, 1952.

[7] Cf. Bultmann, *op. cit.,* 64f.; Dibelius, *A Fresh Approach to the New Testament and Early Christian Literature,* New York, 1936, 47, and *The Message of Jesus Christ,* tr. by F. C. Grant, New York, 1939, 144; and *From Tradition to Gospel,* 178f.; V. Taylor, *Formation of the Gospel Tradition,* London, 1949, 47-48.

[8] Cf. Taylor, *ibid.,* 47; Dibelius, *The Message of Jesus Christ,* 144.

[9] J. Jeremias, *The Eucharistic Words of Jesus,* tr. by A. Ehrhardt, New York, 1966, 61 provides a succinct statement of the way this fact applies to the fourth Gospel.

[10] Statistics from A. Q. Morton and G. H. C. Macgregor, *The Structure of Luke and Acts,* London, 1964, 27.

[11] On the recent efforts to establish the primacy of Matthew see Chapter 4, note 1.

[12] Papias, quoting John the Presbyter, in Eusebius, *Historia Ecclesiastica,* III, 39.

[13] It should be understood that this supposition is made for illustrative purposes only. There is no reason to assume that Mark's account contains any special information from the personal remembrances of Peter, despite Papias' statement.

[14] Mark rivals John as the Gospel whose sources are the most difficult to analyze. In Mark's case the reason, of course, is that it is our earliest Gospel and no sources, even fragmentary, on which it might have been based have survived. It is impossible even to determine whether Mark drew on *any* written materials. However, many scholars have attempted to separate two or more sources in Mark's passion narrative; e.g., Dibelius, *From Tradition to Gospel,* 178f., and

Fresh Approach, 49f., separates an early passion story from the later materials added by Mark from other sources; V. Taylor, *The Gospel According to St. Mark,* London, 1952: "Additional Note J: The Construction of the Passion and Resurrection Narrative," 653–654, finds an older passion account to which Mark added later traditions which came from Simon Peter; W. L. Knox, *The Sources of the Synoptic Gospels,* ed. by H. Chadwick, vol. I: *St. Mark,* Cambridge, 1953, 132f. and E. R. Buckley, "The Sources of the Passion Narrative in St. Mark's Gospel," *J.T.S.* 34 (1933), 138–144 also separate two layers of tradition, one more primitive and authentic than the other. A. T. Cadoux, *The Sources of the Second Gospel,* London, n.d., 185f., 237f. distinguishes three separate strands of tradition. For various theories on the nature of Mark's sources throughout his Gospel see the following recent commentaries in English: P. Carrington, *According to Mark: A Running Commentary on the Oldest Gospel,* Cambridge, 1960; C. E. B. Cranfield, *The Gospel According to St. Mark,* Cambridge, 1959, J. M. C. Crum, *St. Mark's Gospel: Two Stages in Its Making,* Cambridge, 1936; P. Parker, *The Gospel Before Mark,* Chicago, 1953. For a good summary of the problems met in analyzing Mark's sources see H. A. Guy, *The Origin of the Gospel of Mark,* London, 1954; S. E. Johnson, *A Commentary on the Gospel According to St. Mark,* London, 1960, 26–29.

[15] As V. Taylor says, *op. cit.,* 254, among form critics ". . . critical estimates of the original *Grundstock* differ, but the amount of agreement is impressive."

[16] *Op. cit.,* 282–316.

[17] *From Tradition to Gospel,* 178–217.

[18] *Op. cit.,* 303f.

[19] *Op. cit.,* 653f.

[20] *Op. cit.,* 175f.

[21] Cf. Taylor, *op. cit.,* 50: "A single story, as the foundation of all the Gospel accounts, would imply from the beginning a highly organized church governed from one centre. It seems more probable that different communities, whenever it was possible, would have had their own accounts. The probabilities . . . favor the existence of several Passion stories."

[22] Another weakness of this term is its implied emphasis on the creative work of Mark himself. This emphasis is not justified by the evidence. Unfortunately, it is impossible to tell how much personal creativity Mark exercised in composing his passion story (see Chapter 4). It is quite possible that he simply followed his sources faithfully, as Matthew later followed him. Therefore, we should not speak of Mark's account as a new and major stage in the *formation* of the narrative. Much more important is the long development of the passion traditions in the days *before* Mark laid hold of them. Some critics (cf. F. C. Grant, *op. cit.,* 176–179) recognize this by attempting to distinguish various strata within the pre-Markan account itself, describing some as "primary" and some as "secondary but pre-Markan." For this reason, we should dispense with the terms "Markan" and "pre-Markan" as major designations in the growth of the passion narrative. The chief significance of Mark's Gospel in the history of the passion narrative is its effect on the *subsequent* development of that narrative. Mark's account had a dual impact on later Christian interpretation of the trial: (1) it provided a major source for later Gospels (notably our own Matthew and Luke) (2) its circulation tended to inhibit the continuing elaboration of the trial stories. However, it is interesting to note how much the interpretation of the trial continued to change even after the appearance of our Gospels: see Chapter 7.

[23] As Jeremias says with regard to the probable form of the pre-Markan narrative, "An exact determination, let alone a reconstruction of a written source, is quite impossible. It is simply a stage in the development of growing oral traditions, which probably showed very marked local differences." (*The Eucharistic Words of Jesus,* 1966, 65, note 5.)

[24] Paul's letters, of course, do not give us any substantial information about the human circumstances which led to Jesus' death. Paul's concern is with the spiritual meaning of the cross, not its proximate historical causes.

Chapter 4

1 A few years ago C. H. Dodd could say, "The criticism of the Gospels has achieved at least one secure result. Scarcely anyone now doubts that Mark is our primary Gospel" (*New Testament Studies,* Manchester, 1953, 1). But not even that conviction is unanimous: a few scholars have recently revived the attempt to demonstrate the primacy of Matthew. See B. C. Butler, *The Originality of St. Matthew,* Cambridge, 1951; L. Vaganay, *Le Problème Synoptique,* Paris, 1954; W. R. Farmer, *The Synoptic Problem: A Critical Analysis,* New York, 1964. Such attempts usually find an earlier Aramaic Matthew behind both our first and second Gospels. A convenient review of this issue is given by W. Barclay, *The First Three Gospels,* Philadelphia, 1967. Summaries of the present state of Synoptic criticism generally are given in Feine, Behm, Kümmel, *Introduction to the New Testament,* 14th rev. ed., tr. by A. J. Mattill, Jr., Nashville, 1966, 33–60; A. Richardson, *Gospels in the Making,* London, 1938; S. Neill, *The Interpretation of the New Testament, 1861–1961,* Oxford, 1964, 104–122.

2 Unjustly so, in my opinion. The evidence seems persuasive that Luke's Gospel resulted essentially from the addition of Markan material to an already existing Gospel. V. Taylor has been the most energetic spokesman for this battered hypothesis: see particularly, *Behind the Third Gospel: A Study of the Proto-Luke Hypothesis,* Oxford, 1926. Also, B. W. Streeter's pioneering work, *The Four Gospels,* London, 1924; H. Schürmann, *Der Paschamahlbericht, Lk 22 (7–14), 15–18,* and *Jesu Abschiedsrede, Lk 22, 21–38,* vols. 19 and 20 in *Neutestamentliche Abhandlungen,* Münster, 1952 and 1956: F. Rehkopf, *Die lukanische Sonderquelle: Ihr Umfang und Sprachgebrauch,* 1959; J. Jeremias, *The Eucharistic Words of Jesus.* For a full bibliography of authors who defend the Proto-Luke hypothesis in one form or another, see Feine, Behm, Kümmel, *op. cit.,* 92.

3 A clear, although somewhat arbitrary, statement of the case against the Q hypothesis is A. M. Farrer's, "On Dispensing With Q," in *Studies in the Gospels,* Oxford, 1955, 55–86. For a convenient summary of the arguments in favor of Q, see Taylor's article in *New Testament Essays: Studies in Memory of Thomas Walter Manson,* 1959, 246–269.

4 B. W. Bacon comments that the narrative of the arrest as described in Mark is one of the most realistic in the Gospels and its aim almost purely historical. (*The Beginnings of the Gospel Story,* New Haven, 1920, 208.)

5 W. E. Bundy, *Jesus and the First Three Gospels,* Cambridge, Mass., 1955, 514. See also N. A. Dahl, "Die Passionsgeschichte bei Matthäus," *N.T.S.* 2 (1955–56), 17–32.

6 "St. Luke's Passion-Narrative Considered With Reference to the Synoptic Problem," in *Studies in the Synoptic Problem,* ed. by Wm. Sanday, Oxford, 1911, 76–94.

7 As we will see below, Matthew's minor changes and additions are best accounted for by supposing that he had access to various *individual units* of tradition which were not in Mark. Hardly anyone suggests that these Matthean changes reflect the use of another source, in the usual sense of the term. It is interesting that C. H. Dodd should find a second source in Matthew's passion narrative, based on Matthew's change in verb tense (from imperfect to aorist) in the plot story. (*Historical Tradition in the Fourth Gospel,* Cambridge, 1963, 22–24.) For an unusually negative appraisal of Matthew's dependence on Mark in the passion events, see X. Leon-Dufour, "Mt et Mc dans le récit de la Passion," *Biblica* 40 (3,1959), 684–696.

8 The influence of the Old Testament is much stronger in Matthew's passion story than in Mark's; although few examples of this influence are found in the trial events themselves, V. Taylor finds an Old Testament passage, Psalm 31:13, at the base of Matthew's description of the conspiracy. (*From Tradition to Gospel,* 187, note 1.)

9 Another possibility is that, since the temple had actually fallen at the time

Matthew wrote, Jesus' words did not need to be accounted for by false testimony. [10] (1) He omits "made with hands" and "not made with hands" as distinctions of the two temples in view. (2) He puts an oath on the lips of the high priest in demanding an answer from Jesus. (3) He changes Mark's "Son of the Blessed" to "Son of God." (4) He makes Jesus' answer to the high priest read: "Hereafter ($\alpha\pi$' $\alpha\rho\tau\iota$) you shall see the Son of Man . . ." This change is also found in Luke, although Matthew and Luke differ greatly in the words which follow, a fact which seems to preclude the likelihood that they share an earlier copy of Mark which had the statement in this form (cf. Easton, below). It is not certain what Matthew and Luke intended by $\alpha\pi$' $\alpha\rho\tau\iota$; apparently they wished to change Mark's announcement of Jesus' physical return into a reference to his continuing spiritual presence. This change may have been dictated by the fact that these Jewish leaders had *not*, in the years following, seen Jesus return in glory, so that a "spiritualization" of the phrase was necessary. For a review of the critical opinions on this passage see B. S. Easton, "The Trial of Jesus," *American Journal of Theology*, 1915, 447. See also M. Dibelius, *From Tradition to Gospel*, 197–8 for the theological significance of Matthew's version; also B. H. Streeter, *op. cit.*, 321–322, who argues that the agreement of Matthew and Luke here is due only to their editorial activity.

[11] $\kappa\alpha\tau\epsilon\kappa\rho\iota\nu\alpha\nu$

[12] $\epsilon\nu\circ\chi\circ\varsigma$ $\theta\alpha\nu\alpha\tau\circ\upsilon$

[13] Matthew interrupts the Roman trial narrative to record the fate of Judas Iscariot (Mt. 27:3–10), a scene missing in Mark. This is a significant digression from Mark, but is not part of the trial narrative as such and has no bearing on our study. Luke of course has a very different story of Judas' death (Acts 1:15–20).

Chapter 5

[1] B. S. Easton, *The Gospel According to St. Luke*, New York, 1926, provides a detailed analysis of Luke's textual details and its minor linguistic disagreements with the other Gospels in the passion narrative.

[2] Luke's wording can also be interpreted to mean that the officials wanted to move against Jesus because of what might happen among the people *if Jesus were not removed*. This interpretation fits very well into the historical reconstruction suggested in this book. However, this wording seems to have resulted accidentally from the manner in which Luke abridged Mark. The interpretation cited in the text is almost certainly the correct one.

[3] See Luke 22:52; also Acts 4:1; 5:24. Luke also explains Judas' action by saying that Satan had entered into him, and he points out that Judas sought an occasion when Jesus could be betrayed without attracting popular attention.

[4] Luke's other changes are of no special significance. He omits the explanation of the kiss of betrayal, but adds Jesus' words, "Judas, would you betray the Son of Man with a kiss?" He also omits reference to the fact that Jesus' arrest fulfilled the scriptures. For a thorough analysis of Luke's arrest scene, see F. Rehkopf, *op. cit.*

[5] E.g., Blinzler, *op. cit.*, 115: "The most striking departure (in Luke) from Mark's account is the shifting of the trial to daybreak."

[6] In Luke the Jewish crowd is present at the proceedings from the beginning; see Chapter 7 for a discussion of this change.

[7] Sir John Hawkins, *op. cit.*, 78.

[8] The following data are drawn chiefly from A. M. Perry, *The Sources of Luke's Passion Narrative*, Chicago, 1920, 19, 21f., 42f., 62f.; V. Taylor, *Behind the Third Gospel*, 39f., and *Formation of the Gospel Tradition*, 52f.; Sir John Hawkins, *op. cit.*

[9] It is disputed whether 22:69,71 stem from Mark; if Luke took them from Mark he has used them in an entirely different manner.

[10] W. E. Bundy, *op. cit.*, 480.

[11] "The Treatment of His Sources by the Third Evangelist in Luke XXI–XXIV," *Studia Theologica* 8 (2, 1954), 170–171.

[12] For the view that Luke relied on a connected, non-Markan source in the passion narrative see B. Weiss, *Die Quellen des Lukas-evangeliums,* Stuttgart, 1907, 195f.; F. Spitta, *Die synoptische Grundschrift in ihrer Überlieferung durch das Lukas-Evangelium,* Leipzig, 1912, 396–400; F. C. Burkitt, *The Gospel History and Its Transmission,* Edinburgh, 1907, 134f.; J. Jeremias, *The Eucharistic Words of Jesus,* 68–69; "Perikopen-Umstellungen bei Lukas?," *N.T.S.* 4 (2, 1958), 115–119; H. Schürmann, *op. cit.;* F. Rehkopf, *op. cit.;* Morton and Macgregor, *op. cit.,* 28; B. Redlich, *Form Criticism,* New York, 1939, 167; A. Barr, "The Use and Disposal of the Marcan Source in Luke's Passion Narrative," *E.T.* 55 (1943), 227–231; S. Temple, "The Two Traditions of the Last Supper, Betrayal, and Arrest," *N.T.S.* 7 (1, 1960), 77–85; J. B. Tyson, "The Lukan Version of the Trial of Jesus," *Novum Testamentum* 3 (1959), 249f. J. A. Bailey, *The Traditions Common to the Gospels of Luke and John,* Leiden, 1963, finds a very limited non-Markan source, noticeable chiefly in the account of the Sanhedrin proceedings. C. H. Dodd, *Historical Tradition in the Fourth Gospel,* 35–36, notes that of Mark's 17 Old Testament testimonies, Luke incorporates only four, while adding six non-Markan ones.

[13] For the view that *Q* included a passion narrative, see F. C. Burkitt, *op. cit.,* 134; J. V. Bartlet, *op. cit.,* 331f; W. E. Bundy, *op. cit.,* 481.

[14] I.e., the "L" material; cf. Streeter, *op. cit.,* xviii-xix; Taylor, *Behind the Third Gospel,* 7; F. C. Grant, *The Growth of the Gospels,* 104; B. Redlich, *op. cit.,* 167.

[15] Even Luke's account of the mocking is different; its general verbal agreement with Mark is only some eighteen percent (Perry, *op. cit.,* 44–45).

Chapter 6

[1] Clement of Alexandria, quoted by Eusebius, *H.E.* VI,14,7.

[2] See J. Riaud, "La gloire et la royauté de Jésus dans la Passion selon saint Jean," *Bible et Vie Chrétienne* 56 (1964), 28–44; B. W. Bacon, *The Gospel of the Hellenists,* New York, 1933, 226–7; M.-E. Boismard, "La Royauté du Christ dans le quatrième évangile," *Lumière et Vie* 11 (1962), 43–63. J. Blank, "Die Verhandlung vor Pilatus Joh 18,28–19,16 im Lichte johanneischer Theologie," *Biblische Zeitschrift* 3 (1, 1959), 60–81.

[3] In John, of course, the last meal is not a Passover meal and there is no sharing of the bread and wine as representations of Jesus' body and blood; this is replaced by Jesus' washing of the disciples' feet. John uses the last meal as the setting for Jesus' extended discourse and prayer; in John the meal covers five chapters (13–17). The only parallel of significance for our study between John and the Synoptics in the meal is the exposure of Judas as the betrayer, an exposure made much more specific and detailed in John.

[4] John 12:27–28 contains material parallel to the Synoptic Gethsemane scene. However, in this section John pointedly revises the Synoptic picture. In John's version Jesus emphasizes that he will *not* ask for the cup of death to be removed. John is obviously unwilling to let Jesus shy away from the prospect of the cross. On John's omission of the Gethsemane scene, see particularly R. E. Brown, *New Testament Studies,* Milwaukee, 1965, 192–198.

[5] A celebrated problem in John's account concerns the possible dislocation of 18:24. As John's account now stands, Jesus is taken directly to Annas (18:13), whom John identifies as the father-in-law of the high priest, Caiaphas. John relates Peter's first denial of Jesus, then states that the high priest questioned Jesus. But this must refer to Annas, not Caiaphas, because at the end of the examination we read that Annas *then* sent Jesus in bonds to Caiaphas. The confusion is heightened by the fact that nothing takes place at the house of Caiaphas; Jesus is merely led from there to the praetorium. These difficulties are often resolved by supposing that 18:24 (Jesus sent to Caiaphas) belongs immediately after 18:13. The account then reads

that Jesus was taken to Annas, who bound him and sent him to Caiaphas, who questioned him about his teachings and his disciples. *Sin. Syr.* gives the text in just this way. We cannot be certain, but there are good arguments for believing that this reconstruction restores the correct sense. The author of the Fourth Gospel cannot have been confused about the name of the high priest, because twice (18:13 and 18:24) he gives this title to Caiaphas and states that Annas was his father-in-law. Therefore, the statement in 18:19 that the high priest questioned Jesus most logically fits Caiaphas, not Annas. While John could certainly have applied the high-priestly title to Annas because of his past service in the office and his continuing importance in the community (cf. Luke 3:2; Acts 4:6), this would be a very confusing manner of speaking in this section. The argument for this reconstruction is furthered by the fact that, as the text now stands, Caiaphas is mentioned four times in this section but plays no part whatever in the proceedings. It makes little sense for John to put so much emphasis on the name of Caiaphas and then to assign him no role in the story, particularly since John makes special mention of Caiaphas' interest in Jesus (11:49–51; 18:14). The dislocation question has only minor significance for the analysis of Jesus' trial since, no matter which of the two Jewish leaders is believed to have questioned Jesus, the central point is that there was, according to John, only a "private" investigation by these two men, not an investigation by the full Council or even a large portion thereof. However, this problem will continue to arouse interest. In support of the suggested reconstruction see J. Schneider, "Zur Komposition von Joh. 18:12–27. Kaiaphas und Hannas," *Z.N.T.W.* 48 (1957), 111–119; W. R. Church, "The Dislocations in the Eighteenth Chapter of John," *J.B.L.* 49 (1930), 375–383. James Moffatt has offered a slightly different rearrangement ("The Trial of Jesus," in *Dictionary of Christ and the Gospels*, ed. by J. Hastings, New York, 1908, vol. II, 751); see also G. H. C. Macgregor, *The Gospel of John*, in *The Moffatt New Testament Commentary*, New York, 1929, 327–329. I agree with E. Hoskyns and F. N. Davey, *The Fourth Gospel*, London, 1940, vol. II, 607, that preference for the *Sin. Syr.* at this point is very questionable if that reading be thought of as a *survival* of the most primitive reading. However, it is quite reasonable that the attempt of the *Sin. Syr.* to give sense to the passage has resulted in a *restoration* similar to what the original must have been. In defense of the traditional order of verses see A. Mahoney, "A New Look At An Old Problem (John 18,12–14,19–24)," *C.B.Q.* 27 (2,1965), 137–144: see his footnote 9 for extensive bibliography in support of the present order. C. H. Dodd, *Historical Tradition in the Fourth Gospel*, 94, note 2, defends the traditional arrangement and provides an interesting explanation of the apparent confusion. P. Winter accepts the earlier view of J. Wellhausen that Caiaphas was not mentioned at all in the original edition of John; his name was added later as a correction to the name of Annas, whom John (like Luke) had mistakenly thought to be the high priest (*On the Trial of Jesus*, 34f.). Winter also argues that Annas' name was mistakenly introduced because the writer of John confused him with Ananus II, who persecuted Christians a generation after Jesus' death. For a full discussion of John's inclusion of Annas in the proceedings against Jesus, see Chapter 10.

[6] Jesus is presented as an "evildoer" (κακον ποιων). ℵ* reads κακον ποιησας and C*ᵖᶜ κακαποιων.

[7] Determination of the sources and structure of John's Gospel as a whole is a problem on which almost no critical agreement prevails. As J. A. T. Robinson observes, ". . . the effect of reading too much on the Fourth Gospel is to make one feel either that everything has been said about it that could conceivably be said or that it really does not matter what one says, for one is just as likely to be right as anyone else": "The Relation of the Prologue to the Gospel of St. John," *N.T.S.* 9 (1962–3), 120; cited by D. M. Smith, "The Sources of the Gospel of John: An Assessment of the Present State of the Problem," *N.T.S.* 10 (1964), 336–351. This comment applies well to the analysis of John's sources. Among the most important recent studies are: R. Bultmann, *Das Evangelium des Johannes*, Göttingen, 1953; B. Noack, *Zur johanneischen Tradition: Beiträge zur Kritik an der literarkritischen Analyse des vierten Evangeliums*, Copenhagen, 1954; C. H. Dodd, *Interpretation of the Fourth Gospel*, Cambridge, 1953, and *Historical Tradition in the Fourth Gospel*,

op. cit. R. H. Lightfoot, *St. John's Gospel, A Commentary,* Oxford, 1956; C. K. Barrett, *The Gospel According to St. John,* London, 1955; E. C. Hoskyns and F. Davey, *op. cit.,* A. Q. Morton and G. H. C. Macgregor, *The Structure of the Fourth Gospel,* Edinburgh, 1961; W. Wilkens, *Die Entstehungsgeschichte des vierten Evangeliums,* Zürich, 1958; R. E. Brown, *The Gospel According to John, I–XII,* New York, 1966: Brown provides a thorough review of the several approaches to the analysis of John's sources. Brief summaries are provided by D. M. Smith, *op. cit.;* A. M. Hunter, "Recent Trends in Johannine Studies," *E.T.* 71 (1959–60), 164–7, 219–22. For a full bibliography of modern Johannine studies see E. Malatesta, *St. John's Gospel, 1920–1965: A Cumulative and Classified Bibliography of Books and Periodical Literature on the Fourth Gospel,* Rome, 1967.

[8] For the view that John is independent of the Synoptics see P. Gardiner-Smith, *Saint John and the Synoptic Gospels,* Cambridge, 1938; C. H. Dodd, both works cited previously; A. J. B. Higgins, *The Historicity of the Fourth Gospel,* London, 1960; W. Wilkens, *op. cit.;* B. Noack, *op. cit.;* E. Haenchen, "Johanneische Probleme," *Zeitschrift für Theologie und Kirche* 61 (1959), 19–54; R. E. Brown, *The Gospel According to John, I–XII;* R. Bultmann, *Das Evangelium des Johannes;* P. Borgen, "John and the Synoptics in the Passion Narrative," *N.T.S.* 5 (1959), 246–259 (who believes that John knew the Synoptics only second-hand, through oral tradition).

[9] Two lately appreciated characteristics of John's Gospel have led to this judgment: (1) its Semitic background, particularly its linguistic and theological parallels to the Qumran scrolls and (2) its careful topographical notices, which suggest a Palestinian origin for at least part of the material. Although I have seen no statement to this effect, it would seem that if a literary relationship exists between John and any Synoptic, we can no longer exclude the *possibility* that John is the source, not the borrower! However, it is a grave error to leap to the conclusion that John has been restored to a position of equal or near-equal historical value alongside the Synoptics. The possibility that John arose at an early date, or had a Palestinian origin, does not in any way prove that its portrait of Jesus is substantially more accurate than previously supposed. We must remember that John's picture of Jesus is not under suspicion because it was written at a late date; rather, John has been assigned to a late date simply because its portrait of the divine Son of God seems so distant from the Jesus of Nazareth evident in the Synoptics. If we now wish to assign John to an earlier date, we will not thereby alter the reliability of its presentation of Jesus. It is a constant temptation to suppose that by adjusting the date of a Biblical writing forward or backward a few years we automatically reduce or enhance its merit. The arguments against the historicity of John's description of Jesus are not erased by supposing that it was written a few years earlier or a few hundred miles nearer to Jerusalem than we had once supposed. Regrettably, the desire of many commentators to restore faith in John's historical value has caused them to exaggerate the significance of items (1) and (2) listed above.

[10] On the necessity of finding more than superficial parallels between John and the Synoptics in the passion narrative, in order to establish literary interdependence, see the masterly study by Dodd, *Historical Tradition in the Fourth Gospel,* 31–135.

[11] A special relation between Luke and John in the passion narrative, and in their Gospels generally, has been suggested frequently over the years; e.g., P. Parker, "Luke and the Fourth Evangelist," *N.T.S.* 9 (4, 1963), 317–336; J. A. Bailey, *op. cit.;* I. Buse, "St. John and the Passion Narratives of St. Matthew and St. Luke," *N.T.S.* 7 (1, 1960), 65–76; W. J. Harrington, *The Gospel According to St. Luke, A Commentary,* Westminster, Md., 1967; E. Osty, "Les Points de contact entre le récit de la Passion dans Saint Luc et Saint Jean," *Recherches de science religieuse* 39 (1951), 146–154; A. M. Perry, *op. cit.,* 104; V. Taylor, *Formation of the Gospel Tradition,* 53, note 1; B. W. Bacon, *The Gospel of the Hellenists,* 226.

[12] It has been suggested that Luke and John also agree in placing Simon Peter's denial of Jesus before the Jewish proceedings, but this agreement is illusory. In Luke's report there are no proceedings against Jesus until the morning after the arrest, so Luke is forced to relate Simon's denial before these proceedings, since it was known that the denial took place during the night, shortly after the arrest.

In John's version Simon's denials are divided into two parts and are placed both before *and after* the Jewish proceedings. There is no literary parallel between these Gospels at this point.

[13] *Op. cit.*, 226.

[14] Although Luke and John both mention three statements by Pilate that Jesus is innocent, John introduces these statements in a very different way from Luke, and John's overall sequence of events before Pilate is much different from Luke's. The numerical similarity is of little consequence when we compare the two accounts overall. Considering their broad and fundamental differences, it is impossible to imagine that John went through Luke's account counting the number of times in which Pilate mentioned Jesus' innocence, then purposely duplicated that number.

[15] Further, at one point John's version is closer to those of Mark and Matthew than to that of Luke. It agrees. with our first two Gospels in citing an annual custom as the basis for Pilate's offer to release Jesus or Barabbas. This custom is not mentioned in our earliest manuscripts of Luke, and almost certainly was not part of his original work.

[16] It is interesting that C. H. Dodd argues just the opposite, that the Roman trial in John is obviously *political* in character, not religious. (*Historical Tradition in the Fourth Gospel*, 112f.) However, Dodd's larger theme is John's independence of Luke (and the other Synoptics) in the passion events, which is the key point at issue.

[17] It may be that there are evidences in other portions of the passion narrative, or in the rest of the Gospel, that John was familiar with Luke (see particularly the studies of Bailey and Osty cited previously). But since significant parallels are missing in the trial events themselves, this larger question has little relevance for our study. It is quite conceivable that John could have made use of Luke at certain points without being influenced by his account of the trial proceedings.

[18] *Formation of the Gospel Tradition*, 53.

[19] On John's use of a special source or sources in constructing his passion narrative, see e.g. Dodd, *op. cit.;* W. F. Howard and C. K. Barrett, *The Fourth Gospel in Recent Criticism and Interpretation*, London, 1931, 148. (It is interesting that Howard, in "The Gospel According to St. John, Introduction and Exegesis," in *The Interpreter's Bible*, ed. by G. A. Buttrick, vol. VIII, argues that John used a separate source in the passion narrative, but cites the reference to the Roman cohort as the only evidence of it.) See also R. Summers, "The Death and Resurrection of Jesus: John 18-21," *Review and Expositor* 62 (4, 1965), 473-481: J. A. Bailey, *op. cit.*

Chapter 7

[1] For a documentation of this increasing hostility and its effect on the Christian attitude toward the Jewish nation, see J. Parkes, *The Conflict of the Church and the Synagogue*, London, 1934, 47-150; D. R. A. Hare, *The Theme of Jewish Persecution of Christians in the Gospel According to St. Matthew*, Cambridge, 1967, 1-79; C. F. D. Moule, *The Birth of the New Testament*, London, 1962, 105-124. A great many scholars have noted the influence on the trial accounts of the Christian conviction that the Jews were morally responsible for Jesus' death (for which see below). See for example H. Lietzmann, *op. cit.;* C. G. Montefiore, *op. cit.*, I, 351,363f.; A. Loisy, *Les Evangiles Synoptiques*, Paris, 1908, II, 610; B. W. Bacon, *The Beginnings of the Gospel Story*, 210f.; E. C. Colwell, *John Defends the Gospel*, Chicago, 1936, 75f.; R. Bultmann, *The Study of the Synoptic Gospels*, 66; D. W. Riddle, *The Gospels, Their Origin and Growth*, 95; S. J. Case, *Jesus, A New Biography*, Chicago, 1927, 325; C. Guignebert, *Jesus*, tr. by S. Hooke, New York, 1956, 465; W. E. Bundy, *op. cit.*, 514, 532; E. C. Colwell and E. L. Titus, *The Gospel of the Spirit*, New York, 1953, 85f.; P. Winter, *On the Trial of Jesus* (a recurrent theme throughout this book), also "Marginal Notes on the Trial of Jesus,

II," *Z.N.T.W.* 50 (1959), 221–251; H. H. Cohn, "Reflections on the Trial and Death of Jesus," *Israel Law Review* 2 (3, 1967), 332–379. For the contrary view, that apologetic interests had little effect on the Gospel narratives, see J. Blinzler, *The Trial of Jesus*, 40–44.

[2] In Acts 13:27–29 Luke quotes Paul as blaming the Jews for Jesus' death: "Though they could charge him with nothing deserving death yet they asked Pilate to have him killed."

[3] *I Apology* 63:10.

[4] *Dialogue with Trypho* 17:1.

[5] *Ibid.*, 85:2.

[6] *Apology*, 21:18. Italics mine.

[7] M. R. James, *The Apocryphal New Testament*, Oxford, 1924, 90.

[8] *Gospel of Peter* I.1.

[9] Origen also declares that it was not Pilate but the Jewish authorities who sentenced Jesus to death (*Contra Celsum*, ii.34). W. Bauer, *Das Leben Jesu im Zeitalter der neutestamentlichen Apokryphen*, 1909 cites all the references found in the Apocrypha concerning the Jews as the murderers of Jesus; reference from Blinzler, *op. cit.*, 10, note 8. In a spurious letter written centuries after the crucifixion and ascribed to Pontius Pilate, Pilate not only declares his belief in Jesus' innocence but reports that he sent 2,000 troops in an effort to stop the crucifixion! See P. Winter, "A Letter from Pontius Pilate," *Novum Testamentum* 7 (1, 1964), 37–43.

[10] *The Conflicts of the Early Church*, London, 1930, 96–97.

[11] Cf. E. E. Jensen, "The First Century Controversy over Jesus as a Revolutionary Figure," *J.B.L.* 60 (1941), 261–272 (p. 268f.)

[12] *Annals*, XV.44.

[13] στασεως αρχηγετης. Origen, *Contra Celsum*, viii.14. An interesting citation is found in Lactantius (*Div. Inst.* V,3,4; cf. H. P. Kingdon, "Had the Crucifixion a Political Significance?," *Hibbert Journal* 35 (1937), 556–567). It states that one Sossianus Hierocles, governor of Phoenicia and nearby territories about A.D. 220, reported that Jesus ". . . after having been routed (or "refuted," according to one ms.) by the Jews, committed acts of brigandage (*lactronia*) at the head of a band of 900 men." Lactantius says that the governor was *non contra sed ad Christanos*, from which Kingdon concludes that he would have been unlikely to say anything which was not widely believed to be true. This report of Jesus' political activity was probably current in the area and is another example of the use to which non-Christians put the fact of Jesus' execution by a Roman governor.

[14] See the references in note 1 above; also S. G. F. Brandon, *Jesus and the Zealots*, Manchester, 1967, 4f., 221f. On the importance to the early Church of loyalty to the state, see C. E. B. Cranfield, "The Christian's Political Responsibility According to the New Testament," *Scottish Journal of Theology* 15 (2, 1962), 176–192.

[15] As Montefiore says, "It was important to show that though Pilate condemned him, he did so reluctantly, unwillingly, and that the true authors of the condemnation were not the Romans but the Jews. And if the founder was harmless, equally harmless must be his followers." (*The Synoptic Gospels*, vol. I, 371.)

[16] This point is sometimes insufficiently stressed by those who point out the pro-Roman bias of the trial accounts. Goguel notes correctly the priority of the conviction that the Jews were guilty as the key factor in the reshaping of the trial accounts. He also notes that this factor is not due merely to "bias" but harks back to the actual fact that Jewish leaders had led the opposition against Jesus (*The Life of Jesus*, 466.) The Christian stress on Jesus' political innocence, in the same way, sprang primarily from the actual *fact* of his innocence, not merely from the exigencies of apologetic.

[17] On this point see the works cited in note 1 above.

[18] *Op. cit.*, II, 342.

[19] Bundy's judgment is typical: the story is "simply a piece of apologetical and polemical fiction inspired by the bitter prejudice of later Christians." (*Jesus and the First Three Gospels*, 532). Cf. J. A. Fitzmyer, "Anti-Semitism and the Cry of 'All the People' (Mt. 27:25)," *Theological Studies* 26 (1965), 667–671. On the manner in which the Gospels, particularly Matthew, have been affected by Jewish persecution

and a resultant anti-Jewish bias, see the excellent study of D. R. A. Hare, *op. cit.*
[20] See Luke 23:1,4,5,13f., 18f.
[21] *Op. cit.,* 527.
[22] *The Gospel According to St. Luke, 6.*
[23] On John's use of the term "the Jews," see almost any commentary; also G. Baum, *The Jews and the Gospel,* Westminster, Md., 1961, 98f.; also the debate between D. M. Crossan, "Anti-Semitism and the Gospels," *Theological Studies* 26 (1965), 189–214, and G. O'Collins, "Anti-Semitism in the Gospels," *Theological Studies* 26 (1965), 663–6. On John's effort, throughout his passion narrative, to fix the blame for Jesus' death on the Jews, see particularly Colwell, *op. cit.,* 67f.
[24] John places so much emphasis on Pilate's desire to release Jesus, and on his extended appeals to Jesus' Jewish opponents, that it is hard to make good sense out of the pattern of events. See Dodd, *Historical Tradition in the Fourth Gospel,* 97.
[25] This attempt to shift the crucifixion itself from Roman to Jewish hands creates an interesting paradox in John's narrative. In John 18:30–31, Pilate tells the Jews to judge Jesus themselves, but the Jews state that they are not permitted capital powers. In the next verse John makes the editorial observation that this exchange fulfilled Jesus' prophecy about how he was to die. John's meaning is: Jesus had predicted that he would die on a cross; however, crucifixion was not a Jewish means of execution but a Roman one; so Jesus' death at the hands of the Romans (not Jews) fulfilled Jesus' prediction. But when he comes to the end of the scene before Pilate, John contradicts himself by stating that Pilate gave Jesus back to the Jews so that *they* could crucify him. Although John knows that the Jews would never have executed Jesus by putting him on a cross, and has already alluded to that fact, his apologetic desire to place the blame on the Jews overwhelms his knowledge of history and his own earlier statement.

Chapter 8

[1] Our understanding of the Zealots has been advanced in recent years by a number of important studies, particularly M. Hengel, *Die Zeloten: Untersuchungun zur jüdischen Freiheitsbewegung in der Zeit von Herodes I bis 70 n. Chr.,* Leiden, 1961; S. G. F. Brandon, *Jesus and the Zealots, op. cit.* Other useful books and articles are cited in the notes below. A brief review of recent Zealot studies is found in B. Salomonsen, "Some Remarks on the Zealots With Special Regard to the Term 'Qannaim' in Rabbinic Literature," *N.T.S.* 12 (2, 1966), 164–176. Salomonsen gives special attention to the relation of the Zealots and the Pharisees. See also C. Roth, "The Zealots in the War of 66–73," *Journal of Semitic Studies* 4 (4, 1959), 332–355; G. Baumbach, "Zeloten und Sikarier," *Theologische Literaturzeitung* 90 (1965), 727–740.
[2] As H. Rengstorf notes: "Umso beachtlicher ist, dass das Volk mit seinen Sympathien immer auf der Seite der Zeloten gestanden hat . . ." (article on λῃστής in *Theologisches Worterbuch zum Neuen Testament,* Stuttgart, 1942, ed. by G. Kittel, Band IV, 264). Also W. R. Farmer: "The only crucial difference between the Zealot groups and other patriotic Jews who stood outside the collaborating circle of tax collectors, Sadducees, and high-priestly families was over the question, 'When shall our policy of non-collaboration with the occupying powers and of non-fraternization with Jewish collaborators as well as Roman officials and soldiers be changed into the warlike policy of active resistance.' " (*Maccabees, Zealots, and Josephus,* New York, 1956, 182–3.)
[3] *The State in the New Testament,* New York, 1956, 11. See also E. E. Jensen, "The First Century Controversy Over Jesus as a Revolutionary Figure," *J.B.L.* 60, 262.
[4] The chief source for the study of Palestine in the first century B.C. and A.D. is Josephus, *Ant.* XVII–XX and *Bell. Jud.,* I–III, from which the following summary is drawn.
[5] It is impossible to give an exact date to the rise of Zealotism, which was a "spirit

of resistance" as much as a specific movement. See Brandon, *op. cit.*, 26–64 for the development of Zealotism.

[6] See K. Kohler, "Zealots," in *The Jewish Encyclopedia*, ed. by C. Adler *et al.*, New York, 1907, vol. XII, 639; J. Klausner, *Jesus of Nazareth*, 203; Rengstorf, *op. cit.*, 263. The Jewish resistance found its main inspiration in the Maccabean period, in which the Jews had last attained freedom. The theme of Farmer's book, *op. cit.*, is the influence of the earlier Maccabean heroes on the first-century political crises. For the Zealotist activity under the Herods see also S. Mathews, *A History of New Testament Times in Palestine*, 126.

[7] On Josephus' bias see S. Angus, "Zealots," in *Encyclopedia of Religion and Ethics*, ed. by J. Hastings, vol. XII, 854; Farmer, *op. cit.*, 175; Rengstorf, *op. cit.*, 264; Sharman, *op. cit.*, 127.

[8] As J. Wellhausen says, "It was a combination of noble and base elements; superstitious enthusiasts (Acts 21:38), and political assassins . . . were conjoined with honest but fanatical patriots." (*A Sketch of the History of Israel and Judah*, 177.) On the religious motivation of the Zealots see, in addition to the chief works previously cited, C. Roth, "The Zealots—A Jewish Religious Sect," *Judaism* 8 (1, 1959), 33–40, and *The Historical Background of the Dead Sea Scrolls*, New York, 1959); Schürer, *op. cit.*, Div. I, vol. 1, 168f.; J. Klausner, *op. cit.*, 204. It is common to assume that in Jesus' time many of these leaders laid claim to being the awaited Messiah or were so regarded by their followers. So H. G. Friedmann: "From Josephus it appears that in the first century, before the destruction of the Temple, a number of Messiahs arose promising relief from the Roman yoke and finding ready followers." (Article "Pseudo-Messiahs," in *The Jewish Encyclopedia*, vol. X, 251f. See also Sharman, *op. cit.*, 127.) But Josephus never indicates that the people mistook any of these revolutionaries for Messiahs. Of course it is possible that Josephus has hidden the Messianic pretensions of some of these leaders, since he wanted to present all these λῃσταί as mere brigands. But this is mere speculation; we have nothing substantial to justify the notion that Messianic claimants were continually appearing on the scene, as many commentators suppose.

[9] Rengstorf notes correctly: "Bei Josephus ist λῃστής die ständige Bezeichnung der *Zeloten*, die den bewaffneten Kampf gegen die römische Herrschaft mit Einschluss aller derer, die sie fördern, bejahen oder auch nur dulden, zum Inhalt ihres Lebens gemacht haben und für das Ziel der nationalen Freiheit ständig alles, auch das Leben, einsetzen . . ." (*op. cit.*, 263). Good observations about the use of the term Zealots are found in *The Beginnings of Christianity*, vol. I, *Prolegomena* I, Appendix A, 421–5, by the editors, Foakes-Jackson and Lake. They point out that the term "Zealot" does not appear in Josephus until the time of the Jewish War, where it is associated with John of Gischala. Therefore, they challenge the idea that Zealots *per se* had been active in the period since the Herods. But this rigid interpretation of the term "Zealot" obscures more than it explains. Although Josephus does not use this term in the earlier period, the explanation is obviously his refusal to consider these early revolutionists anything but bandits. There can be no doubt that Josephus thought of Judas' work in A.D. 6 as the start of a seditious movement which eventually climaxed in the war of A.D. 66. It is good to be careful about Josephus' titles (cf. M. S. Enslin, "Palestine," in *Interpreter's Bible*, vol. VII, 106), but in order to convey the proper sense of the revolutionary activities, we are not bound to Josephus' own terminology, especially when that terminology is clearly prejudicial. It is proper to apply the name of Zealots to these earlier rebels, because their actions and motivations are identical to those found in the men who later led the nation into war—at which time Josephus belatedly grants them the formal title.

[10] *Ant.* XVIII,i,1, tr. by L. H. Feldman, in *Loeb Classical Library* series, Cambridge, Mass., 1965.

[11] See Chapter 2, particularly the reference in Philo, *Leq. ad. Gaium* 38.

[12] Philo, *ibid.*

[13] See Chapter 9 for the relationship between crucifixion and political crimes; also W. A. Brown, "Cross," in *Dictionary of the Bible*, ed. by J. Hastings, vol. I, 528–9.

[14] Angus, *op. cit.*, 852. See *Bell. Jud.* II,xii,1.

[15] Tacitus, *Annals* XII, 54 has a somewhat different account of this incident. Tacitus

names Felix as procurator of Judaea at this time and Cumanus as governor in Galilee. For the debate concerning these two accounts, see Schürer, *op. cit.,* Div. I, vol. I, 173–4, note 14.

[16] This movement, led by an Egyptian Jew, is also mentioned in Acts 21:38. See note 18 below.

[17] The Sicarii are usually believed to be an especially violent wing of the Zealotist movement; B. Baumbach, *op. cit.,* makes them a separate group who were seeking to exterminate Hellenism in Galilee. The Zealots, by contrast, were centered in Jerusalem and were concerned with the sanctity of the temple, according to Baumbach. On the differentiation between these groups see also S. Zeitlin, "Zealots and Sicarii," *J.B.L.* 81 (4, 1962), 395–398.

[18] Three of the revolutionists named by Josephus in his survey are referred to in Acts. In Acts 5:36,37 Gamaliel, addressing the Sanhedrin, advises that the followers of Jesus be left alone, so that their movement, if not of God, may perish like those led by Judas the Galilean and Theudas. In the latter case Luke apparently thinks of the same Theudas mentioned by Josephus, but he assigns him to the period prior to Judas of Galilee, although Theudas arose at a time subsequent to Gamaliel's speech: Luke's reference seems to be anachronistic. The third revolutionary leader mentioned in Acts is the Egyptian Jew. In Acts 21:38 the Roman tribune who apprehends Paul asks him if he is not that Egyptian who had recently led 4,000 of the "assassins" (σικαριων) into the wilderness. The tribune's question shows how alert the Romans were forced to be over the threat of seditious activity.

[19] In addition to the references already cited, the following are examples of this tendency: R. Bultmann, "The Study of the Synoptic Gospels," 66f.; H. P. Kingdon, *op. cit.,* 558f.; S. Liberty, *The Political Relations of Christ's Ministry,* Oxford, 1916; E. E. Jensen, *op. cit.;* V. G. Simkhovitch, *Toward the Understanding of Jesus,* New York, 1931, 73. Brandon, *op. cit.,* 22f., gives additional bibliography. A handful of radical commentators have claimed that Jesus was a Zealot who actually tried to launch a revolt against Rome; none of these works deserve mention as serious scholarly studies. Brandon, while not claiming that Jesus was a Zealot, does believe that Jesus was sympathetic to the Zealotist cause and had close ties with the movement; See Appendix II.

[20] See the notes in J. Klausner, *From Jesus to Paul,* tr. by W. F. Stinespring, New York, 1943, 437–8; Brandon, *The Fall of Jerusalem and the Christian Church,* 105–6, and *Jesus and the Zealots,* 17, 21f.; Farmer, *op. cit.,* 187–8.

[21] *Op. cit.,* 103.

[22] As C. J. Cadoux remarks, "It would be possible to fill a fair-sized note-book with quotations from exegetes of every period and type to the effect that Jesus entirely excluded political affairs from his orbit." (*The Historic Mission of Jesus,* London, 1941, 163.) See also S. G. F. Brandon, *Jesus and the Zealots,* 280f., 322f.

[23] John 6:15.

[24] ζηλωτην: Mark 3:18 and Matthew 10:4 name him "the Cananaean" (κανavαιov; or κανανιτην in TR Θ of Mark 3:18 and א TR Θ of Matthew 10:4). But the Greek in these cases is apparently only a transcription of the Aramaic word for "Zealot," *Kannai* (קנאי). C. C. Torrey, *The Four Gospels,* New York, 1933, 397, wishes to turn the evidence in the opposite direction: viz., Luke has failed to recognize the name of the town of Cana and has given an incorrect version of the name; Mark and Matthew have the name correctly. This view has little support. But see also K. Lake, "Simon Zelotes," *H.T.R.* 10 (1, 1917), 57–63. In favor of the Zealotist interpretation of Simon's name see C. Daniel, "Esséniens, zélotes et sicaires et leur mention par paronymie dans le N.T.," *Numen* 13 (2, 1966), 88–115.

[25] *The State in the New Testament,* 14f. For a reply to Cullmann's view see D. R. Griffiths, "The Disciples and the Zealots," *E.T.* 69 (1, 1957), 29. For a full discussion of Judas' name see M. de Jonge, "Judas Iskarioth, de Varrader," *Homiletica en Biblica* 18 (5, 1959), 149–156 seq. C. C. Torrey, "The Name 'Iscariot'," *H.T.R.* 36 (1, 1943), 51–62 also discredits the political meaning of the name.

[26] בריונה.

[27] However, there is good linguistic evidence for this theory. The Aramaic בריונה means "rebel," "outlaw," "highwayman," and is assigned in *Gitt.* 56a to the Jewish

war party at the Roman siege of Jerusalem. See M. Jastrow, *A Dictionary of the Targumim, the Talmud Babli and Yerushalmi, and the Midrashic Literature,* New York, 1903. It is quite possible that the Greek βαρ Ιωνα ("Son of Jonah") has misunderstood the Aramaic word for "rebel."

28 Mark 12:13–17par.

29 Matthew 11:12.

30 Luke 12:54–13:9; 13:34f.; 19:41–44; 10:13–15par.

31 Cadoux, *op. cit.,* 168.

32 Mark 13; Matthew 24–25; Luke 21.

33 See H. M. Hughes, "Anti-Zealotism in the Gospels," *E.T.* XXVII (1, 1916), 151–4; also Jensen, *op. cit.,* 263; Cullmann, *op. cit.,* 18–22.

Chapter 9

1 Cf. Jensen, *op. cit.,* 263.

2 See Chapter 11 for a discussion of Barabbas.

3 "The Roman Provincial System," in *The Beginnings of Christianity,* ed. by F. Jackson and Lake, Part I, vol. I, 186.

4 On the political role of the high priests under the procurators, see E. Mary Smallwood, "High Priests and Politics in Roman Palestine," *J.T.S.* 13 (1, 1962), 14–34.

5 Mt. 21:1–9; Mk. 11:1–10; Lk. 19:29–38; Jn. 12:12–18.

6 Mt. 21:8–9; Mk. 11:8–10; Lk. 19:36–38; Jn. 12:12–13. Cf. W. R. Farmer, "The Palm Branches in John 12, 13," *J.T.S.* 3 (1952), 62–66. Farmer argues that the use of palm branches harks back to the Maccabean independence and reflects the political hopes which accompanied Jesus' entry.

7 Zechariah 9:9.

8 Cf. Brandon, *The Fall of Jerusalem and the Christian Church,* 104: "It would therefore appear certain that the presence of Jesus in Jerusalem was marked by a notable demonstration of Messianic enthusiasm, which the authorities, both Roman and Jewish, must inevitably have regarded as a dangerous expression of revolutionary feeling."

9 But see the important remarks by I. Abrahams in *Studies in Pharisaism and the Gospels, op. cit.,* 1917, 82–89. On the outer court generally see also G. Dalman, *Sacred Sites and Ways,* translated by P. Levertoff, New York, 1935, 288f.

10 Cf. *Mishnah Bechoroth* 8:7; *Bab. Talmud, Berakoth* 47b; Ex. 30:13. On the half-shekel tax itself, see the detailed study by J. Liver in *H.T.R.* 56 (3, 1963), 173–198.

11 So Dalman, *op. cit.,* 295.

12 John 2:14.

13 This practice is not attested in the rabbinic literature; see V. Epstein, "The Historicity of the Gospel Accounts of the Cleansing of the Temple," *Z.N.T.W.* 55 (1–2, 1964), 42–58. Epstein, however, offers a highly tendentious explanation of the phenomenon in Jesus' day. See also N. A. Hamilton, "Temple Cleansing and Temple Bank," *J.B.L.* 83 (4, 1964), 365–372.

14 Jesus' words in Mk. 11:17par. are from Isaiah 56:7. The greed of some Sadducean priests is condemned in the *Talmud*; cf. Strack–Billerbeck, *op. cit.,* I, 851, 853; II, 570; references from S. E. Johnson, "The Gospel of Matthew," in *Interpreter's Bible,* Vol. VII, 504.

15 See following note.

16 According to Mark 11:11, on his first day in Jerusalem Jesus went into the temple grounds and "looked around at everything" (περιβλεψαμενος παντα), then left; on the following day he returned and "cleansed" the temple. Matthew and Luke omit reference to the earlier visit; from them one would suppose that Jesus' disruption of the activity took place when he first entered the temple, on arriving in the city. This difference has no great significance, except that Mark's account suggests the possibility that Jesus studied the situation in the temple and then

made his plans to return and upset the trading and selling activity. Mark's story certainly discounts the interpretation that Jesus, on entering the temple, was overcome with sudden indignation and acted on the spur of the moment, unless we suppose that, on his earlier visit, the commercial activity was not in progress, since the hour was late (as Mark explains). It is possible that Matthew and Luke omit this earlier visit since it suggested just such a conscious design in Jesus' actions. Their accounts of the cleansing are briefer than Mark's (see below), and they make some effort to reduce the violence and the extent of Jesus' actions; this omission may be part of that effort. The reason would undoubtedly be the desire to minimize the impression that Jesus had been a man of violence or had done anything flagrantly in violation of law and order. K. Baltzer, "The Meaning of the Temple in the Lukan Writings," *H.T.R.* 58 (3, 1965), 263–277, following Conzelmann's lead, suggests that Luke 19:45 indicates that Jesus came to Jerusalem for the very purpose of cleansing, or indeed taking command of, the temple. This interpretation goes too far.

[17] Many interpreters have sought to avoid the violence and severity of Jesus' action, especially since it seems unbecoming to our normal view of Jesus; so the *Interpreter's Bible* on Matthew, 504: ". . . in the general confusion the benches of the money-changers were overturned." The Gospels, however, make it clear that Jesus purposefully instituted the actions described. H. W. Montefiore, "Josephus and the New Testament," *Novum Testamentum* 4 (2, 1960), 139–160, attempts to locate a parallel between Jesus' act and a reference in Josephus, but there is no basis for this comparison. It is understandable that this brief incident is not recorded in Josephus' histories. Josephus' account of these decades is relatively brief, and is certainly not a comprehensive chronicle of the period. Also, his preoccupation is with those events which illustrate the continuously deteriorating relationship between the Jews and the Romans, particularly major incidents of violence and bloodshed. The incident of the temple-cleansing clearly was not of such magnitude as to attract his attention, and in any case it did not involve any direct or violent confrontation between Jews and Romans. Despite its importance in understanding the arrest and execution of Jesus, it was an incident of minor proportions in the overall history of the Jews of this period. As noted in Chapter 8, Josephus' survey undoubtedly overlooked many significant events from these chaotic years, because of the limits of space.

[18] It seems to me that altogether too little attention has been paid to the almost unavoidable conclusion that Jesus' followers joined in his actions and made his control of the temple grounds possible.

[19] This practice is prohibited in *Berakoth* 9:5; cf. Josephus, *C. Apion* 2:8 I. Abrahams, *op. cit.*, 84–85, suggests that Jesus may actually have been enforcing the Jewish law against such traffic.

[20] Their agreement obviously reflects the historicity of the event; on this see O. Cullmann, "L'opposition contre le Temple de Jerusalem," *N.T.S.* 5 (1958–59), 157–173; S. Mendner, "Die Tempelreinigung," *Z.N.T.W.* 47 (1956), 93–112; V. Epstein, *op. cit.* Mendner argues that Luke's account is the most primitive, and that Mark and Matthew reflect later expansions; see note 16 above.

[21] On John's dating see the full discussions in R. E. Brown, *The Gospel According to John, I–XII*, 117–125, and V. Taylor, *The Gospel According to Saint Mark*, 461–462. As O. Cullmann, *ibid.*, notes, Jesus' opposition to the temple is a central theme in John's Gospel. This fact accounts for John's placement of the cleansing at the beginning of his Gospel, as a dramatization of this theme.

[22] *Ant.* XX,v,3; *Bell. Jud.* II,xii,1. The soldiers who came to Paul's rescue in Acts 21:31 were stationed in Antonia.

[23] See Chapter 12 for a further discussion of the Tower of Antonia.

[24] Mark 11:18par.

[25] On the Messianic significance of Jesus' act, see C. Roth, "The Cleansing of the Temple and Zechariah XIV.21," *Novum Testamentum* 4 (3, 1960), 174–181; also S. E. Johnson, *op. cit.*, 504, for examples of prophetic criticism of the temple.

[26] Cf. Dibelius, *From Tradition to Gospel*, 186; Bultmann, *Die Geschichte der Synoptischen Tradition*, 282; Lightfoot, *History and Interpretation in the Gospels*,

132; Knox, *The Sources of the Synopic Gospels*, vol. I, *St. Mark*, 18; Bundy, *op. cit.*, 482.

[27] E.g., Mk. 2:3–12par.; 2:15–3:6par.; 3:22par.; 7:1–23par.; 8:11–12par.; 8:31par.; 10:2–9par.; Mt. 23:1–36, etc.

[28] Especially Mk. 12:1–40par.; also Mt. 23:1–36.

[29] On this point see J. C. Weber, "Jesus' Opponents in the Gospel of Mark," *Journal of Bible and Religion* 34 (3, 1966), 214–222; H. Conzelmann, *op. cit.*, 78; A. F. J. Klijn, "Scribes, Pharisees, Highpriests and Elders in the New Testament," *Novum Testamentum* 3 (4, 1959), 259–267. J. Blinzler, *The Trial of Jesus*, 51–58, argues that the religious opposition to Jesus throughout his career is the basis of his arrest and trial; this is the traditional interpretation. P. Winter notes that the Pharisees are missing in the passion events and concludes from this that *all* Pharisaic opposition to Jesus in the *earlier* portions of the Gospels is an unhistorical tradition (*On the Trial of Jesus*, 121–6; see also Bultmann, "The Study of the Synoptic Gospels," 34–35). On the Christian misinterpretation of the Pharisees generally, see D. W. Riddle, *Jesus and the Pharisees: A Study in Christian Tradition*, Chicago, 1928. Winter's conclusion is unjustified; it is sufficient to remember that the Gospel's description of the Pharisees is a distorted and prejudicial caricature. Against Winter's view, see H. Merkel, "Jesus und die Pharisäer," *N.T.S.* 14 (2, 1968), 194–208.

[30] For the exception, in John's Gospel, see below. Even John, though he includes the Pharisees in the plot, explains specifically that the conspiracy resulted from political concerns (11:47–53).

[31] Mk. 11:18; Lk. 19:47–48; cf. Mt. 21:15–16.

[32] Mk. 11:27; Mt. 21:23; Lk. 20:1.

[33] Mk. 11:18; 14:2; Mt. 26:5; Lk. 22:2.

[34] P. Winter gives a good summation of the Sadducees' motives: "Faced on one side by growing popular discontent and on the other side by an overwhelming foreign power, they tried to preserve what they could of the residue of Jewish rule. Their fears were real, and were justified. Whether their part in the arrest of Jesus was small or great, they acted from motives they considered to serve the best interests of the nation—and 'the best interests,' as so often, happened to coincide with their own." (*On the Trial of Jesus*, 43.)

[35] Especially Mt. 26:14; see also Jn. 12:6.

[36] *The Quest of the Historical Jesus*, tr. by W. Montgomery, London, 1910, 396–7. For the same view see G. A. Barton, "On the Trial of Jesus Before the Sanhedrin," *J.B.L.* 41 (1922), 208.

[37] Only the most drastically skeptical critics (e.g., Guignebert, *Jesus*, 451–7) suggest that Judas' betrayal is itself a fiction. It is of course incredible that the Church should have created such a story.

[38] Mk. 14:11b; Mt. 26:16; Lk. 22:6.

[39] Rejecting the "longer chronology" of the passion events. According to this theory our Gospels mistakenly compress the last supper, arrest, trial and crucifixion into a twenty-four-hour period, whereas they actually occupied several days. This theory is based on the view that Jesus and his followers celebrated the Passover, their last meal together, on Tuesday evening, not Thursday, since they followed the same solar calendar found in the Book of Jubilees and used by the Essenes of Qumran. (The majority of Jews followed the traditional lunar calendar by which the Passover occurred on Friday of that year, according to this same theory.) Thus the passion events occurred between Tuesday evening and Friday. In the past decade there has been an extensive debate over this theory. I do not go into this chronological problem in detail here because I am convinced that the arguments for this theory are much too weak to overthrow the traditional chronology and I believe that any lengthy discussion of the theory would be an unnecessary digression. Even if this theory were correct it would not seriously affect our understanding of Jesus' trial and execution; no significant changes would be required in the reconstruction I have suggested in this book. As in a modern trial, what matters most is not the length of the proceedings but their nature. It is important to recognize that much of the support for this theory has arisen from a faulty interpretation of the trial itself, particularly the belief that the formal nocturnal Jewish

trial (and Luke's record of the trial before Herod Antipas) are historical. If we accept these two records as authentic, it becomes very difficult to fit all the trial events into the period between the supper in the evening and the beginning of the crucifixion about noon (or 9 A.M.?) of the next day. That is the chief appeal of the longer chronology: it provides more time for all these events to take place. But this approach to the problem is backwards. The solution to the crowded timetable of the trial, as it is described in our Gospels, is not to expand the available time-period but *to reduce the number of events;* that is, to eliminate the formal Jewish trial and the trial before Antipas. The source of this timetable problem is the fact that the early passion story has become overladen with secondary traditions. When we remove these later traditions the problem disappears. There is no good reason why, following a meal with the disciples on Thursday evening, Jesus could not have been arrested on Thursday night, held overnight, subjected to a brief inquiry by the Jewish officials on Friday morning, taken to Pilate immediately afterwards, and sent to the cross by midday. Mlle. Jaubert (see below) and others have argued that the traditional chronology cannot be correct since it would have been illegal for the Sanhedrin both to try and to execute Jesus on the same day. I agree that this rule of procedure was probably in effect in Jesus' day, but Mlle. Jaubert has turned this point the wrong way. Instead of proving that the traditional chronology is faulty, this is merely another indication that the supposed Jewish trial is un-historical. If the Jewish proceedings were only a brief *inquiry,* called to prepare political charges against Jesus, then the Sanhedrin did not violate the above-mentioned rule (if in force) by delivering Jesus immediately to Pilate. Some com-mentators who accept the longer chronology seem to accept the historicity of the Markan trial story *simply because they have now made enough time for it.* But this nocturnal trial can be shown to be unhistorical; see the full discussion in Chapter 10. In short, the timetable problems solved by the longer chronology, as far as the trial is concerned, are largely imaginary. It may be that there are good reasons for believing that Jesus and his disciples followed the sectarian calendar, but the argu-ment will have to stand on other evidence; it cannot be proved by the course of Jesus' prosecution. The following is a selective bibliography of useful writings on this interesting subject. A. Jaubert, *The Date of the Last Supper,* tr. by I. Raf-ferty, New York, 1965; by the same author, "Les séances du sanhédrin et les récits de la passion (suite)," *Revue de l'Histoire des Religions* 166 (2, 1964), 143–169 and 167 (1, 1965), 1–33; "Jésus et le calendrier de Qumrân," *N.T.S.* 7 (10, 1960), 1–30; "Le mercredi oú Jésus fut livré," *N.T.S.* 14 (2, 1968), 145–164. A full discussion of this subject and a highly speculative reconstruction of the trial events, plus a bibliography, is supplied by E. Ruckstuhl, *Chronology of the Last Days of Jesus,* tr. by V. J. Drapela, New York, 1965. See also J. Carmignac, "Comment Jésus et ses contemporains pouvaient-ils célébrer la pâque à une date non officielle?," *Revue de Qumran* 5 (1, 1964), 59–79, who provides a bibliography. P. W. Skehan, "The Date of the Last Supper," *C.B.Q.* 20 (2, 1958), 192–199, largely an exposition of Jaubert's theory, plus some pertinent questions; J. A. Walther, "The Chronology of the Passion Week," *J.B.L.* 77 (1958), 116–122; N. Walker, "Concern-ing the Jaubertian Chronology of the Passion," *Novum Testamentum* 3 (1959), 317–320 and "Yet Another Look at the Passion Chronology," *Novum Testamentum* 6 (1963), 286–289; Walker supports the longer chronology. Against this theory see G. Ogg, "The Chronology of the Last Supper," in *Historicity and Chronology in the New Testament,* 75–96; K. G. Kuhn, "Zum Essenischen Kalender," *Z.N.T.W.* 52 (1–2, 1961), 65–73; E. Kutsch, "Der Kalender des Jubiläenbuches und das Alte und das Neue Testament," *Vetus Testamentum* 11 (1, 1961), 39–47; J. Blinzler, "Qum-ran-Kalender und Passionschronologie," *Z.N.T.W.* 49 (3–4, 1958), 238–251. Brief summary information is provided by E. E. Ellis, "The Gospel of Luke," in *The Century Bible,* New York, 1966, who supplies a bibliography, and J. Finegan, *Hand-book of Biblical Chronology,* 44–57; 285f.

[40] παρα.

[41] Mk. 14:43par.; Acts 4:1–3; 5:17–18.

[42] σπειρα, χιλιαρχος.

[43] E.g., Goguel, *The Life of Jesus,* 468; Zeitlin, *Who Crucified Jesus?*, 155; Cullmann,

op. cit., 45; cf. also V. Taylor, *The Life and Ministry of Jesus,* New York, 1955, 200; P. Winter *On the Trial of Jesus,* 29–30, and "The Trial of Jesus," *Commentary* (3, 1964), 35–41; Howard and Barrett, *The Fourth Gospel in Recent Research,* 134–135.

[44] *Ibid.* Goguel further argues that, if the Romans were involved, the initiative must be assigned to them; therefore, the mention of Jews at the arrest is only a biased perversion of the primitive tradition (p. 469).

[45] E.g., Guignebert, *Jesus,* 460; Loisy, *Quatrième Évangile,* Paris, 1903, 821f.; Macgregor, *The Gospel of John,* 324.

[46] C. H. Dodd, *Historical Tradition in the Fourth Gospel,* 73, notes that σπειρα is also occasionally used to denote a smaller unit of troops, a maniple; but it was normally used of a full cohort. Even the 60–120 men of a maniple make a sizable force, quite large enough for John's dramatic purposes.

[47] Blinzler, *The Trial of Jesus,* 62–70, argues that John may not have been referring to Roman soldiers at all. Despite Blinzler's painstaking study, there is little justification for this view, which requires an unnecessary twisting of the word σπειρα.

[48] A typical statement is found in E. A. McDowell, "Exegetical Notes," *The Review and Expositor* XXXVIII (1, 1941), 44–46. Against this view many scholars have emphasized the literal application of the verse; cf. T. W. Manson, *The Teachings of Jesus,* Cambridge, 1931, 247.

[49] H. Rengstorf, *op. cit.,* 266–7; cf. also E. E. Jensen, *op. cit.,* 266.

Chapter 10

[1] For typical statements of the difficulties of recovering the events see Montefiore, *The Synoptic Gospels,* vol. I, 351; G. Kilpatrick, *op. cit.,* 20; Dibelius, *From Tradition to Gospel,* 188f., 205, 213; Bundy, *op. cit.,* 478; A. Loisy, *Les Évangiles Synoptiques,* vol. II, 596; F. C. Grant, "A Note on Dr. Peritz's Article," *Journal of Bible and Religion,* VII (1939), 177–180.

[2] Cf. Kilpatrick, *op. cit.,* 20, regarding Mark's narrative but applicable to all: "We cannot imagine that it went back to a witness who understood the legal implications of each stage of the proceedings or that it was shaped to answer the questionings of the nineteenth and twentieth centuries."

[3] Acts 4:13.

[4] *Op. cit.,* I, 351.

[5] A. Loisy's suggestion (*op. cit.,* II, 596) that the early Christians were unconcerned about the events needs no refutation; cf. Easton, "The Trial of Jesus," 434: "It is inconceivable that the Jerusalem Christians of the first generation were not informed as to all essentials of the course of events." This is true, but the emphasis must be on *essentials,* not details.

[6] For the judgment that the Mark/Matthew account of a formal Jewish trial is fictitious and that the proceedings were only a hearing in preparation for the trial before Pilate, see Goguel, *op. cit.,* 526f.; Bacon, *Beginnings,* 210f.; Lietzmann, *op. cit.,* 313f.; Dibelius, *The Message of Jesus Christ,* 32, and *From Tradition to Gospel,* 189f.; R. Bultmann, *Geschichte,* 169, 291; Klausner, *op. cit.,* 340f.; Cullmann, *op. cit.,* 41f.; Montefiore, *op. cit.,* I, 352f.; Easton, "The Trial of Jesus," 434f.; R. W. Husband, *op. cit.,* 102f.; Loisy, *Les Évangiles Synoptiques,* II, 608f.; Moffatt, *op. cit.,* 751; Bundy, *op. cit.,* 517f.; Guignebert, *op. cit.,* 463f.; A. E. J. Rawlinson, *op. cit.,* 218f.; Brandt, *Die evangelische Geschichte,* 53; Cadoux, *The Sources of the Second Gospel,* 181f., 240f.; A. H. McNeile, *op. cit.,* 397; Lightfoot, *History and Interpretation in the Gospels,* 140f.; W. L. Knox, *op. cit.,* I, 132f.; J. Jacobs, "Jesus of Nazareth," *The Jewish Encyclopedia,* ed. by C. Adler *et al.,* vol. VII, 166; H. Danby, "The Rabbinical Criminal Code," 60f.; A. T. Cadoux, *op. cit.,* 237; V. Taylor, *The Gospel According to St. Mark,* 659, 661; E. R. Buckley, "The Sources of the Passion Narrative in St. Mark's Gospel," 139f.; Brandon, *Jesus and the Zealots,* 221f.; T. A.

Burkill, "The Trial of Jesus," 1f.; P. Winter, *On the Trial of Jesus*, 23f., and "Luke xxii 66b–71," *Studia Theologica* 9 (2, 1955), 112–115, and "Markus 14:53b, 55–64 ein Gebilde des Evangelisten," *Z.N.T.W.* 53 (3–4, 1962), 260–263; G. Braumann, "Markus 15,2–5 und Markus 14,55–64," *Z.N.T.W.* 52 (3–4, 1961), 273–278; C. E. B. Cranfield, *op. cit.*, 439f., B. Redlich, *St. Mark's Gospel*, London, 1948, 170; F. V. Filson, *A Commentary on the Gospel According to St. Matthew*, London, 1960, 282–284.

[7] The argument holds even if we suppose that Matthew is the earlier source and that Mark copied from him; see the earlier reference to this issue in Chapter 4. The point is that one Evangelist has copied the other.

[8] A. T. Cadoux, *Sources of the Second Gospel*, London, n.d., 644, says that even in Mark there is no formal condemnation and judicial sentence. However, although Mark's language may be imprecise, he certainly thinks of a conviction and death sentence.

[9] Mk. 14:50; Mt. 26:56. John (18:15f.) claims that Simon Peter and "another disciple" followed Jesus and gained access into the court of the high priest, where Jesus was questioned.

[10] See Chapter 7, note 1.

[11] The difficulty of finding some logical use for this morning meeting is exemplified in E. Ruckstuhl, *The Chronology of the Last Days of Jesus*, 41–46.

[12] The Synoptics, of course, indicate that the last supper was a Passover meal; John, that the Passover was the following day. For the proposed "longer chronology" of the passion week, see note 39, Chapter 9.

[13] See Chapter 1, discussion of the Mishnaic rules.

[14] Cf. A. Jaubert, "Les Séances du sanhédrin et les récits de la passion (suite)," *op. cit.*

[15] J. Blinzler has argued that the Jewish trial did not violate the Sanhedrin's rules since, in Jesus' day, the Sanhedrin operated under the harsh code of the Sadducees, rather than the more humanitarian code of the Pharisees ("Das Synedrium von Jerusalem und die Strafprozessordnung der Mischna," 54–65.) But the Sanhedrin was strongly Pharisaic in the years before the war of A.D. 66–72, and there is no justification for supposing that the Council observed *only* rules agreeable to the Sadducees; there is also no reason to imagine that even Sadducaic rules would have allowed for any such flagrant injustices as described in Mark's account.

[16] *The Beginnings of the Gospel Story*, New Haven, 1920.

[17] The artificiality of Mark's picture is underlined by the fact that in John's Gospel the Jewish accusations of blasphemy are not in the trial narrative at all, but in Chapter 10. We can safely conclude that Mark has simply taken a unit of early Christian tradition and transferred it into the trial chambers, where it becomes pivotal for explaining Jesus' death. See R. E. Brown, "Incidents That Are Units in the Synoptic Gospels but Dispersed in John," *C.B.Q.* XXIII (2, 1961), 143–160. As Brown notes, since the disciples did not have an exact record of the trial proceedings, it would have been natural for them to transfer into the trial narrative all threats and accusations made *earlier* against Jesus, which they considered the explanation of his death.

[18] For this view, see G. Kilpatrick, *op. cit.*

[19] For examples of detailed studies of the blasphemy charge see J. Blinzler, *The Trial of Jesus*, 125–134; Kilpatrick, *op. cit.*, 9–16; M. J. La Grange, *The Gospel of Jesus Christ*, vol. II, London, 1938, 244–6; P. Lamarche, "Le 'blasphème' de Jésus devant le sanhédrin," *Recherches de Science Religieuse* 50 (1, 1962), 74–85; T. F. Glasson, "The Reply to Caiaphas (Mark xiv. 62)," *N.T.S.* 7 (1, 1960), 88–93; O. Linton, "The Trial of Jesus and the Interpretation of Psalm CX," *N.T.S.* 7 (3, 1961), 258–262; T. Horvath, "Why Was Jesus Brought to Pilate?", *Novum Testamentum*, XI (3, 1969), 174–184. For a summary of the most common viewpoints see H. Mantel, *op. cit.*, 275f.

[20] This view predominates in most nonprofessional studies of the trial and appears in some serious works. A typical noncritical analysis adopting this view is F. J. Powell, *The Trial of Jesus Christ*, London, 1949. Among the competent scholarly works defending this viewpoint are: G. A. Barton, "On the Trial of

Jesus before the Sanhedrin," *J.B.L.* 41 (1922), 205–211; G. Kilpatrick, *op. cit.*; E. Dabrowski, *Proces Chrystusa w swietle historyczno-Krytycznym*, Poznan, 1965 (reviewed in *C.B.Q.*, Jan., 1967).

[21] This theory that the charges were switched would be completely unwarranted even if the Jewish trial were historical. The only thing which suggests such a reversal is the fact that the Jewish and Roman trials in Mark and Matthew are completely discontinuous and irreconcilable.

[22] H. H. Cohn suggests a novel interpretation of the authorities' intentions in the hearing: they were seeking evidence to *acquit* Jesus so that the Romans would not punish him for political crimes. According to Cohn, this effort was frustrated by Jesus' Messianic claims at the inquiry. ("Reflections on the Trial and Death of Jesus," *Israel Law Review* 2 (3, 1967), 332–379.)

[23] What Bacon says of Mark is true of all the Synoptics: they make ". . . the Jewish Sanhedrin responsible for what was really a secret plot of the priestly clique of Annas." (*Beginnings*, 208.) Cf. G. A. Barton, ". . . it was the Sadducean priesthood, over whom Annas ruled as a sort of Ecclesiastical boss, that secured the condemnation of Jesus" (*op. cit.*, 208).

[24] P. Winter comments, "The magnification of the importance of those who played an adverse part in the final proceedings against Jesus would be calculated by the Evangelist to enhance the significance of Jesus." (*On the Trial of Jesus*, 29.) It is surprising that Winter does not see that John added Roman soldiers to the arrest-party for exactly the same reason; Winter defends the historicity of this reference (see note 27, Chapter 9).

[25] This is Luke's version; it is clearly to be preferred to the claim in Mark/Matthew that the Sanhedrin members taunted and reviled Jesus. See Knox, *op. cit.*, Vol. I, 132; Montefiore, *op. cit.*, Vol. II, 613; Taylor, *Behind the Third Gospel*, 49; Winter, "The Treatment of His Sources by the Third Evangelist," 162. Luke's version is not an adaptation of Mark's account; it rests on a separate tradition. Only six of Luke's 27 words parallel Mark's; see V. Taylor, *ibid.*; also Perry, *Sources*, 44.

Chapter 11

[1] R. W. Husband, *op. cit.*, 140–141 has summarized the evidence to this effect from Tacitus (*Agr.* 9), Cicero (*Ad Att.* 5,21,9; 6,2,4–5; 6,4,1), and Julius Caesar (*B.G.* I,54; VI,44; VIII,46). See also Strack-Billerbeck, *op. cit.*, II, 822; Sherwin-White, *op. cit.*, 14.

[2] A great many scholars have called attention to the fact that the Roman trial is political, not religious, in character and that Jesus died as a political criminal. In addition to the works cited elsewhere see Bultmann, *The Study of the Synoptic Gospels*, 66f.; Lietzmann, *op. cit.*, 320; Cullmann, *op. cit.*, 11–12, 34f.; S. J. Case, *Jesus: A New Biography*, 323–325; S. Zeitlin, *op. cit.*, 159f.; H. P. Kingdon, *op. cit.*, 556f.; E. E. Jensen, *op. cit.*, 264; Farmer, *Maccabees, Zealots, and Josephus*, 197f.; S. Liberty, *The Political Relations of Christ's Ministry*, 140f.; C. K. Barrett, *Jesus and the Gospel Tradition*, London, 1967. J. S. Kennard, "The Jewish Provincial Assembly," *op. cit.* A gross overstatement of the political character of Jesus' life and death is given by R. Eisler, *The Messiah Jesus and John the Baptist*, tr. by A. H. Krappe, New York, 1931, and Ἰησοῦς βασιλεὺς οὐ βασιλεύσας, 2 vols., Heidelberg, 1929–1930. (So also J. S. Kennard, *Politique et religion chez les Juifs au temps de Jesus et dans l'église primitive*, Paris, 1927.) Eisler's theory is based largely on his reconstruction of the orginal text of the Slavonic Josephus. Eisler argues that Jesus embraced a political form of Messiahship, led an armed mob from the Mount of Olives into Jerusalem, sparked a rebellion against the Romans, occupied the Temple and was finally suppressed by the Romans with the aid of special troops from Caesarea. Refutation of these views, should any be required, may be found in S. G. F. Brandon, *The Fall of Jerusalem, op cit.*, 115f., and in J. M. Creed, "The Slavonic

Version of Josephus' History of the Jewish War", *H.T.R.* 25 (1932), 277–319.

[3] A good illustration of the attitude of Roman officials toward questions of native religious infractions is found in the case of Gallio, Paul, and the Jews of Corinth, Acts 18:12–17.

[4] This fact is so well recognized as to require little demonstration. Cf. Lietzmann, *op. cit.,* 321; Kilpatrick, *op. cit.,* 8; Cullmann, *op. cit.,* 42; Winter, *On the Trial of Jesus,* 62–66. See generally C. W. Wilston, "The Roman Law of Treason under the Early Principate," *Journal of Roman Studies* 45 (1955), 73–81.

[5] This fact also is universally recognized. For examples of the employment of this means of execution for political offenses, cf. Josephus, *Ant.* XVII,x,10; XX,v,2; *Bell. Jud.* II,v,2; II,xii,6; V,vi,1.

[6] Cf. J. Klausner, *op. cit.,* 348, notes that in the Gospels Pilate ". . . is suddenly turned into a tender, pacific being, sparing of bloodshed and anxious to save a 'just man perishing through his righteousness.' "

[7] τω θεληματι αυτων, Lk. 23:25.

[8] I know of no satisfactory explanation of the charge that Jesus encouraged his fellow Jews not to pay their taxes to Rome. The usual presumption is that this, like the other charges, was falsely concocted by the priests. But it is much more reasonable to suppose that the priests built their charges around things which Jesus had actually said and done. To suppose that the priests made up their charges gratuitously misses the point that they actually believed him dangerous. The best explanation is apparently that the priests supposed, because of something which Jesus had said or done, that he opposed the payment of any tribute to Rome. It is quite possible that the little pericope giving Jesus' words, "Render unto Caesar . . ." made its way into the Gospel records as a rebuttal to this claim.

[9] συλεγεις. It is interesting that the words are identical in all four Gospels. These words were doubtless repeated over and over again in the early days of the Church in describing the Roman trial.

[10] Cf. Bultmann, *The Study of the Synoptic Gospels,* 66: "To those who stood outside it, this movement must have appeared like any of the other Messianic movements which in those decades convulsed the Jewish people and finally led to the war with Rome and the destruction of Jerusalem. The Roman procurators suppressed such movements with blood, and Jesus fell a victim to the intervention of the procurator Pilate."

[11] For an attempt to explain this omission see Knox, *The Sources of the Synoptic Gospels,* I, 137–139; also Streeter, "On the Trial of Our Lord before Herod—A Suggestion," in *Studies in the Synoptic Problem,* 229–231.

[12] Streeter, *ibid.,* 231.

[13] Cf. J. B. Tyson, "Jesus and Herod Antipas," *J.B.L.* 79 (3, 1960), 239–246.

[14] See Dibelius, "Herodes und Pilatus," *Z.N.T.W.,* 1915, 113f.; J. M. Creed, *The Gospel According to St. Luke,* London, 1930, 280; Montefiore, II, 619; Bultmann, *Geschichte,* 294. The influence of the Old Testament in the shaping of the passion narrative has been noted in a great many studies; see, for example, Dibelius, *A Fresh Approach to the New Testament and Early Christian Literature,* New York, 1936, 47–48, and *From Tradition to Gospel,* 184f.; Dodd, *History and the Gospel,* London, 1938, 60f. and 80f., and *Historical Tradition and the Fourth Gospel,* 31–49, the latter being an exceptionally thorough and useful study of the Old Testament testimonies.

[15] It has been suggested that the point of the Herod tradition is that another ruler found Jesus *innocent.* It is possible that this meaning was drawn from the story in the early Church, but the desire to involve a Jewish judge in the proceedings seems to me a much more basic motive of this unit.

[16] This suggestion is from Creed, *op. cit.,* 280.

[17] The most commonly noted passages are the reference in Livy V.13 to the temporary parole of prisoners at the Lectisternium at Rome and a first century papyrological reference to the release of a prisoner by the prefect at the demand of the populace. The continual attempt (and failure) to locate parallels to the Gospel story are cited in most studies of the Barabbas incident; a particularly detailed account is provided by H. A. Rigg, "Barabbas," *J.B.L.* 64 (1945), 417–

456, especially 421–426. A figure supposedly paralleling Barabbas is found in Philo's story (*In Flacc.* vi.36–39) concerning a *mimus* by Alexandrians of Agrippa I on the occasion of his arrival in Alexandria from Rome after his appointment as king of Judaea. An imbecile named "Carabas" was made a mock king and was paraded before Agrippa. For a discussion of Carabas in this connection see J. G. Frazer, *The Golden Bough,* 3d ed., Part VI, London, 1913, 418f. For the supposed relation of this figure to the Barabbas of the Gospels see A. Loisy, *Les Évangiles Synoptiques,* II, 653f. Rebuttal to this imagined parallel is given by Montefiore, *The Synoptic Gospels,* I, 379 and Rigg, *ibid.,* 423, where a complete bibliography is supplied.

[18] So Rigg, *ibid.,* 421, 423: "It is admitted that the Barabbas incident stands alone. Nowhere has there ever been found an extra-Biblical parallel or precedent for the so-called 'custom' . . . (No attempt) has ever met with more than occasional approval and all of them have sooner or later been rejected as groundless, inadequate, or inappropriate." Cf. Strack-Billerbeck, *op. cit.,* I, 1031. In defense of the custom see Blinzler, *The Trial of Jesus,* 205f., 218–221. P. Winter, *On the Trial of Jesus,* 91–99, rejects it.

[19] John alone (18:39) specifies the Passover as the occasion. Mark and Matthew may intend the same by the phrase κατα δε εορτην but their words could mean "at this feast during this year," or "annually at this feast," or "at any or all feasts." The first possibility is almost certainly prohibited by the grammatical force of απελυεν (Mk. 15:6), απολυειν (Mt. 27:15), which apparently designate repeated practice. See Rigg, *op. cit.,* 420, note 11. Although Rigg notes that the words cited need not represent the imperfect of custom and so be translated "used to," he agrees that "No matter how one translates the imperfects, something seems to have been done that implies reasonable customary procedure. In any case, whatever was done was done in such a way that it was not considered either unique or even unusual. On that the Gospel accounts are unanimous" (p. 426)—excepting Luke, of course. Repeated practice is also indicated by κατα, which would normally be distributive. The most common-sense interpretation is that Mark, Matthew and John all regard it as a Passover custom.

[20] For example, Bultmann, *Geschichte,* 164; Goguel, *The Life of Jesus,* 516–520; Guignebert, *Jesus,* 468–470; Loisy, *op. cit.,* 642–644.

[21] For a defense of the incident, once it has been stripped of its later accretions (particularly the custom), see Montefiore, *The Synoptic Gospels,* I, 372f.; Brandt, *Die Evangelische Geschichte,* 94f.; Bertram, *op. cit.,* 67.

[22] Ιησουν βαραββαν in Θ and other Greek mss. of the Caesarean recession, also *Syr. Sin., Syr. Pal., and Origen (Matt.).* See Rigg, *op. cit.,* 429 for attestations of the reading in Syriac literature.

[23] So A. C. Clark, *The Primitive Text of the Acts and Gospels,* 41; also P. Schmiedel, "Barabbas," in *Encyclopedia Biblica,* New York, 1899, ed. by Cheyne and Black, vol. I, 476.

[24] The list of scholars who accept this reading as correct is now long; cf. Streeter, *The Four Gospels,* 136; Rawlinson, *St. Mark,* 228–229; C. S. C. Williams, *Alterations to the Text of the Synoptic Gospels and Acts,* Oxford, 1951, 31–33; Rigg, *op. cit.,* 429f. Rigg turns the argument to very different use, however; he claims that "Jesus Barabbas" was a second name for Jesus of Nazareth, not a second person. He argues that Jesus was presented to Pilate under these two separate names, a theory which, to my knowledge, has never found any support from any quarter. In support of "Jesus Barabbas" see also H. Meynell, "The Synoptic Problem: Some Unorthodox Solutions," *Life of the Spirit* 17 (1963), 451–459; R. C. Nevius, "A Reply to Dr. Dunkerley," *E.T.* 74 (8, 1963), 255.

[25] On the supposition that the other two insurrectionists who died alongside Jesus had been involved in the same movement.

[26] στασις, Mark 15:7.

[27] This question is sometimes debated, with reference to the amnesty custom. It is hard to believe that such a custom, if historical, could have applied to criminals already convicted and sentenced; cf. R. W. Husband, "The Pardoning of Prisoners by Pilate," *American Journal of Theology* 21 (1917), 110–116.

²⁸ On this reconstruction see Rawlinson, *op. cit.*, 228–229.

²⁹ Against the Gospel picture of a Jewish crowd crying for Jesus' death see D. M. Crossan, "Anti-Semitism and the Gospels," *Theological Studies* 26 (2, 1965), 189–214. On Jesus' popularity with the people gathered in Jerusalem see G. Rau, "Das Volk in der lukanischen Passionsgeschichte, eine Konjektur zu Lk. 23:13," *Z.N.T.W.* 56 (1–2, 1965), 41–51.

Chapter 12

¹ Mk. 15:25. It is possible that Mark employed an artificial time scheme in reporting the crucifixion events: crucifixion at the third hour, darkness at the sixth hour (15:33), death at the ninth hour (15:34f.). This time sequence seems too neat to be precise, and it is unlikely that the exact hours were observed as the events occurred. See the full discussion in J. Blinzler, *op. cit.*, 265f.

² Jn. 19:14. N. Walker, "The Reckoning of Hours in the Fourth Gospel," *Novum Testamentum* 4 (1960), 69–73, suggests that the conflict may be only apparent; John may use the Roman method of calculating the hour, beginning with midnight. The "sixth hour" would then be 6 A.M., which would correspond to Mark's reference.

³ E.g., Josephus, *Bell. Jud.* II,xiv,8, where the procurator Gessius Florus resided and sat in judgment at the palace. In Philo, *Leg. ad Gaium*, 38–39, the palace is specifically mentioned as the residence of Pilate in Jerusalem.

⁴ *Bell. Jud.* V,v,8.

⁵ Gr. πραιτωριον, Lat. *praetorium*. The word first designated the praetor's tent, later any site where a praetor sat in judgment. In the provinces, a praetorium might be any place where a governor conducted governmental affairs, and particularly his residence. See the discussion in V. Taylor, *The Gospel According to St. Mark*, 585; also C. Kopp, *The Holy Places of the Gospels*, New York, 1963, 365; W. Sanday, *Sacred Sites of the Gospels*, Oxford, 1903, 54; P. Benoit, "Prétoire, Lithostroton et Gabbatha," *R.B.* 59 (1952), 531–550. Mark says, "the palace, that is, the praetorium." Here the word palace (αυλη) does not (necessarily) designate Herod's palace; Mark uses the term as a synonym for "praetorium," and the word could as well apply to Antonia.

⁶ John states that when Pilate was ready to pronounce sentence he sat down (or made Jesus sit down; see note 13 below) on the judgment seat (βημα) at a place called The Pavement (Gr. λιθοστρωτον), the Hebrew word being Gabbatha (Gr. Γαββαθα), a transliteration of an Aramaic word, probably גבחתא, "open space." The word Gabbatha indicates a raised area paved with stones, such as a terrace (the prefix Gab- indicating elevation). Just such a large paved area has been uncovered outside the Tower of Antonia. This pavement originally covered some 2,200 square yards and some of the remaining stones are still etched with lines made by Roman soldiers for use in some unknown game. It is tempting to conclude that this pavement must be the very one mentioned by John, and thus to identify the Tower as the locale of the trial. This identification has been made by several scholars, most notably the distinguished L.-H. Vincent; cf. Vincent and F.-M. Abel, *Jérusalem nouvelle*, Paris, 1914, III, 562f.; Vincent, "Le Lithostrotos Évangélique," *Revue Biblique* 59 (1952), 513–530. However, it is unlikely that this pavement had been constructed at the time of Jesus. On this recently discovered pavement see A. Parrot, *Golgotha and the Church of the Holy Sepulchre*, London, 1957. The *Ecce Homo* arch was of course erected subsequent to the time of Jesus; it dates from the reign of Hadrian in the second century. See also Kopp, *op. cit.*, 372–373.

⁷ Good summaries of this much discussed question, with extensive references to the pertinent literature, are given by G. Dalman, *op. cit.*, 335f. (It is interesting that while Dalman favors the palace as the praetorium, his English translator has added

204 THE EXECUTION OF JESUS

a note [p. 342] favoring Antonia!); Vincent and Abel, *ibid.*; Kopp, *ibid.*; P. Benoit (note 5 above); J. Blinzler, *The Trial of Jesus,* 173f. See also the better Biblical encyclopedias on "Praetorium," "Gabbatha," "lithostroton," etc.

8 Some of whom had probably been recruited in Sebaste (Samaria). Cf. S. Perowne, *The Later Herods: The Political Background to the New Testament,* London, 1958, 28.

9 Cf. *Bell. Jud.* II,xiv,9; also Philo, *Ad Flacc.* v–vi. A commonly noted parallel involving a certain Carabas (see Chapter 11, note 17) is described in J. G. Frazer, *The Golden Bough,* vol. III, 138f. V. Taylor, *The Gospel According to St. Mark,* 646–648, provides a detailed discussion of this and other ancient parallels to the scourging of Jesus.

10 Mark says a whole battalion (σπεῖρα) was involved in the scourging.

11 See the references in Strack-Billerbeck, *op. cit.,* I, 587.

12 τίτλος, Jn. 19:19.

13 According to John, the charge was written in three languages: Hebrew, Latin and Greek. Some mss. of Luke (א* A C³ D W θ) have picked up this Johannine claim. John also states that the chief priests sought, to no avail, to have Pilate change the *titulus* to, "This man said, I am King of the Jews" (19:20–22). John obviously conceives of this incident as an ironic tribute to Jesus' kingship. The same irony may be in view in John's description of the judgment scene before Pilate. John says, "When Pilate heard these words, he brought Jesus out *and sat down* on the judgment seat . . ." (19:13). The verb ἐκάθισεν may be understood transitively, "he *made him* (Jesus) sit down on the judgment seat. . . ." See I. de la Potterie, "Jésus roi et juge d'après Jn 19, 13: Ἐκάθισεν ἐπὶ βήματος," *Biblica* 41 (3, 1960), 217–247. If this reading is correct, John sees Pilate's act as an ironic testimony to Jesus' kingship.

14 It is frequently observed that John may have omitted reference to Simon of Cyrene because of a Docetic claim that Simon had actually substituted for Jesus on the cross. (See Irenaeus, quoting Basilides, in *Adv. Haer.* I.19.2,5). It seems unlikely that, at the time when the fourth Gospel was written, this claim would have been a concern. Even if so, the more convincing explanation is John's desire to avoid any suggestion of Jesus' weakness.

15 Mark identifies Simon by naming his sons, Alexander and Rufus, evidently because their names were known to his readers. Matthew and Luke ignore this reference.

16 ἠγγάρευσαν is here a technical word signifying forced service.

17 This seems to be the meaning of 23:29: "For behold, the days are coming when they will say, 'Blessed are the barren, and the wombs that never gave suck!' "

18 Interpreting 23:31: "For if they do this when the wood is green, what will happen when it is dry?" Parallels are found in the rabbinic literature. Luke 23:30 is from Hosea 10:8. On the women following Jesus, see Zech. 12:10–14. On the possible primary and secondary elements in these Lukan verses see W. Käser, "Exegetische und theologische Erwägungen zur Seligpreisung der Kinderlosen Lc. 23:29b," *Z.N.T.W.* 54 (3–4, 1963), 240–254.

19 (1) The earthquake and opening of the graves at Jesus' death (27:51b–53) (2) the placement of special guards at Jesus' tomb, at the request of the Jewish officials (27:62–66) (3) the bribery of these guards after the resurrection (28:11–15). Numbers 2 and 3 are part of a single tradition, split by Matthew for insertion into Mark's story. On all these items, see the text below.

20 John 19:20; Heb. 13:12.

21 Greek Γολγοθα, transliterating the Aramaic גלגלתא, and translated by κρανίον (Lk. 23:33).

22 Other conjectures are (1) that the site received its name from the bodies of those executed at the site, although it is highly unlikely that the Jews would have allowed bodies to remain unburied (2) that it was so named because Adam's skull was buried at this site. A detailed examination of these conjectures, with all pertinent ancient references, is provided by C. W. Wilson, "Golgotha and the Holy Sepulchre," *Palestine Exploration Fund Quarterly,* 1902, 66f. Wilson's series of articles in the 1902–03 volumes is a mine of carefully researched information on

the crucifixion site and related subjects. The notion that Golgotha was a hill (see text below) does not appear until the sixth century.

[23] The story is told by Eusebius in *Life of Constantine*, III, 25–28.

[24] For a concise discussion of this famous subject see Dalman, *op. cit.*, 346f.; Parrot, *op. cit.*, who leans heavily on Dalman and especially Vincent; Wilson, *op. cit.*, vol. 1902, 376f. and vol. 1903, 51f.; R. H. Smith, "The Tomb of Jesus," *Biblical Archeologist* 30 (3, 1967), 74–90. There is nothing to support the so-called "Gordon's Calvary," named for Gen. "Chinese" Gordon, who championed this site. Gordon's Calvary, a hill near Jeremiah's Grotto, northeast of the Damascus Gate, was first suggested as the site of Golgotha by Otto Thenius in 1849, chiefly because of the hill's resemblance to a skull, although this was not the basis of Gordon's identification. It was once argued that the Church of the Holy Sepulchre cannot be at the actual site of Golgotha, since it is not outside the city wall (the "second" wall) of Jesus' time. But it is now virtually certain that this traditional site was outside the wall. The site of Constantine's edifice was selected because, according to tradition, St. Helena, Constantine's mother, there discovered the cross of Jesus.

[25] Cicero, *In. Verr.* 1.5.61,62; *Quint.* VIII.4 Josephus, *Bell. Jud.* II.xiv.8,9 considered it scandalous that the procurator Florus had crucified Jewish citizens of noble rank. See also J. J. Collins, "The Archeology of the Crucifixion," *C.B.Q.* 1939, 154–159.

[26] Deut. 21:23: "Hanging" here may originally have signified not crucifixion but the hanging of bodies after death; cf. C. W. Wilson, *op. cit.*, vol. 1902, 154, n.3. However, this law is understood as applying to crucifixion in Gal. 3:13 and was probably so interpreted by Jews in the time of Jesus.

[27] Detailed information on crucifixion and crosses is available from a large number of studies. Good summaries are found in the following encyclopedia articles: H. E. Dosker, "Cross," in *International Standard Bible Encyclopedia*, ed. by Jas. Orr *et al.*, New York, 1939, 760–762; J. C. Lambert, "Crucifixion," in *Dictionary of the Bible*, ed. by J. Hastings *et al.*, New York 1909, 170; D. Smith, "Crucifixion," in *A Dictionary of Christ and the Gospels*, ed. by J. Hastings *et al.*, New York, 1906, 397–399. Precise information on the history of crucifixion is given by J. W. Hewitt, "The Use of Nails in the Crucifixion," *H.T.R.* 25 (1932), 29–45. See Blinzler, *op. cit.*, 263f.

[28] Mt. 27:37; Lk. 23:38. But see the discussion in Blinzler, *ibid.*

[29] H. Branscomb, *The Gospel of Mark*, in *Moffatt New Testament Commentary*, London, 1937, 292. Cf. *Bell. Jud.* V,vi,1 on the severity of the pain suffered in crucifixion. Eusebius, *H.E.* viii.8 mentions that crucified martyrs often remained alive until they died from hunger.

[30] Indirectly, in 20:27, where Jesus shows the nail prints to Thomas. No reference is made to nails in the crucifixion story itself. In Luke 24:39(40) the marks of crucifixion in Jesus' hands and feet are implied. But cf. J. W. Hewitt, *op. cit.*

[31] Cf. *Sanh.* 43:1, wine and frankincense given to a man crucified. Also Prov. 31:6.

[32] Psalm 69:21: "They gave me also gall for my meat, and in my thirst they gave me vinegar to drink." (Auth. Ver.) Gall (Gr. χολη; Heb. ראש.) Gall was a liquid derived from a bitter, perhaps poisonous plant.

[33] See notes in the text below. The vinegar (οξος) of Mk. 15:36 and Lk. 23:36 may designate *posca*, the sour wine drunk by soldiers of the time. V. Taylor, *The Gospel According to St. Mark*, 594f., gives a detailed study of the vinegar offered Jesus on the cross.

[34] It is interesting that an apparent misunderstanding by the author of the fourth Gospel has affected his version of the division of clothing. Psalm 22:18 reads: ". . . they divide my garments among them, and for my raiment they cast lots." John seems to have misinterpreted the Hebrew parallelism as referring to two separate acts. To bring this scene into closer harmony with the psalm, John therefore states that the soldiers divided his garments among themselves, but that they could not divide the tunic, which was seamless, so they cast lots for it. This Johannine passage is an excellent minor example of the effect of the Old Testament, particularly Psalm 22, on the crucifixion traditions.

[35] Cf. Acts 12:4.

[36] Later editors sought to find a Scriptural parallel to the death of the other two

men. Θ λ φ TR it vg sy^p add, ". . . and the scripture was fulfilled which says, 'He was reckoned with the transgressors.'" (Mk. 15:28; cf. Is. 53:12.)

[37] It is often suggested that the reference to passers-by indicates that a road lay nearby. However, this is of no help in identifying the site today, and it is more likely that the reference to passers-by was derived from Ps. 22:7.

[38] It is interesting that the reference to Jesus' own destruction of the temple, which appears here again, is so central in the tradition. It seems possible that during his last days in Jerusalem Jesus made some statement concerning the destruction of the temple which, in the early days of the Church, was quoted by some Jews as a claim that Jesus personally intended to destroy the temple. Such a (supposed) claim would naturally have been a cause for animosity and debate between the first Christians and their Jewish brethren.

[39] See the discussion of Luke's sources in the passion narrative in Ch. 5. On Luke's use of a non-Markan source in the crucifixion narrative particularly see V. Taylor, The Gospel According to St. Mark, 587f., 653f.; Behind the Third Gospel, 54f; also J. Jeremias, "Perikopen-Umstellungen bei Lukas?," op. cit., 115–119. Luke's independence of Mark is noticeable not only in the new material added by Luke (most of which is noted in the text), but even more in his Markan omissions. Luke omits (1) the name of Golgotha (2) the wine offered to Jesus and rejected by him (3) the time of the crucifixion (4) the railing of the passers-by (5) part of the chief priests' taunts (6) "My God, my God . . ." and the misunderstanding concerning Elijah. See V. Taylor, Behind the Third Gospel, 55–56. Taylor sees Markan insertions only in 23:26, 34b, 44f., and perhaps 49b. On the friendliness of the Jews toward Jesus in Luke's passion narrative, see G. Rau, "Das Volk in der lukanischen Passionsgeschichte, eine Konjektur zu Lk. 23:13," Z.N.T.W. 56 (1965), 41–51.

[40] Cf. also Lam. 1:12; 2:15; Is. 51:23.

[41] B D W Θ sy^s sa bo.

[42] It is also interesting that these words of Jesus closely parallel Stephen's words in Acts 7:60: "Lord, do not hold this sin against them." Jesus' final cry in Luke, "Father, into thy hands . . ." also parallels Stephen's, "Lord Jesus, receive my spirit."

[43] Despite interesting differences, Luke is obviously dependent on Mark here. Mark designates the "chief priests" and Luke says "the rulers," but both think of the leading Jewish officials. Matthew, to broaden the Jewish guilt, adds the scribes and elders. Matthew follows the same pattern in 27:62, adding the Pharisees to the chief priests who demand a guard at Jesus' tomb. See note 79 below.

[44] As time passed, these insults came to be associated more with the Jews than the Romans. For example, Mark and Matthew make no mention of verbal abuse by the soldiers. Their record may represent a later stage of the tradition than Luke's source.

[45] On the significance of "paradise" (παραδεισος) see the discussion by A. R. C. Leaney, A Commentary on the Gospel According to St. Luke, London, 1958, 285–287; also P. Grelot, "'Aujourd'hui tu seras avec moi dans le Paradis' (Luc, XXIII, 43)." R.B. 74 (2, 1967), 194–214.

[46] There is considerable textual confusion in v. 39, but of no great significance.

[47] However, Matthew (27:54) implies that several of those with the centurion shared in his statement, and that their comment was spurred by the miraculous signs rather than by Jesus' demeanor. Subsequent Christian traditions elaborated the reaction of the soldier, asserting that he later became a disciple.

[48] As E. C. Colwell notes, the scriptural testimonies in John arose from John's effort to dignify the cross and to show that it was not an unexpected defeat but a long-predicted part of God's plan (John Defends the Gospel, op cit., 86–87).

[49] Or perhaps John had to make the garment seamless so as to necessitate the casting of lots, in accordance with Psalm 22:18; see note 34 above. On the seamless robe of the high priest see Ex. 31:10; Lev. 21:10; see C. K. Barrett, The Gospel According to St. John, op. cit., 457–458.

[50] On the possible Messianic significance of the words "I thirst," see J. N. Spurrell, "An Interpretation of 'I Thirst,'" Church Quarterly Review 167 (1966), 12–18.

[51] It is sometimes suggested that "hyssop" (υσσωπῳ) is a mistaken rendering of

"javelin" ($\nu\sigma\sigma\omega$). This solution is intriguing, but it is more likely thate $\nu\sigma\sigma\omega\pi\psi$ is original, because of John's interest in the paschal imagery. See discussion in J. N. Sanders, *The Gospel According to St. John,* New York, 1968, 409.

[52] Only in John does Jesus actually take the drink. The reason for this difference is not clear, except that John does not conceive of the drink as a mockery, as in the Synoptics, but as help.

[53] In order to make this scene possible, John is forced to draw the women near the cross, whereas the Synoptic tradition places them at a distance. There can be very little doubt that John's version is secondary. A detailed examination is provided by A. Dauer, "Das Wort des Gekreuzigten an seine Mutter und den 'Jünger, den er liebte.' Eine traditionsgeschichtliche und theologische Untersuchung zu Joh 19,25–27," *Bib. Zeit.* 11 (2, 1967), 222–239.

[54] An interesting problem surrounds these words. Mark quotes the entire sentence in Aramaic, including the Aramaic "Eloi, Eloi" (אלהי). Matthew changes the divine name to the Hebrew form, "Eli" (אלי), as found in the Scriptures. Although we would expect Mark's reading to be the earlier, it is difficult to see why the cry, "Eloi" would have been misunderstood for "Elijah." The misunderstanding is more natural if Matthew's version is correct. A logical explanation is that Jesus actually said, "Eli," but that Mark, transcribing the divine name, naturally thought of Aramaic, Jesus' own tongue. Matthew, then, has corrected the wording, restoring the Hebrew. In Codex D Jesus speaks the entire sentence in Hebrew, exactly as in the original psalm. See M. Rehm, "Eli, Eli, lamma sabachthani," *Bib. Zeit.* 2 (2, 1958), 275–278; F. Zimmerman, "The Last Words of Jesus," *J.B.L.* 66 (1947), 465–466; T. Boman, "Das letzte Wort Jesu," *Studia Theologica* 17 (2, 1963), 103–119, which makes the novel suggestion that Jesus spoke not from Psalm 22 but Psalm 118:28. See also note 56 below. J. Bligh, "Typology in the Passion Narrative," *Heythrop Journal* 6 (3, 1965), 302–309, suggests a symbolic relationship between Elijah and the miraculous signs at the crucifixion.

[55] Adopting Matthew's reading. Mark is obscure; this Gospel seems to indicate that the man offering the drink spoke in restraint of himself.

[56] This incident adds further credibility to the Gospel record. If we imagine that these words of Jesus arose secondarily, we then have to suppose that the Church also added the misunderstanding, which seems incredible. I suggest that another explanation is possible, although it is based wholly on conjecture. It may be that Jesus actually did cry out to Elijah, as would have fit Jewish practice. This cry would have been remembered by the earliest Christians, but would have been an uncomfortable remembrance, since it would not have seemed fitting for Jesus, superseding the prophets and dying in accordance with God's will, to have cried out to Elijah for help. Therefore, the tradition might have been altered, borrowing the words of Psalm 22 and substituting "Eli, Eli" for Elijah, with the explanation that those nearby had simply misunderstood Jesus. This would account for the hearers' supposed mistake, and would coincide with the view that Psalm 22 was a controlling factor in the creation of the crucifixion narrative. My preference is for the view expressed in the text, but this seems a likely alternative.

[57] $\tau\epsilon\tau\epsilon\lambda\epsilon\sigma\tau\alpha\iota$. Dodd, *The Interpretation of the Fourth Gospel,* 437 provides a good discussion of the theological significance of this final word.

[58] $\epsilon\phi'$ $o\lambda\eta\nu$ $\tau\eta\nu$ $\gamma\eta\nu$ may be understood in either sense.

[59] Luke (23:45) evidently thinks of an eclipse, but this would have been impossible at the full-moon season of Passover. Cf. Amos 8:9: "'And on that day,' says the Lord God, 'I will make the sun go down at noon, and darken the earth in broad daylight.'" Cf. also Is. 60:12.

[60] Less probably, a curtain separating the holy place and the courtyard.

[61] Mary Magdalene is named in each Gospel. Mark and Matthew add Mary the mother of James and Joses (Joseph), whom Luke also mentions in the resurrection narrative. Mark mentions Salome, but Matthew changes this to "the mother of the Sons of Zebedee." It is uncertain whether he means Salome or some other person. Luke does not identify any women by name except in the resurrection narrative, where he adds Joanna and other unidentified women. John, of course,

adds Mary the Mother of Jesus, plus Mary's sister. He then mentions Mary the wife of Clopas, and it is not clear whether this is Mary's sister, just referred to, or an additional person.

[62] Luke (23:49) also speaks of "acquaintances" (γνωστοι) at the cross, but these clearly do not mean the inner circle of disciples or Luke would have said so.

[63] Deut. 21:22,23. See also *Bell. Jud.* IV,v,2, where crucified bodies were lowered from crosses on the day of crucifixion, to permit burial before sundown. Cf. Strack-Billerbeck, *op. cit.,* I, 1047; reference from J. S. Kennard, *op. cit.,* 228, note 2.

[64] Mk. 15:43; Jn. 19:31,42.

[65] This practice of *crurifragium* was not uncommon; cf. Cicero, *Phil.* XIII.12. However, the Synoptics know nothing of such a request to Pilate. Mark's account (15:44) indirectly contradicts John's. Mark states that, rather than having given instructions to speed Jesus' death, Pilate was apparently surprised to learn (from Joseph of Arimathea) that Jesus had died at an early hour.

[66] Although the reference seems to be to Ps. 34:20, it is possible that John thinks primarily of Ex. 12:46 (cf. Num. 9:12) and the paschal lamb, whose legs were not broken. See G. A. Barton, "'A Bone of Him Shall Not Be Broken,' John 19:36," *J.B.L.* 49 (1930), 13–19. For a defense of the historicity of John's claim concerning the legs being unbroken, see W. D. Davies, *Invitation to the New Testament,* New York, 1967, 492–493.

[67] Zech. 12:10.

[68] See Blinzler, *op. cit.,* 258f.

[69] It is often identified with Ramah (Ramathaim), the birthplace of Samuel. J. S. Kennard, *op. cit.,* 229–230, supplies a list of scholars who have doubted the historicity of the Joseph story. Such doubts are wholly unjustified. Joseph is a central part of the record; his role is central, not peripheral, in the accounts; the slight confusion of details concerning him merely reflects the gradual elaboration of the primitive tradition; and, despite claims to the contrary, his presence in the story serves no theological or apologetic interest of importance.

[70] 19:42: "So because of the Jewish day of Preparation, as the tomb was close at hand, they laid Jesus there."

[71] Kennard, *op. cit.,* concludes a very useful study of the burial with the strange suggestion that Joseph's burial of Jesus was a *second* burial, and that the empty-tomb story arose because Jesus' followers did not realize that Joseph had removed the body from its first resting place. Obviously, this theory violates the whole thrust of the Gospel records, in which Joseph provides a very quick burial, immediately after the crucifixion. If one wants to explain the empty tomb by a displacement of the body, he must hypothesize a removal *from* Joseph's tomb, not *to* that tomb.

[72] A graphic portrayal—literally and figuratively—of these tombs is provided by A. Parrot, *op. cit.,* 45–46; see also Vincent and Abel, *op. cit.,* 89f.; R. H. Smith, *op. cit.,* 85f.

[73] The ledges were either chiseled straight into the rock, forming a recess similar to a modern burial vault, or were hewn laterally into the rock, so that one side of the body was exposed.

[74] Cf. *Sanh.* 46,47. Harvie Branscomb observes that Jesus' burial in a fresh tomb was not, therefore, a mark of honor, but of further humiliation (*op. cit.,* 303).

[75] Mk. 15:46 says that Joseph bought the shroud that day, which would suggest (as John says, against the Synoptics) that the crucifixion day was not the Passover. However, this reference is weak evidence for John's view. It is better to suppose that Mark's detail is simply inaccurate. Perhaps that is why the other Synoptists omit it.

[76] One hundred pounds (!) of myrrh and aloes, an extraordinary amount, far more than would have been used.

[77] Mark and Luke themselves disagree concerning the women's obtaining of the anointing oils. In Luke, as noted, the women prepare these ointments immediately after the burial. In Mark, the women do not purchase the ointments until the day after the Sabbath. The reason for their delay is clearly the lateness of the hour after the crucifixion.

[78] The Synoptics are certainly to be preferred here. John probably added the anointing by Joseph (and Nicodemus) because it seemed undignified for Jesus to be hurriedly buried without the proper observances.

[79] The inclusion of the Pharisees, who have not appeared earlier in Matthew's passion narrative, reflects the lateness of this tradition. See note 43 above.

[80] See K. Smyth, "The Guard Posted on the Tomb," *Heythrop Journal* 2 (2, 1961), 157–159.

Conclusion

[1] J. Blinzler, *op. cit.*, 138, note 52, provides an extensive bibliography. Most writers who claim that the trial was illegal base their judgment on the Mark/Matthew Sanhedrin trial, and many rely on *Mishnah Sanhedrin* for proof. A good example is H. M. Cheever, "The Legal Aspects of the Trial of Christ," *Bibliotheca Sacra* 60 (1903), 495–509. See also A. Taylor Innes, *The Trial of Christ*, Edinburgh, 1899; Septimus Buss, *The Trial of Jesus Illustrated from the Talmud and Roman Law*, London, 1906; S. Rosenblatt, "The Crucifixion of Jesus from the Standpoint of Pharisaic Law," *J.B.L.* 1956, 315–321. The specific illegalities of the trial by rabbinic standards are summarized in Strack-Billerbeck, *op. cit.*, 818f. and H. Danby, *op. cit.*, 54–55. Some writers have attempted to prove the illegality of the trial by reference to general legal principles; cf. G. Rosadi, *The Trial of Jesus*, New York, 1905. For a full bibliography of such studies and a refutation of this approach see Juster, *op. cit.*, II, 134f.

[2] A few writers defend the legality of the proceedings even though they authenticate the Sanhedrin trial recorded in Mark/Matthew. So J. Blinzler, *op. cit.*, who claims that the Sanhedrin conscientiously observed all legal formalities. Blinzler cites the disagreement of the witnesses as proof that the testimony was not prearranged. He also argues that the trial was legal in that only the more severe legal code of the Sadducees was operative in the time of Jesus. On the legality of the trial see also M. Radin, *The Trial of Jesus of Nazareth*, Chicago, 1931, 39; A. H. McNeile, *The Gospel According to St. Matthew*, London, 1915, 398. Most scholars who believe that the Jewish proceedings were only a hearing accept their legality.

[3] Sherwin-White, *op. cit.*, 14–24 provides a valuable discussion of the legality of the Roman proceedings from the standpoint of Roman provincial practice.

[4] For a full discussion of *laesa majestas* and its application to the trial see Buss, *op. cit.*, 208–212.

[5] See Goguel, *op. cit.*, 526; Guignebert, *op. cit.*, 471–2. Guignebert notes, "It is not likely that Pilate, or any other procurator, would have troubled to base his decision on a statute. He was responsible for the maintenance of order and would take what measures he thought necessary to that end, by virtue of his general powers."

APPENDIX I

THE PASSION NARRATIVE IN MARK (CHS. 14–15)

Note: the text is supplied only for those portions of the narrative which have direct bearing on Jesus' arrest, trial and execution.

1. THE PLOT AGAINST JESUS' LIFE (14:1–2)

It was now two days before the Passover and the feast of Unleavened Bread. And the chief priests and the scribes were seeking how to arrest him by stealth, and kill him; for they said, "Not during the feast, lest there be a tumult of the people."

2. Jesus' anointing by a woman in nearby Bethany (14:3–9)

3. THE BETRAYAL BY JUDAS ISCARIOT (14:10–11)

Then Judas Iscariot, who was one of the twelve, went to the chief priests in order to betray him to them. And when they heard it they were glad, and promised to give him money. And he sought an opportunity to betray him.

4. The preparation and eating of the last supper (14:12–25)

5. The brief scene at the Mount of Olives (14:26–31)

6. Jesus' anxiety in the Garden of Gethsemane (14:32–42)

7. JESUS' ARREST (14:43–52)

And immediately, while he was still speaking, Judas came, one of the twelve, and with him a crowd with swords and clubs, from the chief priests and the scribes and the elders. Now the betrayer had given them a sign, saying, "The one I shall kiss is the man; seize him and lead him away safely." And when he came, he went up to him at once, and said, "Master!" And he kissed him. And they laid hands on him and seized him. But one of those who stood by drew his sword, and struck the slave of the high priest and cut off his ear. And Jesus said to them, "Have you come out as against a robber, with swords and clubs to capture me? Day after day I was with you in the temple teaching, and you did not seize me. But let the scriptures be fulfilled." And they all forsook him and fled. And a young man followed him, with nothing but a linen cloth about his body; and they seized him, but he left the linen cloth and ran away naked.

8. THE JEWISH PROCEEDINGS AGAINST JESUS (14:53–15:1a)

And they led Jesus to the high priest; and all the chief priests and the elders and the scribes were assembled. And Peter followed him at a distance, right into the courtyard of the high priest; and he was sitting with the guards, and warming himself at the fire. Now the chief priests and the whole council sought testimony against Jesus to put him to death; but they found none. For many bore false witness against him, and their witness did not agree. And some stood up and bore false witness against him, saying, "We heard him say, 'I will destroy this temple that is made with hands, and in three days I will build another, not made with hands.' " Yet not even so did their testimony agree. And the high priest stood up in the midst, and asked Jesus, "Have you no answer to make? What is it that these men testify against you?" But he was silent and made no answer. Again the high priest asked him, "Are you the Christ, the Son of the Blessed?" And Jesus said, "I am; and you will see the Son of Man sitting at the right hand of Power, and coming with the clouds of heaven." And the high priest tore his mantle, and said, "Why do we still need witnesses? You have heard his blasphemy. What is your decision?" And they all condemned him as deserving death. And some began to spit on him, and to cover his face, and to strike him, saying to him, "Prophesy!" And the guards received him with blows.

(9. Peter's denial of Jesus, 14:66–72)

And as soon as it was morning the chief priests, with the elders and scribes, and the whole council held a consultation.

10. THE ROMAN PROCEEDINGS AGAINST JESUS (15:1b–15)

And they bound Jesus and led him away and delivered him to Pilate. And Pilate asked him, "Are you the King of the Jews?" And he answered him, "You have said so." And the chief priests accused him of many things. And Pilate again asked him, "Have you no answer to make? See how many charges they bring against you." But Jesus made no further answer, so that Pilate wondered.

Now at the feast he used to release for them any one prisoner whom they asked. And among the rebels in prison, who had committed murder in the insurrection, there was a man called Barabbas. And the crowd came up and began to ask Pilate to do as he was wont to do for them. And he answered them, "Do you want me to release for you the King of the Jews?" For he perceived that it was out of envy that the chief priests had delivered him up. But the chief priests stirred up the crowd to have him release for them Barabbas instead. And Pilate again said to them, "Then what shall I do with the man whom you call the King of the Jews?" And they cried out again, "Crucify him." And Pilate said to them, "Why, what evil has he done?" But they shouted all the more, "Crucify him." So Pilate, wishing to satisfy the crowd, released for them Barabbas; and having scourged Jesus, he delivered him to be crucified.

11. The scourging by the soldiers (15:16–20)

12. The crucifixion (15:21–47)

13. The resurrection (16:1–8)

APPENDIX II

THREE MODERN STUDIES
OF THE TRIAL OF JESUS

The two most significant studies of Jesus' trial in the past generation have come from two widely-known Biblical scholars, Josef Blinzler and Paul Winter. These studies are of such importance, and are so opposed in their methods and conclusions, that it seems worthwhile to add a special note concerning them, particularly with reference to the views expressed in the present book.

Also, S. G. F. Brandon, the noted British scholar, has recently produced another major analysis of the trial which has not yet attracted the wide attention accorded the above two works. Since Brandon's book appeared too late to be taken adequately into account in the body of this study, I have added a brief summary of it at the end of this note.

Blinzler's book (*Der Prozess Jesu,* Regensburg, Germany, 1959; English translation *The Trial of Jesus,* Westminster, Md., 1959, tr. by I. and F. McHugh) is a remarkable encyclopedia of information concerning the trial and the relevant literature. To him we owe a great debt of gratitude for his painstaking scholarship in providing the best reference work available on this monumental problem. It is unlikely that any other writer in this century will catalogue so much helpful information concerning the trial. Blinzler's work is especially useful in citing many European books and journal articles—particularly from earlier periods—which might otherwise be overlooked by American students.

Blinzler's own interpretation of the trial can best be described as one based on an extremely conservative approach to the Gospel sources. In his study, Blinzler does not, so far as I have detected, discredit as unhistorical or even inaccurate a single reference in any Gospel on any matter relating to the trial. His method is to interweave the four accounts and to explain away any apparent contradictions, often by subtleties of interpretation. This method is pursued to such an extent that Blinzler's work sometimes gives appearance of being a defense of the Gospels more than an analysis of them. In this connection he denies that apologetic interests had any serious influence on the shaping of the Gospel records and also denies that the Old Testament had any influence even in the forming of the crucifixion stories.

Blinzler's interpretation of the trial is also conditioned, at the outset, by a very unusual and certainly remarkable evaluation of a non-Gospel source, a letter from one Mara bar Sarapion, a Syrian Stoic. The letter cannot be accurately dated, but may be as late as the third century A.D. and to my knowledge has never figured seriously in any other evaluation of the trial. The surviving portion of Mara's letter makes reference only to the fact that "the Jews" (?) had executed "their wise king" (?); this is the extent of the letter's "evidence." There is no assurance that this "wise king" was Jesus of Nazareth; more important, there is not the slightest reason for assuming that the author's statement is based on any primitive or valuable information concerning the trial. He is far removed from the scene, he writes probably 100 years or more after the event, and his reference is, to say the least, vague. Yet solely on the basis of this obscure reference, Blinzler discounts three of the five possible interpretations of the relative guilt of the Jews and the Romans for Jesus' death, and states that no interpretation of the trial which discounts the major complicity of the Jews can be correct. This is surely a most questionable criterion for such an important judgment, particularly as a premise for the whole study.

Blinzler's interpretation of the events may be summarized briefly as follows, with emphasis on the points of disagreement with my own view. (The reader should of course consult Blinzler's work for a full appreciation of his thesis.)

The Jews arrested Jesus because of widespread opposition to him by *all* the various groups identified in the Gospels. Following the arrest, the Jewish Sanhedrin subjected Jesus to a formal trial. (Blinzler accepts Mark's description of the nighttime Jewish trial as an exact, verbatim record, and minimizes the other Gospel variations from Mark. He states, for example, that the basic difference in Luke's report of the Jewish proceedings is simply the transfer of the trial to daybreak.) The Sanhedrin convicted Jesus of blasphemy, not because of his remarks concerning the temple, but because of his self-designation as the Messiah. The Sanhedrin also passed a formal death sentence against Jesus, but since they lacked the power to carry out executions on their own authority they were forced to take Jesus to Pilate. Pilate, however, was bound to judge Jesus by Roman laws, not Jewish, and in any case he would have had no interest in a blasphemy charge. Therefore, the Jews contrived to change the charge to one of high treason. (Blinzler also accepts the Gospel records of the Roman trial as a precise, verbatim record of the proceedings.) Pilate, after sending Jesus to Herod Antipas, condemned Jesus; he was convinced of Jesus' innocence, but was coerced by the Jewish officials and crowd.

Blinzler has thus given the definitive statement to a view which might be called the traditional or "conservative" interpretation since, with minor variations, it is by far the most common theory among conservative exegetes. Once one has accepted the Markan "nighttime trial" as historical, the remaining interpretations are largely predetermined. The issue then becomes simply: why did the Jews take Jesus to Pilate, and on what grounds? The answers usually given are: they took him because they could not execute Jesus themselves (Jn. 18:31), and they trumped up political charges in order to get Pilate to execute Jesus, since he would not have been concerned with religious charges. An occasional variation is the suggestion that Pilate was asked merely to ratify the Jewish sentence, and that he did so, though this view is extremely hard to defend in the light of Jesus' execution by Roman soldiers, employing a Roman means of death, with a Roman charge over his head, rather than by Jewish means, Jewish executioners and Jewish charges. See the discussion of these points in my Chapters 1, 10 and 11.

The differences between Blinzler's views and my own are obvious and need not be elaborated. It is sufficient to note that my own interpretation is contrary to Blinzler's at almost every point. I should like simply to mention three areas in which it seems to me that Blinzler's very scholarly and valuable work might have been strengthened.

First, Blinzler makes no effort to trace the development of the passion or trial narratives in the period before they appeared in our four Gospels, some 40–70 years after the events. He virtually ignores all the questions raised by form-critical or any other study of the pre-Gospel stage of Christian traditions. I believe that, whatever one's view of the reliability of the Gospels, one is almost bound to reckon with the extremely important work which has been done over the last century in analyzing the development of early Christian traditions prior to the writing of the Gospels. This element is missing or extremely limited in Blinzler's study.

In the same way, Blinzler engages in almost no source-analysis of any kind in evaluating the four Gospel accounts: there are only infrequent comments about the intricate literary interrelation of the Gospels. Blinzler does not feel it necessary to analyze in depth the often perplexing and interesting variations in the Gospel stories. I believe his presentation of his views would have been strengthened if he had based them more fully on careful source-analysis and comparison of the minor and major differences in the Gospels.

Finally, I feel that Blinzler has been overly defensive in his admission of apologetic material in the accounts. The identification of apologetic material is, of necessity, a matter of judgment, and Blinzler states fully his reasons for disallowing major apologetic influence. Yet I believe the evidence is overwhelming that the Gospels show concrete evidence of the desire to fix the blame on the Jews, and to absolve the Romans, beyond what history will bear, and that this is so obvious in some instances as to be almost beyond the necessity of debate.

None of these comments is intended to discredit Dr. Blinzler's very able contribution nor the importance of his study. As Vincent Taylor comments in the Preface to his commentary on Mark, ". . . we learn most from those from whom we are compelled to differ."

.   .   .   .   .

Paul Winter's book (*On the Trial of Jesus, Studia Judaica, Forschungen zur Wissenschaft des Judentums I,* Berlin, 1961) is not a full analysis of the trial but a series of individual studies on several of its aspects.

Winter's interpretation of the trial and his approach to the Gospel material is directly contrary to Blinzler's. Winter has virtually no faith in the accuracy of the trial narratives, but regards them almost entirely as products of the later apologetic and doctrinal needs of the Church. According to Winter, Jesus' death is to be explained by the political opposition of the Romans to Jesus' acts; religious opposition had nothing to do with the trial and execution. Indeed, the supposed opposition of the Pharisees to Jesus *during his ministry* itself is entirely imaginary; it is a fiction created by the developing Church as a result of the conflict between the early Christians and the Jews. Even the arrest was engineered by the Romans; Winter defends at length John's reference to Roman soldiers in the arrest scene.

Winter discounts the record of a nocturnal Jewish trial, ascribing this story to the anti-Semitic tendencies of the early Church. He argues that the Jews did have the power of capital punishment, which would have been exercised had Jesus been tried on religious charges. But this power was of no consequence in a political trial; the Jews simply delivered Jesus to Pilate for judgment.

Despite major differences, there are some close similarities between Winter's book and my own, so much so that I feel some comment on this fact is in order. As noted in the Preface, my own study of the trial originated as a doctoral dissertation completed in 1960. This dissertation included several references to Dr. Winter's very useful journal articles, particularly on the subject of Luke's sources (see Bibliography). By the time his book on the trial was published in 1961, I had turned my attention away from this subject and did not return to it until 1968. Only then did I inquire into the relevant literature since 1960, an inquiry which led to a study of Winter's book. I was struck by the harmony of many of our views, and by the coincidence of language in some sections. I mention this fact now only to avoid the inference that I might have been so ungrateful as to make use of any of his material without proper acknowledgment. I have limited this usage entirely to some references, especially two or three very apt quotations, in my footnotes. Any other harmony in the two books is purely coincidental. Needless to say, Dr. Winter did not make any use of my unpublished dissertation in the preparation of his own excellent book. I can only add that I am pleased to find points of agreement between my book and his very suggestive study; these agreements increase my confidence about the description of Jesus' trial given in these pages.

Of the key differences between Winter's book and my own, four bear mention here.

I consider Winter unduly skeptical, indeed nihilistic, in his evaluation of the Gospel sources. For Winter the Gospels are in the main unhistorical tracts dominated, especially in the passion narrative, by anti-Jewish, pro-Roman sentiments and by the theological convictions of the early Church. I have indicated the areas where I feel the Gospel records have been seriously affected by these interests, but my assessment is much less skeptical than Winter's. On Winter's premises it becomes very difficult to make any analysis whatever of the trial. Unless the Gospels can be trusted as to the main outline of events, and to many of the actual details, historical inquiry into Jesus' death is *ipso facto* impossible.

Winter's investigation also appears to be motivated to considerable extent by a desire to absolve the Jews of all responsibility for

Jesus' death. While a careful investigation will certainly yield this result, this aim must not be allowed to become the motive of an inquiry; a study of the trial must proceed with as much detachment as possible, and the facts must be allowed to determine the conclusions, however desirable or undesirable. As Blinzler seems determined *a priori* to establish the accuracy of the Gospels, so Winter seems determined *a priori* to establish the innocence of the Jews. I agree with his assessment of the responsibility, but this assessment must be the result, not the purpose, of the investigation. Winter's book frequently seems to take on the tone of a polemic rather than an inquiry.

Third, I cannot accept Winter's conclusion that there is no historical basis for the Gospel record of a significant clash between Jesus and representatives of the Pharisees during his ministry. It goes without saying that the Gospel depiction of Pharisaism in general is a caricature: certainly the Gospels have dramatized this conflict so as to place the Pharisees in the worst possible light, and they clearly reflect the tendency to broaden the Jewish hostility to Jesus and to push this hostility back to his earliest days. But these facts do not justify the view that the conflict between the Pharisees and Jesus has been created out of whole cloth in the emerging Church. It is sufficient to note that the Pharisees were not responsible for Jesus' death, that his beliefs were much closer to theirs than to any other party, including the Essenes, and that the conflicts reflected in the Gospels developed only over certain issues—and perhaps with individual Pharisees. This is adequate corrective to the mistaken impression that all the Pharisees waged religious warfare with Jesus throughout his ministry, and that they were instrumental in causing his death.

Finally, although I regard the issue as beyond certainty (see Chapter 1), I disagree with Winter's contention that the Jews retained full judicial powers under the Romans. However, I agree with him that the issue is somewhat academic in the light of the actual proceedings against Jesus, which were politically inspired and were of a political nature.

Despite these and other disagreements with Winter's view, I

think he has performed a very valuable service, particularly because he bases his views on serious analysis of the primitive development of the passion narrative, even though, as stated, his conclusions as to the reliability of this narrative seem unduly negative. He has also been helpful in emphasizing adequately—perhaps too adequately —the very intense desire of the Christians, for apologetic reasons, to shift the responsibility for Jesus' death away from Pilate and the Romans. It must certainly become established as axiomatic that Christians were under great pressure, in the first and second centuries, to defend the Church against the most difficult charges and attacks in the Roman world, and that the Gospel descriptions of Jesus' death clearly reflect the Church's desire to explain that death in terms which would relieve, rather than exacerbate, that pressure. This point is also made with force and clarity in the work noted below.

.   .   .   .   .

The recent book by S. G. F. Brandon (*The Trial of Jesus of Nazareth,* New York, 1968) should be read in conjunction with two of his other important works, *The Fall of Jerusalem and the Christian Church* and *Jesus and the Zealots* (see Bibliography). These two presage some of the views expressed in his study of the trial, particularly his emphasis on the profound effect which the fall of Jerusalem had on the development of Christianity, and on Jesus' close ties with the revolutionary movement in Judaea. The following is a brief summary of some of the key views in Brandon's latest book.

Brandon begins by showing that, in contrast to Paul, most early Jewish Christians had an interest in the historical facts of Jesus' life, and that this interest is reflected in the records of the trial. According to Brandon, the earliest Jewish-Christian tradition of the trial made no effort to show that Jesus was innocent of sedition; indeed, the suggestion that Jesus had died as a political martyr tended to enhance Jesus in the eyes of Jews and Jewish-Christians alike. The chief aim of this early Jewish-Christian tradition was to show that Jesus' death did not negate his claim to Messiahship. This tradition was, in effect, an apologetic directed toward Jews. To defend Jesus' Messiahship, this tradition denied that Jesus had predicted the destruction of the temple, and in this primitive account of his trial it was shown that only false witnesses bore this testimony against Jesus.

Mark, however, wrote in the aftermath of the temple's destruction, and in the midst of the Christian effort to gain acceptance in the Roman world. His chief concern was to show that Jesus was innocent of sedition. He also wished to dissociate Jesus from Judaism, and he claimed that Jesus had in fact correctly predicted the temple's fall. In these two respects Mark altered the early Jewish-Christian tradition, giving a wholly new interpretation to Jesus' death, one aimed at describing Jesus as politically innocuous. The other Gospels followed suit, introducing relatively minor changes into Mark's version.

To complete his picture of the distinction between Judaism and Jesus, Mark also extended the Jewish opposition to Jesus back to the beginnings of Jesus' ministry, and made that opposition entirely religious in nature. He also emphasized that Jesus had been condemned by the Jewish court on religious grounds.

The truth, according to Brandon, is that Jesus was executed for sedition; the only question is, was this conviction justified? Very few writers have answered this question affirmatively, since this view assumes that Jesus was actually a political revolutionary, but Brandon largely accepts this interpretation. In *Jesus and the Zealots* Brandon stops short of claiming that Jesus was himself a Zealot who sought the violent overthrow of Rome; he does so again in this work. But he indicates again that Jesus was sympathetic to the Zealot cause and, even more strikingly, he claims that the "temple incident" was actually a frontal assault by Jesus on the Jewish religious leaders in their citadel of power and was intended to overthrow these religious leaders. He equates Jesus' action with the Zealot attempt to seize the temple in A.D. 66. According to Brandon, Jesus failed in his revolutionary effort and, uncertain of what to do next, remained briefly in Jerusalem while considering a return to Galilee. However, the Jewish officials arrested Jesus before he left the city and instigated proceedings against him during the night. These proceedings constituted an investigation aimed at learning the details of Jesus' plot and also at learning the names of Jesus' co-conspirators in the temple assault. The Jewish officials then presented Jesus to Pilate as the leader of a rebellion, and evidently explained to the governor that Jesus, rather than Barabbas, was the man guilty of leading the uprising. Pilate accepted the charges against Jesus and had him crucified.

Alongside this rather novel reconstruction of the events, Brandon provides other material, including a review of the political history of the period (Chapter 2), a description of the relation between Christianity and Judaism before and after A.D. 70 (Chapter 3), and a brief summary of the trial traditions in later Christian writings and Christian art (Chapter 7). On the question of judicial competence Brandon states, without a lengthy examination, that the Jews did have the right to try and to execute capital crimes, subject to the procurator's confirmation. As noted, however, he denies that the Jewish proceedings against Jesus constituted a formal trial.

Again the points of difference with my own view are clear. I cannot accept Brandon's thesis that Jesus went to Jerusalem with revolutionary intent toward the religious establishment, nor that the temple incident was the main thrust of this revolutionary effort, nor that he "failed" and was contemplating a return to Galilee, nor that the nocturnal investigation was aimed solely at digging out the facts about this abortive *coup*. This interpretation of the arrest and trial calls for a radical reassessment of the mission and methods of Jesus—one which, I think, is very unlikely to gain much support.

Probably the most thought-provoking part of Brandon's book is his suggestion concerning Mark's radical revision of the early Jewish-Christian interpretation of the trial. Here again, however, I find myself at odds with his views. Brandon's emphasis on the creative role of Mark makes this one author responsible for the fundamental interpretation of the trial found, supposedly, in all four Gospels. I must consider this a serious overstatement of Mark's personal editorial role in the shaping of the trial narratives. In my view, it is clear that the earliest trial stories underwent significant changes *before* they found their way into our Gospels, and Mark's account should be regarded more as a reflection of a gradually developed interpretation than as a disjunctive and quite new interpretation. I have raised the suggestion (see my Chapter 10) that Mark might possibly have been the first author to transform the nighttime investigation into a formal trial, but there is little reason to make of Mark an innovator on a broad scale. I prefer to think of Mark's Gospel, including his passion narrative, as a *reflection* of the development of early Christian traditions, not a primary source of that development.

In this connection, Brandon also seems to suggest that the story of a full-scale Jewish *trial* goes back to the days of the earliest Jewish-Christian tradition, although he states that Mark reinterpreted the nature of that trial. With this I must disagree; the evidence is compelling that the Jewish investigation was reinterpreted as a trial only in the later stages of the tradition. Brandon seems to take no notice of the very large number of scholars who have argued against the primitiveness of this supposed nocturnal trial.

I find another major disagreement in the fact that Brandon, somewhat like Blinzler, does slight justice to the differences found in the other three Gospels. He treats them (except perhaps John, which he describes as "theatre" rather than "history") merely as minor revisions of Mark. Of Luke he says, ". . . the differences (with Mark) in his account are only of a minor nature and do not seriously challenge Mark's presentation" (p. 116) and he adds that Luke seems only to have "drastically abbreviated" Mark's account (p. 119). I have emphasized why I feel it is a serious mistake to overlook the very significant differences from Mark found in Luke and John.

Finally, Brandon argues that Mark introduced a morning meeting of the Sanhedrin as an explanation of the switch from religious charges to political ones. I have stated in Chapter 10 why I feel this common suggestion must be discredited. It seems manifestly wrong to assign this explanation to the morning meeting when Mark himself did not do so, and when he gives no suggestion of any such tactic. As I have stated, if Mark understood the meeting in this sense, he certainly missed an excellent opportunity to say so. This omission is all the more important since it would have fit Mark's plans perfectly to show that the political charges were illegitimate and had been conjured up by the scheming Jewish officials. It is hard to see why he would have avoided such an explanation of the morning meeting had it occurred to him. Rather, Mark mentions this morning meeting simply because it was a fixed part of the tradition as he received it. After he had interjected the story of a supposed nighttime trial, this morning meeting became superfluous, but Mark includes it as an established section of the trial narrative. He can give no explanation of it, and does not seek to do so. The presence of this unexplained and pointless "morning meeting" is one of the best literary evidences that the nocturnal "trial" story was a late interjection into the narrative. It was either an isolated tradition received by Mark and included by him, or was possibly a creation of his own hand. It was not, however, a part of the most primitive record.

The above represents a summary of some of Brandon's major themes. Brandon's inquiry leads him down a great many avenues, some of which seem remote from the study of the trial itself, and his account is not always the easiest to follow because of these diverse investigations. But, like his earlier works, it will certainly reward the careful reader, particularly because of Brandon's expert knowledge of the historical period surrounding the ministry of Jesus and the birth of the Church. While I doubt that Brandon's interpretation of the last days of Jesus will be widely accepted, he has again made an important contribution to New Testament studies.

BIBLIOGRAPHY
OF MODERN AUTHORS

The following abbreviations are used for the most frequently cited journals:

Bib. Zeit. — Biblische Zeitschrift
C.B.Q. — Catholic Biblical Quarterly
E.T. — Expository Times
H.T.R. — Harvard Theological Review
J.B.L. — Journal of Biblical Literature
J.T.S. — Journal of Theological Studies
N.T.S. — New Testament Studies
R.B. — Revue Biblique
Z.N.T.W. — Zeitschrift für Neutestamentliche Wissenschaft

Abrahams, I., "Sanhedrin," *Encyclopedia of Religion and Ethics,* ed. by J. Hastings, Edinburgh, 1921, vol. XI, 184–185.

—— *Studies in Pharisaism and the Gospels,* First Series, Cambridge, 1917.

Angus, S., "Zealots," *Encyclopedia of Religion and Ethics,* ed. by J. Hastings, Edinburgh, 1922, vol. XII, 849–855.

Arnold, W. T., *The Roman System of Provincial Administration,* Oxford, 1914.

Bacher, W., "Sanhedrin," *Dictionary of the Bible,* ed. by J. Hastings, New York, 1911, vol. IV, 397–402.

Bacon, B. W., *The Beginnings of the Gospel Story,* New Haven, 1920.

—— *The Gospel of the Hellenists,* New York, 1933.

Bailey, J. A., *The Traditions Common to the Gospels of Luke and John,* Leiden, 1963.

Baltzer, K., "The Meaning of the Temple in the Lukan Writings," *H.T.R.* 58 (3,1965), 263–277.

Barclay, W., *The First Three Gospels,* Philadelphia, 1967.

Barnes, T. D., "The Date of Herod's Death," *J.T.S.* 19 (4,1968), 204–209.

Barr, A. "The Use and Disposal of the Marcan Source in Luke's Passion Narrative," *E.T.* 55 (1943), 227–231.

Barrett, C. K., *The Gospel According to St. John,* London, 1955.

—— *Jesus and the Gospel Tradition,* London, 1967.

Bartlet, J. V., "The Sources of St. Luke's Gospel," *Studies in the Synoptic Problem*, ed. by W. Sanday, Oxford, 1911.

Barton, G. A., " 'A Bone of Him Shall Not Be Broken,' John 19:36," *J.B.L.* 49 (1930), 13–19.

—— "On the Trial of Jesus before the Sanhedrin," *J.B.L.* 41 (1922), 205–211.

Baum, G., *The Jews and the Gospel*, Westminster, Md., 1961.

Baumbach, G. "Zeloten und Sikarier," *Theologische Literaturzeitung* 90 (1965), 727–740.

Beare, F. W., *The Earliest Records of Jesus*, Nashville, 1962.

Benoit, P., "Prétoire, Lithostroton et Gabbatha," *R.B.* 59 (1952), 531–550.

Bertram, G., *Die Leidengeschichte und der Christuskult*, Göttingen, 1922.

Beyschlag, K., "Das Jakobusmartyrium und seine Verwandten in der frühchristlichen Literatur," *Z.N.T.W.* 56 (3–4,1965), 149–178.

Black, M., "The Arrest and Trial of Jesus and the Date of the Last Supper," *New Testament Studies: Essays in Memory of Thomas Walter Manson, 1893–1958*, ed. by A. J. B. Higgins, Manchester, 1959, 19–33.

Blank, J., "Die Verhandlung vor Pilatus Joh 18,28–19,16 im Lichte johanneischer Theologie," *Bib. Zeit.* 3 (1,1959), 60–81.

Bligh, J., "Typology in the Passion Narrative," *Heythrop Journal* 6 (3,1965).

Blinzler, J., "Qumran-Kalender und Passionschronologie," *Z.N.T.W.* 49 (3–4,1958), 238–251.

—— "Das Synedrium von Jerusalem und die Strafprozessordnung der Mischna," *Z.N.T.W.* 52 (1–2,1961), 54–65.

—— *The Trial of Jesus*, tr. by I. and F. McHugh, Westminster, Md., 1959.

Boismard, M.-E., "La Royauté du Christ dans le quatrième évangile," *Lumière et Vie* 11 (1962), 43–63.

Boman, T., "Das letzte Wort Jesu," *Studia Theologica* 17 (2,1963), 103–119.

Borgen, P., "John and the Synoptics in the Passion Narrative," *N.T.S.* 5 (1959), 246–259.

Bornkamm, G., Barth, G., and Held, H. J., *Tradition and Interpretation in Matthew*, tr. by P. Scott, Philadelphia, 1963.

Brandon, S. G. F., *The Fall of Jerusalem and the Christian Church*, London, 1951.

—— *Jesus and the Zealots*, Manchester, 1967.

—— *The Trial of Jesus of Nazareth*, New York, 1968.

Branscomb, H., *The Gospel of Mark* in *Moffatt New Testament Commentary*, London, 1937

Braumann, G., "Markus 15,2-5 und Markus 14,55-64," *Z.N.T.W.* 52 (3-4, 1961), 273-278.

Brown, R. E., *The Gospel According to John, I-XII*, in *The Anchor Bible*, New York, 1966.

—— "Incidents That Are Units in the Synoptic Gospels but Dispersed in John," *C.B.Q.* XXIII (2,1961), 143-160.

—— *New Testament Studies*, Milwaukee, 1965.

Brown, W. A., "Cross," *Dictionary of the Bible*, ed. by J. Hastings, I, 528-529.

Büchler, A., *Das Synhedrion in Jerusalem*, Vienna, 1902.

Buckley, E. R., "The Sources of the Passion Narrative in St. Mark's Gospel," *J.T.S.* 34 (1933), 138-144.

Bultmann, R., *Das Evangelium des Johannes*, Göttingen, 1953.

—— *Die Geschichte der synoptischen Tradition*, Göttingen, 1921.

—— "The Study of the Synoptic Gospels," in *Form Criticism: A New Method of New Testament Research*, tr. by F. C. Grant, Chicago, 1934.

Bundy, W. E., *Jesus and the First Three Gospels*, Cambridge, 1955.

Burkill, T. A., "The Competence of the Sanhedrin," *Vigiliae Christianae* 10 (1956), 80-96.

—— "The Trial of Jesus," *Vigiliae Christianae* 12 (1958), 1-18.

Burkitt, F. C., *The Gospel History and Its Transmission*, Edinburgh, 1907.

Buse, I., "St. John and the Passion Narratives of St. Matthew and St. Luke," *N.T.S.* 7 (1,1960), 65-76.

Butler, B. C., *The Originality of St. Matthew*, Cambridge, 1951.

Cadoux, A. T., *The Sources of the Second Gospel*, London, n.d.

Cadoux, C. J., "The Politics of Jesus," *Congregational Quarterly* (1,1936), 61.

—— *The Historic Mission of Jesus*, London, 1941.

Carmignac, J., "Comment Jésus et ses contemporains pouvaient-ils célébrer la Pâque à une date non officielle?," *Revue de Qumran* 5 (1,1964), 59-79.

Carrington, P., *The Primitive Christian Calendar*, Cambridge, 1952.

—— *According to Mark: A Running Commentary on the Oldest Gospel*, Cambridge, 1960.

Case, S. J., *Jesus: A New Biography*, Chicago, 1927.

Chavel, C. B., "The Releasing of a Prisoner on the Eve of Passover in Ancient Jerusalem," *J.B.L.* 60 (1941), 273-278.

Cheever, H. M., "The Legal Aspects of the Trial of Christ," *Bibliotheca Sacra* 60 (1903), 495–509.

Church, W. R., "The Dislocations in the Eighteenth Chapter of John," *J.B.L.* 49 (1930), 375–383.

Cohn, H. H., "Reflections on the Trial and Death of Jesus," *Israel Law Review* 2 (3,1967), 332–379.

Collins, J. J., "The Archeology of the Crucifixion," *C.B.Q.* 1939, 154–159.

Colwell, E. C., *John Defends the Gospel,* Chicago, 1936.

—— "Popular Reaction Against Christianity in the Roman Empire," *Environmental Factors in Christian History,* ed. by J. T. McNeill *et al,* Chicago, 1939.

—— and Titus, E. L., *The Gospel of the Spirit,* New York, 1953.

Conzelmann, H., *The Theology of St. Luke,* tr. by G. Buswell, London, 1960.

Corbishley, T., "The Chronology of the Reign of Herod the Great," *J.T.S.* 36 (1935), 22–32.

Cranfield, C. E. B., *The Gospel According to St. Mark,* Cambridge, 1959.

—— "The Christian's Political Responsibility According to the New Testament," *Scottish Journal of Theology* 15 (2,1962), 176–192.

Creed, J. M., *The Gospel According to St. Luke,* London, 1930.

—— "The Supposed 'Proto-Lukan' Narrative of the Trial Before Pilate: A Rejoinder," *E.T.* (May,1935), 378–379.

—— "The Slavonic Version of Josephus' History of the Jewish War," *H.T.R.* 25 (1932), 277–319.

Crossan, D. M., "Anti-Semitism and the Gospels," *Theological Studies* 26 (1965), 189–214.

Crum, J. M. C., *St. Mark's Gospel: Two Stages in Its Making,* Cambridge, 1936.

Cullmann, O., "L'opposition contre le Temple de Jerusalem," *N.T.S.* 5 (1958–1959), 157–173.

—— *The State in the New Testament,* New York, 1956.

Dabrowski, E., *Proces Chrystusa w swietle historyczno-krytycznym,* Poznan, 1965 (reviewed in *C.B.Q.,* Jan., 1967).

Dahl, N. A., "Die Passionsgeschichte bei Matthäus," *N.T.S.* 2 (1955–1956), 17–32.

Dalman, G., *Sacred Sites and Ways,* tr. by P. Levertoff, New York, 1935.

Danby, H., "The Bearing of the Rabbinical Criminal Code on the Jewish Trial Narratives in the Gospels," *J.T.S.* 21 (1920), 51–76.

Daniel, C., "Esséniens, zélotes et sicaires et leur mention par paronymie dans le N. T.," *Numen* 13 (2,1966), 88–115.

Dauer, A., "Das Wort des Gekreuzigten an seine Mutter und den 'Jünger, den er liebte,'" *Bib. Zeit.* 11 (2,1967), 222–239.

Davies, W. D., *Invitation to the New Testament*, New York, 1967.

Deissman, G. A., *Light from the Ancient East*, tr. by L. R. M. Strachan, New York, 1927.

Dibelius, M., *A Fresh Approach to the New Testament and Early Christian Literature*, New York, 1936.

—— *From Tradition to Gospel*, tr. by B. L. Woolf, Tübingen, 1919.

—— "Herodes und Pilatus," *Z.N.T.W.* (1915), 113–126.

—— *The Message of Jesus Christ*, tr. by F. C. Grant, New York, 1939.

—— "The Structure and Literary Character of the Gospels," *H.T.R.* 20 (3,1927), 151–170.

Dodd, C. H., *Historical Tradition in the Fourth Gospel*, Cambridge, 1963.

—— *History and the Gospel*, London, 1938.

—— *Interpretation of the Fourth Gospel*, Cambridge, 1953.

—— *New Testament Studies*, Manchester, 1953.

Dosker, H. E., "Cross," *International Standard Bible Encyclopedia*, ed. by James Orr *et al*, New York, 1939, 760–762.

Duckworth, H. T. F., "The Roman Provincial System," *The Beginnings of Christianity*, ed. by F. J. Foakes-Jackson and K. Lake, London, 1920seq., Part I, vol. 1, 186f.

Easton, B. S., *The Gospel According to St. Luke*, New York, 1926.

—— *The Gospel Before the Gospels*, New York, 1928.

—— "The Trial of Jesus," *American Journal of Theology* 19 (1915).

Eisler, R., Ἰησοῦς βασιλεὺς οὐ βασιλεύσας, Heidelberg, 1929.

—— *The Messiah Jesus and John the Baptist*, tr. by A. H. Krappe, New York, 1931.

Ellis, E. E., "The Gospel of Luke," in *The Century Bible*, New York, 1966.

Enslin, M. S., "Palestine," in *Interpreter's Bible*, ed. by G. Buttrick *et al*, vol. VII, 100–113.

Epstein, V., "The Historicity of the Gospel Accounts of the Cleansing of the Temple," *Z.N.T.W.* 55 (1–2,1964), 42–58.

Farmer, W. R., *Maccabees, Zealots, and Josephus*, New York, 1956.

—— "The Palm Branches in John 12,13," *J.T.S.* 3 (1952), 62–66.

—— *The Synoptic Problem: A Critical Analysis*, New York, 1964.

Farrer, A. M., "On Dispensing With Q," *Studies in the Gospels*, Oxford, 1955, 55–86.

Feine, P., Behm, J., Kümmel, W. G., *Introduction to the New Testament*, 14th ed., tr. by A. J. Mattill, Jr., Nashville, 1966.

Filmer, W. E., "The Chronology of the Reign of Herod the Great," *J.T.S.* 17 (2,1966), 283–298.

Filson, F. V., *A Commentary on the Gospel According to St. Matthew,* London, 1960.

—— *Origins of the Gospels,* New York, 1938.

Finegan, J., *Handbook of Biblical Chronology,* Princeton, 1964.

Fitzmyer, T. A., "Anti-Semitism and the Cry of 'All the People' (Mt. 27:25)," *Theological Studies* 26 (1965), 667–671.

Foakes-Jackson, F. J. and Lake, K., "The Zealots," *The Beginnings of Christianity,* ed. by F. J. Foakes-Jackson and K. Lake, London, 1920, Part I, vol. I, Appendix A.

Frazer, J. G., *The Golden Bough,* 3d ed., Part VI, London, 1913.

Friedmann, H. G., "Pseudo-Messiahs," *The Jewish Encyclopedia,* ed. by C. Adler *et al.,* New York, 1901seq., vol. X, 251–255.

Gardiner-Smith, P., *Saint John and the Synoptic Gospels,* Cambridge, 1938.

Glasson, T. F., "The Reply to Caiaphas (Mark xiv. 62)," *N.T.S.* 7 (1,1960), 88–93.

Goguel, M., *Les Sources du Récit Johannique de la Passion,* La Roche-sur-Yon, 1910.

—— *The Life of Jesus,* tr. by Olive Wyon, New York, 1933.

Goodenough, E. R., *The Jurisprudence of the Jewish Courts in Egypt,* New Haven, 1929.

Grant, F. C., *The Earliest Gospel,* New York, 1943.

—— *The Growth of the Gospels,* New York, 1933.

—— "A Note on Dr. Peritz's Article," *Journal of Bible and Religion* VII (1939), 177–180.

—— "On the Trial of Jesus: A Review Article," *Journal of Religion* 44 (3,1964), 230–237.

Greenidge, A. H., "Procurator," *Dictionary of Greek and Roman Antiquities,* London, 1901, vol. II.

Grelot, P., "'Aujourd'hui tu seras avec moi dans le Paradis' (Luc. XXIII, 43)," *R.B.* 74 (2,1967), 194–214.

Griffiths, D. R., "The Disciples and the Zealots," *E.T.* 69 (1,1957), 29.

Guignebert, C., *Jesus,* tr. by S. Hooke, New York, 1956.

Guy, H. A., *The Origin of the Gospel of Mark,* London, 1954.

Haddad, G., *Aspects of Social Life in Antioch in the Hellenistic Period,* New York, 1949.

Hamilton, N. A., "The Temple Cleansing and Temple Bank," *J.B.L.* 83 (4,1964), 365–372.

Hare, D. R. A., *The Theme of Jewish Persecution in the Gospel of Matthew*, Cambridge, 1967.

Harrington, W. J., *The Gospel According to St. Luke, A Commentary*, Westminster, Md., 1967.

Hawkins, Sir John, *Horae Synopticae*, Oxford, 1909.

—— "St. Luke's Passion-Narrative Considered with Reference to the Synoptic Problem," *Studies in the Synoptic Problem*, ed. by W. Sanday, Oxford, 1911, 76–94.

Hengel, M. *Die Zeloten: Untersuchungen zur jüdischen Freiheitsbewegung in der Zeit von Herodes I bis 70 n. Chr.*, Leiden, 1961.

Herford, R. Travers, "Zealots," *The Universal Jewish Encyclopedia*, ed. by I. Landman, New York, 1943, vol. X, 630–631.

Hewitt, J. D., "The Use of Nails in the Crucifixion," *H.T.R.* 25 (1932), 29–45.

Higgins, A. J. B., *The Historicity of the Fourth Gospel*, London, 1960.

Hoenig, S. B., "Sanhedrin," *The Universal Jewish Encyclopedia*, ed. by I. Landman, New York, 1943, vol. IX, 361–363.

—— *The Great Sanhedrin*, New York, 1953.

Hoskyns, E. and Davey, F. N., *The Fourth Gospel*, London, 1940.

Horvath, T., "Why Was Jesus Brought to Pilate?", *Novum Testamentum* XI (3,1969), 174–84.

Howard, W. F., *The Gospel According to St. John*, in *The Interpreter's Bible*, ed. by G. Buttrick, vol. VIII.

Howard, W. F. and Barrett, C. K., *The Fourth Gospel in Recent Criticism and Interpretation*, London, 1955.

Hughes, H. M., "Anti-Zealotism in the Gospels," *E.T.* XXVII (1,1916), 151–154.

Hunter, A. M., "Recent Trends in Johannine Studies," *E.T.* 71 (1959–1960), 164–167, 219–222.

Husband, R. W., "The Pardoning of Prisoners by Pilate," *American Journal of Theology* 21 (1917), 110–116.

—— *The Prosecution of Jesus*, Princeton, 1916.

Innes, A. Taylor, *The Trial of Jesus Christ*, Edinburgh, 1899.

Jacobs, J., "Jesus of Nazareth," *The Jewish Encyclopedia*, ed. by C. Adler *et al.*, New York, 1904, vol. VII, 160–173.

James, M. R., *The Apocryphal New Testament*, Oxford, 1924.

Jastrow, M., *A Dictionary of the Targumim, the Talmud Babli and Yerushalmi, and the Midrashic Literature*, New York, 1903.

Jaubert, A., *The Date of the Last Supper*, tr. by I. Rafferty, New York, 1965.

—— "Jésus et le calendrier de Qumrân," *N.T.S.* 7 (10,1960), 1–30.

—— "Le mercredi où Jésus fut livré," *N.T.S.* 14 (2,1968), 145–164.

—— "Les séances du sanhédrin et les récits de la passion (suite)," *Revue de l'Histoire des Religions* 166 (2,1964), 143–169 and 167 (1,1965), 1–33.

Jensen, E. E., "The First Century Controversy Over Jesus as a Revolutionary Figure," *J.B.L.* 60 (1941), 261–272.

Jeremias, J., *The Eucharistic Words of Jesus,* tr. by A. Ehrhardt, New York, 1966.

—— *Jerusalem zur Zeit Jesu,* Göttingen, 1958.

—— "Perikopen-Umstellungen bei Lukas?," *N.T.S.* 4 (2,1958), 115–119.

—— "Zur Geschichtlichkeit des Verhörs Jesu vor dem hohen Rat," *Z.N.T.W.* 43 (1950–1951), 145–150.

Johnson, S. E., *A Commentary on the Gospel According to St. Mark,* London, 1960.

—— *The Gospel According to Matthew,* in *The Interpreter's Bible,* ed. by G. Buttrick, vol. VII.

de Jonge, M., "Judas Iskarioth, de Verrader," *Homiletica en Biblica* 18 (5,1959), 149–156seq.

Juster, J., *Les Juifs dans l'Empire Romain,* Paris, 1914, vols. I and II.

Käser, W., "Exegetische und theologische Erwägungen zur Seligpreisung der Kinderlosen Lc. 23:29b," *Z.N.T.W.* 54 (3–4,1963), 240–254.

Kennard, J. S., "The Jewish Provincial Assembly," *Z.N.T.W.* 53 (1962), 25–51.

—— *Politique et religion chez les Juifs au temps de Jesus et dans l'église primitive,* Paris, 1927.

Kiddle, M. "The Passion Narrative in St. Luke's Gospel," *J.T.S.* 36 (1935), 267–280.

Kilpatrick, G. D., *The Origins of the Gospel According to St. Matthew,* Oxford, 1946.

—— *The Trial of Jesus,* London, 1953.

Kingdon, H. P., "Had the Crucifixion a Political Significance?," *Hibbert Journal* 35 (1937), 565–567.

Klausner, J., *From Jesus to Paul,* tr. by W. F. Stinespring, New York, 1943.

—— *Jesus of Nazareth,* tr. by H. Danby, New York, 1925.

Klijn, A. F. J., "Scribes, Pharisees, Highpriests and Elders in the New Testament," *Novum Testamentum* 3 (4,1959), 259–267.

Knox, W. L., *St. Mark,* in *The Sources of the Synoptic Gospels,* ed. by H. Chadwick, vol. I, Cambridge, 1953.

Kohler, K., "Zealots," *The Jewish Encyclopedia,* ed. by C. Adler *et al,* New York, 1907, vol. XX, 639–643.

Kopp, C., *The Holy Places of the Gospels,* New York, 1963.

Kraeling, C., "The Episode of the Roman Standards in Jerusalem," *H.T.R.* 35 (1942), 263–289.

――――― "The Jewish Community at Antioch," *J.B.L.* 51 (1932), 130–160.

Kuhn, K. G., "Zum Essenischen Kalender," *Z.N.T.W.* 52 (1–2,1961), 65–73.

Kutsch, E., "Der Kalender des Jubiläenbuches und das Alte und das Neue Testament," *Vetus Testamentum* 11 (1,1961), 39–47.

La Grange, M. J., *The Gospel of Jesus Christ,* tr. by members of the English Dominican province, London, 1938, vol. II.

Lake, K., "Simon Zelotes," *H.T.R.* 10 (1,1917), 57–63.

Lamarche, P., "Le 'blasphème' de Jésus devant le sanhédrin," *Recherches de Science Religieuse* 50 (1,1962), 74–85.

Lambert, J. C., "Crucifixion," in *Dictionary of the Bible,* ed. by J. Hastings, New York, 1909, 170.

Lauterbach, J. S., "Sanhedrin," *The Jewish Encyclopedia,* ed. by G. Adler *et al,* New York, 1905, vol. XI, 41–46.

Leaney, A. R. C., *A Commentary on the Gospel According to St. Luke,* London, 1958.

Leon-Dufour, X., "Mt et Mc dans le récit de la Passion," *Biblica* 40 (3,1959), 684–696.

Liberty, S., "The Importance of Pontius Pilate in Creed and Gospel," *J.T.S.* 45 (1944), 38–56.

――――― *The Political Relations of Christ's Ministry,* Oxford, 1916.

Lietzmann, H., "Der Prozess Jesu," *Sitzungsberichte der Preussischen Akademie der Wissenschaften,* Berlin, 1931.

Lightfoot, R. H., *History and Interpretation in the Gospels,* London, 1935.

――――― *St. John's Gospel: A Commentary,* Oxford, 1956.

Linton, O., "The Trial of Jesus and the Interpretation of Psalm CX," *N.T.S.* 7 (3,1961), 258–262.

Liver, J., "The Half-Shekel Offering in Biblical and Post-Biblical Literature," *H.T.R.* 56 (3,1963), 173–198.

Loisy, A., *Les Évangiles Synoptiques,* Paris, 1908, vol. II.

――――― *Le Quatrième Évangile,* Paris, 1903.

Macgregor, G. H. C., *The Gospel of John,* in *Moffatt New Testament Commentary,* New York, 1929.

Mahoney, A., "A New Look at an Old Problem (John 18,12–14, 19–24)," *C.B.Q.* 27 (1,1965), 137–144.

Malatesta, E., *St. John's Gospel, 1920–1965: A Cumulative and Classified Bibliography of Books and Periodical Literature on the Fourth Gospel,* Rome, 1967.

Manson, T. W., *The Teachings of Jesus,* Cambridge, 1931.

Mantel, H., *Studies in the History of the Sanhedrin,* Cambridge, Mass., 1961.

Marxsen, W., *Der Evangelist Markus,* Göttingen, 1956.

Mathews, S., *A History of New Testament Times in Palestine,* New York, 1913.

Mattingly, H., "Procurator," *The Oxford Classical Dictionary,* ed. by M. Carey *et al,* Oxford, 1949, 733.

McDowell, E. A., "Exegetical Notes," *The Review and Expositor* 38 (1,1941), 44–46.

McNeile, A. H., *The Gospel According to St. Matthew,* London, 1915.

Mendner, S., "Die Tempelreinigung," *Z.N.T.W.* 47 (1956), 93–112.

Merkel, H., "Jesus und die Pharisäer," *N.T.S.* 14 (2,1968), 194–208.

Moffatt, J., "The Trial of Jesus," *Dictionary of Christ and the Gospels,* ed. by J. Hastings, New York, 1908, vol. II, 749–759.

Mommsen, T., *The Provinces of the Roman Empire from Caesar to Diocletian,* New York, 1887, vol. II.

Montefiore, C. G., *The Synoptic Gospels,* London, 1927, vols. I and II.

Montefiore, H. W., "Josephus and the New Testament," *Novum Testamentum* 4 (2,1960), 139–160.

Morton, A. Q., and Macgregor, G. H. C., *The Structure of the Fourth Gospel,* Edinburgh, 1961.

—— *The Structure of Luke and Acts,* London, 1964.

Moule, C. F. D., *The Birth of the New Testament,* London, 1962.

Neill, S., *The Interpretation of the New Testament, 1861–1961,* Oxford, 1964.

Nilsson, M., *Imperial Rome,* tr. by G. C. Richards, London, 1926.

Niven, W. E., *The Conflicts of the Early Church,* London, 1930.

Noack, B., *Zur Johanneischen Tradition: Beiträge zur Kritik an der literarkritischen Analyse des vierten Evangeliums,* Copenhagen, 1954.

O'Collins, G., "Anti-Semitism in the Gospels," *Theological Studies* 26 (1965), 663–666.

Ogg, G., "The Chronology of the Last Supper," *Historicity and Chronology in the New Testament,* ed. by D. E. Nineham, London, 1965, 75–96.

Olmstead, A. T., *Jesus in the Light of History,* New York, 1942.

O'Neill, E., "Procurator," *Encyclopedia Britannica,* Chicago, 1947, vol. 18, 548.

Osty, E., "Les Points de contact entre le récit de la Passion dans Saint Luc et Saint Jean," *Recherches de science religieuse* 39 (1951), 146–154.

Parker, P., *The Gospel Before Mark*, Chicago, 1953.

—— "Luke and the Fourth Evangelist," *N.T.S.* 9 (4,1963), 317–336.

Parkes, J., *The Conflict of the Church and the Synagogue*, London, 1934.

Parrot, A., *Golgotha and the Church of the Holy Sepulchre*, London, 1957.

Patton, C. S., *Sources of the Synoptic Gospels*, New York, 1915.

Perowne, S., *The Later Herods: The Political Background to the New Testament*, London, 1958.

Perrin, N., *What Is Redaction Criticism?*, Philadelphia, 1969.

Perry, A. M., *The Sources of Luke's Passion Narrative*, Chicago, 1920.

de la Potterie, I., "Jésus roi et juge d'après Jn 19,13: Ἐκάθισεν ἐπὶ βήματος," *Biblica* 41 (3,1960), 217–247.

Rau, G., "Das Volk in der lukanischen Passionsgeschichte, eine Konjektur zu Lk. 23:13," *Z.N.T.W.* 56 (1965), 41–51.

Rawlinson, A. E. J., *St. Mark*, in *Westminster Commentaries*, ed. by W. Lock, London, 1925.

Redlich, B., *Form Criticism*, New York, 1939.

—— *St. Mark's Gospel*, London, 1948.

Rehkopf, F., *Die lukanische Sonderquelle: Ihr Umfang und Sprachgebrauch*, Tübingen, 1959.

Rehm, M., "Eli, Eli, lamma sabachthani," *Bib. Zeit.* 2 (2,1958), 275–278.

Rengstorf, H., "λῃστής," *Theologisches Wörterbuch zum Neuen Testament*, Stuttgart, 1942, ed. by G. Kittel, Band IV, 262–267.

Riaud, J., "La gloire et la royauté de Jésus dans la Passion selon saint Jean," *Bible et Vie Chrétienne* 56 (1964), 28–44.

Richardson, A., *Gospels in the Making*, London, 1938.

Riddle, D. W., *The Gospels: Their Origin and Growth*, Chicago, 1939.

—— *Jesus and the Pharisees: A Study in Christian Tradition*, Chicago, 1928.

Riesenfeld, H., *The Gospel Tradition and Its Beginnings: A Study in the Limits of Formgeschichte*, London, 1957.

Rigg, H. A., "Barabbas," *J.B.L.* 64 (1945), 417–456.

Robertson, A. T., *Luke the Historian in the Light of Recent Research*, New York, 1920.

Ross, A. H. (pseudonym Frank Morison), *And Pilate Said*, New York, 1940.

Roth, C., "The Cleansing of the Temple and Zechariah XIV.21," *Novum Testamentum* 4 (3,1960), 174–181.

————*The Historical Background to the Dead Sea Scrolls,* New York, 1959.

———— "The Zealots—A Jewish Religious Sect," *Judaism* 8 (1,1959), 33–40.

———— "The Zealots in the War of 66–73," *Journal of Semitic Studies* 4 (4,1959), 332–355.

Ruckstuhl, E., *Chronology of the Last Days of Jesus,* tr. by V. J. Drapela, New York, 1965.

Salomonsen, B., "Some Remarks on the Zealots With Special Regard to the Term 'Qannaim' in Rabbinic Literature," *N.T.S.* 12 (2,1966), 164–176.

Sanday, W., *Sacred Sites of the Gospels,* Oxford, 1903.

Sanders, J. N., *The Gospel According to St. John,* New York, 1968.

Schmidt, K. L., *Der Rahmen der Geschichte Jesu,* Berlin, 1919.

Schmiedel, P., "Barabbas," *Encyclopedia Biblica,* ed. by Cheyne and Black, New York, 1899, vol. I, 476.

Schneider, J., "Zur Komposition von Joh. 18:12–27. Kaiaphas und Hannas," *Z.N.T.W.* 48 (1–2,1957), 111–119.

Schürmann, H., *Der Paschamahlbericht, Lk 22,(7–14), 15–18,* and *Jesu Abschiedsrede, Lk 22,21–38,* vols. 19 and 20 in *Neutestamentliche Abhundlungen,* Münster, 1952, 1956.

Schürer, E., *The Jewish People in the Time of Jesus Christ,* Edinburgh, 1901.

Sharman, H. B., *The Teaching of Jesus about the Future,* Chicago, 1909.

Sherwin-White, A. N., "The Trial of Christ," *Historicity and Chronology in the New Testament,* ed. by D. E. Nineham, London, 1965.

———— *Roman Society and Roman Law in the New Testament,* Oxford, 1963.

Sieffert, F., "Zealots," *The New Schaff-Herzog Encyclopedia,* Grand Rapids, Mich., 1950, vol. XII, 497–498.

Simkhovitch, V. G., *Toward the Understanding of Jesus,* New York, 1931.

Skehan, P. W., "The Date of the Last Supper," *C.B.Q.* 20 (2,1958), 192–199.

Smallwood, E. Mary, "High Priests and Politics in Roman Palestine," *J.T.S.* 13 (1,1962), 14–34.

Smith, D., "Crucifixion," *A Dictionary of Christ and the Gospels,* ed. by J. Hastings, New York, 1906, vol. I, 397–399.

Smith, D. M., "The Sources of the Gospel of John: An Assessment of the Present State of the Problem," *N.T.S.* 10 (1964), 336–351.

Smith, R. H., "The Tomb of Jesus," *Biblical Archeologist* 30 (3,1967), 74–90.

Smyth, K., "The Guard Posted on the Tomb," *Heythrop Journal* 2 (2,1961), 157–159.

Spitta, F., *Die synoptische Grundschrift in ihrer Überlieferung durch das Lukas-Evangelium,* Leipzig, 1912.

Spurrell, J. N., "An Interpretation of 'I Thirst,' " *Church Quarterly Review* 167 (1966), 12–18.

Stevenson, G. H., "The Imperial Administration," *Cambridge Ancient History,* ed. by J. B. Bury *et al,* Cambridge, 1923seq., vol. X, ch. VII.

Strack, H. L. and Billerbeck, P., *Kommentar zum Neuen Testament aus Talmud und Midrasch,* München, 1928.

Streeter, B. H., *The Four Gospels,* London, 1924.

—— "On the Trial of Our Lord before Herod—A Suggestion," *Studies in the Synoptic Problem,* ed. by W. Sanday, Oxford, 1911, 229–231.

Summers, R., "The Death and Resurrection of Jesus: John 18–21," *Review and Expositor* 62 (4,1965), 473–481.

Taylor, V., *Behind the Third Gospel, A Study of the Proto-Luke Hypothesis,* Oxford, 1926.

—— *The Formation of the Gospel Tradition,* London, 1949.

—— *The Gospel According to St. Mark,* London, 1952.

—— *The Life and Ministry of Jesus,* New York, 1955.

—— "The Original Order of Q," *New Testament Essays: Studies in Memory of Thomas Walter Manson, 1893–1958,* ed. by A. J. B. Higgins, Manchester, 1959, 246–269.

Temple, S., "The Two Traditions of the Last Supper, Betrayal and Arrest," *N.T.S.* 7 (1,1960), 77–85.

Torrey, C. C., *The Four Gospels,* New York, 1933.

—— "The Name 'Iscariot,' " *H.T.R.* 36 (1,1943), 51–62.

Tyson, J. B., "Jesus and Herod Antipas," *J.B.L.* 79 (3,1960), 239–246.

—— "The Lukan Version of the Trial of Jesus," *Novum Testamentum* 3 (1959), 249–258.

Vaganay, L., *Le Problème Synoptique,* Paris, 1954.

Vincent, L.-H., "Le Lithostrotos Évangélique," *R.B.* 59 (1952), 513–530.

Vincent, L.-H. and Abel, F.-M., *Jérusalem nouvelle,* Paris, 1914.

Walker, N., "Concerning the Jaubertian Chronology of the Passion," *Novum Testamentum* 3 (1959), 317–320.

—— "The Reckoning of Hours in the Fourth Gospel," *Novum Testamentum* 4 (1960), 69–73.

—— "Yet Another Look at the Passion Chronology," *Novum Testamentum* 6 (1963), 286–289.

Walther, J. A., "The Chronology of the Passion Week," *J.B.L.* 77 (1958), 116–122.

Weber, J. C., "Jesus' Opponents in the Gospel of Mark," *Journal of Bible and Religion* 34 (3,1966), 214–222.

Weiss, B., *Die Quellen des Lukas-evangeliums*, Stuttgart, 1907.

Wellhausen, J., *A Sketch of the History of Israel and Judah*, London, 1891.

Wilkens, W., *Die Entstehungsgeschichte des vierten Evangeliums*, Zürich, 1958.

Williams, C. S. C., *Alterations to the Text of the Synoptic Gospels and Acts*, Oxford, 1951.

Wilson, C. W., "Golgotha and the Holy Sepulchre," *Palestine Exploration Fund Quarterly*, vols. 1902–1903, 66seq.

Wilston, C. W., "The Roman Law of Treason under the Early Principate," *Journal of Roman Studies* 45 (1955), 73–81.

Winter, P., "A Letter from Pontius Pilate," *Novum Testamentum* 7 (1,1964), 37–43.

―――― "Luke xxii 66b–71," *Studia Theologica* 9 (2,1955), 112–115.

―――― "Marginal Notes on the Trial of Jesus, II," *Z.N.T.W.* 50 (3–4, 1959), 221–251.

―――― "Markus 14:53b,55–64: Ein Gebilde des Evangelisten," *Z.N.T.W.* 53 (3–4, 1962), 260–263.

―――― *On the Trial of Jesus, Studia Judaica, Forschungen zur Wissenschaft des Judentums I*, Berlin, 1961.

―――― "Sadokite Fragments IX,1," *Revue de Qumran* 6 (1,1967).

―――― "The Treatment of His Sources by the Third Evangelist in Luke XXI–XXIV," *Studia Theologica* 8 (2,1954), 138–172.

―――― "The Trial of Jesus," *Commentary* 38 (3,1964), 35–41.

―――― "The Trial of Jesus and the Competence of the Sanhedrin," *N.T.S.* 10 (4,1964), 494–499.

―――― "Sources of the Lucan Passion Narrative," *E.T.* 68 (1956), 95.

Zeitlin, S., "The Political Synedrion and the Religious Sanhedrin," *Jewish Quarterly Review* 36 (1945), 109–140.

―――― *Who Crucified Jesus?*, New York, 1942.

―――― "Zealots and Sicarii," *J.B.L.* 81 (4,1962), 395–398.

Zimmerman, F., "The Last Words of Jesus," *J.B.L.* 66 (1947), 465–466.

INDEX

For main subjects consult also Table of Contents

Acts, book of, 10, 12, 76f., 82, 137
Agrippa I, 20 passim, 88
Alexandria, 9, 31
Ananus I, 7
Ananus II, 12
Annas, 66, 73, 116, 127f.
Antioch (Syria), 31
Antipas, 4, 57, 58, 71, 78, 131, 136f., 141, 147
Antonia, Tower of, 100, 146
Archelaus, 4, 87
Arimathea, see Joseph of Arimathea
Arrest of Jesus
    in Mark, 45
    in Matthew, 48
    in Luke, 55
    in John, 65f.
    reconstructed, 106f.
Athens, 31
Augustus, 5, 13, 20

Bar Cochba, 89
Barabbas, 47, 58, 81, 131, 139f.

blasphemy, 10, 46, 50, 56, 123f.
burial of Jesus, 162f.

Caesarea, 19, 129
Caiaphas, 7, 48, 66, 96, 116
Caligula, 20
Calvary, 151
capital powers, see Sanhedrin
Celsus, 79
centurion at cross, 156
chief priests, 7, 44, 47, 55, 102f., 126, 164
Church of the Holy Sepulchre, 151
"cleansing" of temple, 97f.
cohort, see Roman soldiers
Constantine, 151, 152
corban, 19
cross, shape of, 152
crucifixion
    nature of, 130, 147, 152f.
    political consequences of Jesus', 79f.
Cumanus (procurator), 89

Cyrene, 9, 13, 148

Dead Sea Scrolls, 9
disciples, the, 65, 119, 165
    in temple cleansing, 99
    political activists among, 92

Ecce Homo arch, 146
Egypt, 13
Elijah, 159
Ephesus, 31
Essenes, 9

Fadus (procurator), 88f.
Felix (procurator), 89
Festus (procurator), 89
form criticism, 27f.

Galilean, Galilee, 4, 22, 44, 91, 97,
    129, 162
Garden of Gethsemane,
    see Gethsemane
Gerizim (Mt.), 19, 88
Gethsemane, 34, 35, 45, 48, 55, 65,
    105, 113
Golgotha, 34, 133, 149, 151f., 153
Gospel of Peter, The, 78, 138

half-shekel tax, 98
Herod Agrippa I, see Agrippa I
Herod Antipas, see Antipas
Herod the Great, 4, 20, 87, 97, 146
Hezekias, 87
high priests(s), see also chief priests,
    6f, 45f., 49, 55, 57, 81, 86, 102,
    108, 123, 127f.
high priest's daughter, burned, 9, 11
hyssop, 157

James, brother of Jesus, 9, 12
"Jesus Barabbas," 141f.
Jewish proceedings
    in Mark, 45f.
    in Matthew, 48f.
    in Luke, 55f.
    in John, 66f.
    reconstructed, 113f.
Jewish trial, see Jewish proceedings
John (the disciple), 158

Joseph of Arimathea, 162 passim
Josephus, 5, 9, 11, 12, 20, 21, 85, 86f.
Judaea, 4f., 7
    Roman government of, 6f.
Judas Iscariot, 35, 44, 45, 48, 54,
    64f., 92, 104f.
Justin Martyr, 78

Kidron (brook), 65
king, Jesus' claim to be, 50, 51, 57,
    126f., 134f., 147, 148

laesa majestas, 170
Last Supper, 34, 35, 44, 54f., 65
legates, 5
"lestes" (lestai), 45 ($\lambda\eta\sigma\tau\eta s$), 87
    passim, 110f., 140
"longer chronology" of passion
    events, 196f., (note 39)
lynchings, 10, 11f.

Maccabean, Maccabees, 4
Mary Magdalene, 160
Mary, Mother of Jesus, 157
Mishnah, 9, 10, 11, 122, 168
mocking, see scourging
Mount Gerizim, see Gerizim
Mount of Olives, 45, 55

Nicodemus, 122, 162, 164

oral traditions behind Gospel
    records, 29f.

palace (Herod's), 146
passion narrative, nature of, 28f.
Passover, 35, 44, 64, 68, 89, 95f., 122,
    125, 129, 140, 142, 146, 161
Paul, 10, 17, 77
Perea, 89
Peter, 17, 32, 34f., 45, 55, 66, 77,
    120, 163
Pharisees, 6, 7, 86, 97, 101f., 108,
    164, 167
Philip (son of Herod I), 4
Philo Judaeus, 9. 11, 20 passim
Pilate
    character of, 17f., 131f.
    conduct of Roman trial, chiefly
        129f. (see also Roman trial)

early Christian attitude
   toward, 76f.
governmental powers of, 5f.
Pilate's wife, 49f., 81
plot against Jesus, 35, 44, 48, 64, 70,
   102f.
Pompey, 4
Pontius Pilate, see Pilate
praetorium, 129, 138, 140, 142, 146f.
Preaching of Peter, The, 77
procurator
   nature of office, 5
   powers of, 5f.
provinces, nature of Roman, 5
Psalm 22, influence of in crucifixion
   stories, 151, 154 passim

"Q" source, 43, 61
Quadratus, 89

ratification theory (of Roman trial),
   15, 130
responsibility for Jesus' death, 76f.,
   171f.
Roman Empire, early Christian
   problems in, 178f.
Roman insignia in Jerusalem, 18f.
Roman soldiers (at arrest), 66, 73,
   107f.
Roman trial
   in Mark, 46f.
   in Matthew, 49f.
   in Luke, 57f.
   in John, 67f.
   reconstructed, 129f.
Rome (city), 31, 32, 42, 123, 130

Sadducean, Sadducees, 6, 7, 86, 96,
   97, 101 passim, 120, 132, 168
Samaritans, 18, 22, 88, 89
Sanhedrin
   membership of, 6f.

nature of, 6f.
powers of, 7f.
"trial," historicity of, 115f.
scourging by soldiers, 34, 35, 46, 47,
   49, 55, 58, 122, 137, 146, 147f.
Scripture fulfilled (in passion
   events), 45, 55, 111, 137f.,
   150 passim
Sicarii, 89, 92
Simon Peter, see Peter
Simon of Cyrene, 148f.
Simon the leper, 44
Simon the Zealot, 93
Stephen, 10, 12, 18, 19, 77
Synoptic relations, 41f., 47f., 53f.,
   58f., 68f
Syria, 19, 78

Tacitus, 79
Talmud, 9, 14
temple (of Jerusalem), 9, 11, 45, 49,
   89, 97f., 134, 160
Tertullian, 78
Theudas, 88f.
Tiberius Alexander (procurator), 89
Tiberius Caesar, 20, 79
titulus, 148, 152
Tomb of Jesus, 163f.
Torah, 89
Tower of Antonia, see Antonia
two-document hypothesis, 43

Ventidius Cumanus, see Cumanus
Via Dolorosa, 146
Vitellius, 19, 20

women at cross, 160f., 164

Zealotism, Zealots, 86f.